MARTIAL VALOR
—FROM—
BEOWULF
TO VIETNAM

ALFREDO BONADEO

Copyright © 2024 Alfredo Bonadeo.

1st Edition 2010.

Edited by Barbara Bates Bonadeo.

All rights reserved. No part of this book may be reproduced, stored, or transmitted by any means—whether auditory, graphic, mechanical, or electronic—without written permission of both publisher and author, except in the case of brief excerpts used in critical articles and reviews. Unauthorized reproduction of any part of this work is illegal and is punishable by law.

ISBN: 979-8-89419-000-6 (sc)
ISBN: 979-8-88640-021-2 (hc)
ISBN: 979-8-89419-236-9 (e)

Because of the dynamic nature of the Internet, any web addresses or links contained in this book may have changed since publication and may no longer be valid. The views expressed in this work are solely those of the author and do not necessarily reflect the views of the publisher, and the publisher hereby disclaims any responsibility for them.

One Galleria Blvd., Suite 1900, Metairie, LA 70001
(504) 702-6708

CONTENTS

Introduction v

Reputation 1

Violence 28

Degradation 62

Cause 82

Against Death 101

Killing Heroics 145

Endnotes 183

INTRODUCTION

When Aristotle declared that "courage is noble, and, accordingly, its end is noble too,"[1] the notion of valor as a value in itself was engendered. Thomas Carlyle still echoed the ancient philosopher's view: "It is an everlasting duty, valid in our day as in that [of the Norsemen], the duty of being brave... A man shall and must be valiant." Carlyle had doubts about the legitimacy of an exceedingly violent kind of valor, for example that of the Norsemen, "wild, bloody valour." Nonetheless, he approved of it, just because it was valor: "Yet valour of its kind; better, I say, than none."[2] Konrad Lorenz, like Carlyle, recognized the value of valor, conceding that valor may be a virtue, even a manly one. But he cautioned that violence, which often goes along with it, may undermine its value, since valor is "traditionally associated with waging war,"[3] an activity that shows a variety of vices side by side some virtues. Less than noble ends have indeed justified the use of valor. It has been used to enhance the reputation of individuals and classes, to excuse crimes, and to achieve political ends. The Japanese Bushido code produced rape, massacre, and torture, one historian argued, but in the Second World War, it inspired a heroism in the Japanese soldier that has impressed many people who had reasons to hate the Japanese.[4]

If valor is a value in itself regardless of the end for which it is used, then any end could be justified in the name of valor. Nations have sometimes fought to show heroism rather than to uphold a just cause. Historical and military realities have often been justified and magnified by the valor that politicians and soldiers have displayed. But in the end the cause of the action in which valor is used defines its value and legitimacy. Under what circumstances is valor a virtue or a vice?

The idea and practice of valor changed from the Middle Ages to contemporary times. In the Middle Ages and in the Renaissance, valor was valued as an end in itself. The resolve to act and to display courage was intense, the value of life irrelevant, and loss of life was significant mainly for enhancing heroism. In later ages, wars required large armies and the demand for heroism increased. But the attachment to life has increased too, because men are now aware of the power of heroism to deprive them of life.

Whereas valor was once sought for one's own glorification, In modern times, it is sought as a property essential to the fighting capability, the winning and surviving of the combatant. In earlier times, valor was the undisputed prerogative of all men of chivalry; now it is a rare quality. In modern times military men covet it but find it hard to summon because it often requires sacrifices that many are unwilling to make. True valor has become "expensive." Unfortunately, it has been replaced by naked violence.

REPUTATION

Born at the dawn of the modern age, *Beowulf* is aptly defined as heroic history.[5] Its protagonist covets valor as a means to prove and establish his reputation as a hero, a reputation that in his warrior society transcends all other values. In this society, heroism governs the lives of men and commonwealths.

Young, strong, and brash, Beowulf is known as "the man whose name was known for courage" (340),[6] and when he fights, he is for real. He travels to Heorot, the great mead hall in Denmark, for the ostensible purpose to free the Danes from the ravages of the monster Grendel and his mother. But the true reason is something else. He shows little interest in the hopes of the Danish people, the liberation from the monster and re-establishment of normal life. He even shows his lack of regard for the Danish warriors when he tells them that the monster "can trample down you Danes / to his heart's content, humiliate and murder / without fear of reprisal" (599-601). Beowulf is in Heorot to display his bravery. His heroism is known by his contemporaries, but not as much as he would like. The monsters give him the chance to reassert and reinforce his fame.

He places considerable value on the coming fight with Grendel. It will be the crowning achievement of his star-studded career. To make sure that his valor will shine, and thus his reputation, he decides to fight the monster without any weapon, hand to hand. Before the fight he confirms this intention, "I prove myself with a proud deed" (637). Later, when Beowulf will take on Grendel's mother, he tells King

Hrothgar that the fight will be another occasion for displaying his valor and achieving glory, "Life is short and there is no time to lose. For every one of us, living in this world / means waiting for our end. Let whoever can / win glory before death," (1386-88). When his sword fails to bite into the monster's flesh, and Beowulf suffers a minor setback, he gets hold of himself by "thinking about / his name and fame." From this, he receives a jolt of energy enabling him to discard his sword and grapple with the monster bare-handed, doing exactly what "must a man do / who intends to gain enduring glory" (1530-31, 1534-35).

It is noteworthy that Beowulf's encounters with Grendel and his mother emphasize the heroism of his performance rather than its fruit, the restoration of normal life for the Danes. Beowulf "was granted / the glory of winning," and he "was happy with his nightwork / and the courage he had shown" (826-27).

Already on the way back from the lake to Heorot, the retainers sing Beowulf's virtue: his deeds

> were praised over and over again.
> Nowhere, they said, north or south
> between the two seas or under the tall sky
> on the broad earth was there anyone better
> to raise a shield or to rule a kingdom (856-60).

At the court King Hrothgar's minstrel celebrates Beowulf's deeds, which are sung in well-fashioned lines, stressing the excellence of the hero, not the end result of his performance—peace and security for the Danish community. His "courage was proven, his glory was secure." (1646). Hrothgar acknowledges what Beowulf craves, his fame as a valiant warrior: "Beowulf, my friend, / your fame has gone far and wide, / you are known everywhere" (1703-05). The apotheosis of Beowulf occurs on his return home where the chief and the people recognize that on Danish soil he successfully fought "to win glory / and prove [his] worth" (2133-34).

Even so, the deeds done and the valor shown in Heorot are not enough to quench Beowulf's thirst for glory. When age and weakness ought to induce him to desist from fighting, he decides instead to challenge the dragon in his own homeland to show that his prowess is undiminished, proclaiming that he has "no dread at all" of the dragon, which is known for its courage and strength. Beowulf fights for the "glory of winning," and his resolve is so compelling that he claims the right to fight the dragon single-handedly, just as he had fought Grendel's mother earlier. He refuses his thanes' offer of help in the hope of getting all the credit, "I shall win the gold / by my courage," (2514, 2535-36).

In the Middle Ages, valor held great value as an agent of reputation, so much so that in *The Song of Roland* its display supplants sound military strategy and forfeits victory. As King Marsiliun's forces close in on the French rear guard at Roncesvalles, Oliver surveys the enemy horde and reports to Roland on the Saracens' overpowering strength: "Never on earth has such a hosting been,"[7] a hundred thousand of them. Thrice Oliver entreats Roland to blow the Olifant to bring Charlemagne and his army back and get the help that the rear guard desperately needs; thrice Roland refuses. Each of his three refusals to sound the Olifant is followed by his resolve to shed a lot of enemy blood independently from the military results:

> I'll smite great strokes with Durendal my sword,
> I'll dye red high to the hilt with gore (83).
> Rather will I with Durendal strike out
> With this good sword, here on my baldrick bound;
> From point to hilt you'll see the blood run down (84)
> I'll strike a thousand and then seven hundred strokes,
> Blood-red the steel of Durendal shall flow (85).

What keeps Roland from asking for help is not the belief that his force alone would be able to prevail, but the fear of impairing his reputation. He thinks that calling for help would be a sign of cowardice on his part. He responds to Oliver's pleading with an emotional and energetic refusal: "Madman were I and more, / And in fair France my fame would suffer scorn; May never God allow / That I should cast dishonor on my house." Oliver speaks again of the enemy's superiority, this time emphatically, pointing out that the Saracens "cover all the mountains and the vales" (83, 84, 86). Roland again refuses to blow the Olifant and justifies his refusal with the necessity of serving the emperor the way he thinks he ought to be served, "If the King loves us, it is for our valour's sake." Roland is resolved to stand and fight to prove his valor; the display of valor counts more than victory, and he will fight valiantly, but will lose the battle and all his men.

Roland's resolve to fight is irrational, and Oliver, a personage remarkable for his display of wisdom, indicts him for the indiscriminate use of the chivalric virtues that have plunged him and the French into a hopeless battle. When the disagreement between Oliver and Roland reaches its climax with the poet's statement that "Roland is valiant and Oliver is wise" ("Rollant est proz e Oliver est sage," 87), Oliver admonishes:

> There is a wise valor, and there is recklessness:
> Prudence is worth more than foolhardiness.
> Through your overweening you have destroyed the French;
> Never shall we do service to Charles again.
> Had you but given some heed to what I said,
> My lord had come, the battle had gone well,
> And King Marsiliun had been captured or dead.
> Your prowess, Roland, is a curse on our heads (131).

In the aftermath of the battle, the dying hero turns to his sword and worshipfully intones: "Ah, Durendal! So bright, so brave, so gay! / How dost you glitter and shine in the sun's rays!" He faces death worshipping and glorifying his real God—Durendal, the agent of his heroic career:

> With this I won him [Charlemagne] Anjou and Britayn;
> With this I won him Poitou, and conquered Maine;
> With this I won him Normandy's fair terrain,
> And with it won Provence and Acquitaine,
> And Lombardy and all the land Romayne,
> Bavaria too, and the whole Flemish state,
> And Burgundy and all Apulia gained (172).

The Durendal that in the past has performed so valiantly, enhancing the glory and power of imperial France, could do no wrong at Roncesvalles. Durendal's toil, reputation, and achievements set the seal of valor on the slaughter and loss that was Roncesvalles. Heroic exhilaration coincides with the moment in which valor reaches closure and immortalizes the hero's reputation.

Roland's decision to stand and fight at Roncesvalles echoes the mentality and practice of the age, which prescribed the "exercise of courage" independently from need.[8] Already Aristotle's idea of the nobility of valor's purpose is compromised.[9] A recent study of the "Chansons de geste," chronicles, didactic treatises, panegyrics, and epitaphs shows that from the twelfth century on, the exercise of courage was the chief requirement of knightly life. It was necessary for the noble warrior to perform "many acts of great courage and hardy enterprises," not so much for the welfare of the individual, the family or community, but to gain "honour, glory, and posthumous renown."[10] Valor was the blood of the chivalric class. Whether valor was used for a bad or good cause mattered little; what mattered was the display and the reputation accruing to the valiant knight.

This ethos, which ruled the upper classes, explains to an extent Count Roland's decision to stand against an enemy who will destroy both the Christian paladin and his rear guard. In the Middle Ages the preoccupation with valor was not confined to great personages who, like Roland played a prominent role in public life. Valor, (its original meaning increasingly imperiled), played a role in ordinary lives also. A man could distinguish himself by being valiant. Chroniclers and poets often represented the excitement and fulfillment that deeds of valor yielded. "When battle is joined," wrote Bertrand de Born, "let all men of good lineage think of naught but the breaking of heads and arms." He told his readers that he found "no such savor in food, or in wine, or in sleep" as in "seeing men great and small go down on the grass beyond the fosses; in seeing at last the dead, with the pennoned stumps of lances still in their sides."[11]

In Arthurian literature, personal valor takes over the epic narrative, as the knight goes through trials and adventures to show his chivalric worth. "Aventure" is the knight's key test, and the test can be passed only by showing valor, which establishes the worth of an individual. The decision of young Alexander, Cligés's future father, to travel from Greece to Arthur's court epitomizes the relevance of valor to personal power. Alexander, who felt unable to rule his father's empire because he had no chivalric virtues ("I am not brave and wise enough") he says, travels to King Arthur's court to gain the virtue he needs to rule. He will apply himself "to the whetstone and to the real true test, whereby my prowess shall be proved."[12] Calogrenant explains his presence in the forest of Broceliande by his resolve to test himself for no other purpose than proving himself valiant. He is looking, he declares, for "some adventure whereby to test my prowess and my bravery."[13] In the romance of Erec and Enide, Erec proved his valor by challenging the custom of the sparrohawk, and won Enide's heart, but at the court, he becomes neglectful of his virtue, a reprehensible vice, for in the chivalric world a life divorced from fighting and bravery induces degeneration. The knights at the court murmured that it was a great misfortune that "such a valiant man as he was" now is loathed to even bear arms. A reputation for valor must be constantly renewed. Enide herself pressures him into resuming the wandering life in search of adventures for his reputation's sake. Erec complies and eventually earns King Arthur's approval.[14] The pleasure of love and family traps Yvain, and threatens his reputation, too. He is saved by Gawain, who urges Yvain to show his valor, "to frequent the lists, to share in the onslaught, and to contend with force, whatever effort it may cost!"[15] Adventures, dangers, and valiant exploits are the very blood of chivalric life, regardless of their results. And the roots that generate them must be kept alive. No matter how many adversaries the knights of Chrétien de Troyes's romances dispose of, the forest and towns are left alive with evil characters. Chivalric valor is needed to oppose them. But what matters is the display, not peace and order in the communities. The knight needs an enemy, not merely to tame the forest wilderness. He needs the daemonic dwarfs, the outlaws, and giants in order to have a reason to fight and display his prowess. What matters is not the righting of the wrong in society, but the triumph of the knight's valor. Valor is the very blood of his life. "Bravery is what a baron's reputation and position depend on."[16] His success modifies nothing of life in the forest, the world that needs to be tamed to improve the life of the community. The forest, "locus of the physical and the chaotic,"[17] and the court, the place of courteous behavior, remain mutually exclusive worlds.

The chivalric spirit that places the worth of valor above historical or social contingencies re-emerges in the Renaissance, and the poet, Ludovico Ariosto, mocked it. He portrays Rinaldo, one of the two "beacons" of Charlemagne's martial strength and wisdom, deviating in a most theatrical and absurd way from his duty to Charlemagne who has dispatched him to Britain to recruit fresh troops for the Christian cause. Rinaldo is distracted by personal chivalric pursuits. When his ship is thrown by a gale onto the shores of the Darnantes Wood, instead of doing the repairs needed to continue his journey and accomplish his mission, he lands and sets out to explore the Wood. He knows that the Darnantes Wood is the setting of famous chivalric deeds by the knights of the Round Table. Here "so often the clash of arms resounded amid the ancient shady oaks." He also knows that the place is rich in chivalric tradition. Through it travel "knights errant renowned for their prowess" from all over Britain, and from other lands near and far. "Great deeds were accomplished here by Tristan,

Lancelot, Galahad, Arthur, and Gawain, and other famous knights of the new Round Table," (IV:51-53). They capture Rinaldo's imagination and lure him into imitating the knights of old for no other reason than to prove himself as valiant as they. Rinaldo sets out through the forest, looking for "novel adventures" (IV:52, 54). The poet taunts him, "The man of little valour should not adventure there [wood], for where he seeks honour he shall find death." This deviation from the mission that Charlemagne had entrusted him measures the intensity of his need to enhance his reputation, to prove by some noteworthy feat that he "was deserving of praise.[18]

The European romances that stirred a "radical" individualistic quest for honor gained through feats of arms, touched the English imagination. As a result, the image of the knight as a man of martial prowess dominated the new chivalry in England, so much that showing prowess became the goal while the political and military considerations that prowess might serve were ignored.[19] The chivalric tradition provided the knight with the basis for self-deception.[20]

The tradition influenced Shakespeare's portrayal of the "glorious defeat" suffered by the Talbots in France, a defeat that extinguished English heroism, at least momentarily.[21] In an early play "such heroism as the English displayed," occur during the years that encompass the Henry VI trilogy.[22] Shakespeare concentrates on two historical figures, the Talbots, father and son. In Henry VI, Part I, "valiant" Talbot the elder fights a lengthy skirmish, performing amazing deeds of valor. His "undaunted spirit" is an inspiration for all Englishmen who bravely rush into battle (1.1.120-21, 28). He is instrumental in establishing England's reputation for valor on French soil. But the bravery of the legendary soldier fails to produce any results beneficial to the English cause. When he suffers a spear wound, the city of Orleans is lost, and his forces are surrounded.

Adversity strikes when Somerset and York in England withhold military help, showing that not the strength of French arms, but the fraud of politicians works against Talbot and his men. However, the scheming of the English politicians is not an historical reality. It is a Shakespearean invention designed to enhance Talbot's reputation for valor, as he now faces a superior enemy. Rather than disheartening him, the enemy's clear superiority stimulates Talbot to fight, and because he is the underdog, his courage in battle will be magnified.[23]

Shakespeare conjures up an aura that places in full view the decision of the Talbots to fight in order to enhance their heroic reputation. The scene in which father and son decide to make their last, heroic stand is tense and decisive. Their strategy is dictated by emotion rather than by intelligent plans, by the egos of the two warriors rather than by considerations about the military advantages or disadvantages that may come to the English. Defeat is certain. Retreat or surrender is deemed cowardice. "Is my name Talbot? And am I your son? And shall I fly?" John asks horrified at the consequence of avoiding battle and saving himself, "To make a bastard and a slave of me! / The world will say, he is not Talbot's blood." The coming battle without any hope of victory renders the Talbots' resolve to act like heroes admirable, but it also reveals the futility of their heroism. The elder Talbot cares about his reputation even more than his son does, "My age was never tainted with such shame." At the English camp near Bordeaux, the father welcomes his son "unto a feast of death." He predicts that both of them "are sure to die." John embraces death, "Here on my knee I beg mortality." Both resolve "side by side together [to] live and die," and in the midst of the battle they reaffirm their common will, "Let's die in pride." The death of "valiant John" is an occasion for old Talbot to celebrate valor, "Triumphant death," he exclaims, "young Talbot's valor makes me smile at thee." The moment of their death, after their valor has been fully displayed in futile battle, turns into valor's final triumph, "In that sea of blood my boy did drench / His over-mounting spirit, and there died" (4.5.7-54; 4.6.57; 4.7.2-4, 14-15). The epilogue pays tribute to English valor in the midst of lives sadly wasted.

Heroism proved irrelevant in achieving military ends or diplomatic gains for England. The valor of the legendary Talbots, displayed for the benefit of heroism, was sterile. It compromised the English forces and their hold over France. Their defeat coincided with the beginning of the decline of England's hegemony, a trend so unfortunate that could make Henry V, her erstwhile conqueror, "burst his lead and rise from death" (1.1.65).

However, it was not merely the European romances to influence Shakespeare's imagination. It was also something inherent in the politics and aristocracy of England, the belief that valor was essential to her prestige and standing. If Shakespeare himself "certainly was not a warmonger,"[24] the same cannot be said of one of his notable creations, Henry V. His belief in valor as an aristocratic and national value is strong enough to send him to war if only to assert it. Driven by a burning ambition to imitate his ancestors' reputation, the king masks his war of conquest in France as a righteous enterprise. He contrives what he undoubtedly believes is a noble cause—upholding the reputation of his forebears and goes to war to keep faith in a supposed tradition of valor running through his lineage.

In the beginning of *Henry V*, the king's counselors try to pave his path to war by telling him that he has a claim on the French crown and that the Salic Law is no obstacle. After the Archbishop of Canterbury makes a muddled discourse on this Law and English rights, Henry appears confused; he asks his counsellors: "May I with right and conscience make this claim?" (1.2.100). They tell him that he is in the right. At this point, some critics note, his doubts about claiming the French crown dissipate, and he resolves to invade France. To stress this resolve the critics quote the passage beginning with Henry's words "Now are we well resolved."[25] However, the expression of this resolve follows, not the assurance by the clergymen about the validity of the king's claim, but a lengthy disquisition on valor that comes right after the assurance. In the end his resolve to go to war depends not on the clergymen's assurance, but on that disquisition. Henry's claim to the French crown and his decision to go to war are made on the basis of the imperative to bring back to life the valor of his ancestors. "Gracious Lord," the bishop of Canterbury preaches to the king:

> Stand for your own, unwind your bloody flag,
> Look back into your mighty ancestors;
> Go, my dread lord, to your great-grandshire's tomb,
> From whom you claim; invoke his warlike spirit,
> And your great-uncle's, Edward the Black Prince,
> Who on the French ground played a tragedy,
> Making defeat on the full power of France,
> Whiles his most mighty father on a hill
> Stood smiling to behold his lion's whelp
> Forage in blood of French nobility (1.2.104-114).

The Bishop of Ely supports Canterbury, alluding to the Lancasters' military reputation and glory, and urges Henry to reenact their history of courage and bloodshed, and keep alive their reputation for valor:

> Awake remembrance of these valiant dead
> And with your puissant arm renew their feats.
> You are their heir; you sit upon their throne;
> Th e blood and courage that renowned them
> Runs in your veins (1.2.119-123).

The lesson that the counselors try to teach Henry, and one which he readily grasps, is that he is the offspring of valiant ancestors, and that he too must show his valor. His ancestors place on him an obligation to imitate their virtue, and to do so, he must go to war against France. Besides, the Duke of Exeter reminds the king, his nephew, that the greats of the world hold valor in high esteem and their eyes are on the king, waiting to see if he is capable of matching his forebears' standards:

> Your brother kings and monarchs of the earth
> Do all expect that you should rouse yourself,
> As did the former lions of your blood (1.2.126-128).

It was not hard to persuade Henry, for reputation was also a personal concern of his. Going to war would give him the opportunity to fix a problem, his well-known reluctance to do deeds of valor, a shortcoming that had vexed even his father. In Part I, Henry IV, the king showed admiration for the virtue that was missing in his son by praising Hotspur's fame, "the theme of honour's tongue." Hotspur, the "incarnation of valor," had been busy performing glorious deeds all his life.[26] He is a peculiar hero, valiant but somewhat deranged, as heroism obsesses him in strange ways. Visions of valiant deeds grip him even in his sleep. "In thy faint slumbers," Lady Percy reveals to him,

> I by thee have watched,
> And heard thee murmur tales of iron wars;
> Speak terms of manage to thy bounding steed;
> Cry 'Courage! To the field!' (2.3.50-53).

The martial deeds he plans to do are enough to stir up the frenzy of words and dreams that keep his spirit warring while his body rests, "We must have bloody noses and cracked crowns," he replies to his wife puzzled by his ranting (2.3.96). Hotspur's penchant for doing deeds of valor gave the king a good reason to express displeasure with his unheroic son. In his heart of hearts, he rejects him:

> O that it could be proved
> That some night-tripping fairy had exchanged
> In cradle-clothes our children where they lay,
> And called mine Percy, his Plantagenet!
> Then would I have his [Northumberland's]
> Harry, and he mine (1.1.81-90).

When the news of "gallant Hotspur's exploits at Holmedon reaches London, Henry IV launches on the praise of Hotspur's reputation and berates Harry, inferior in martial spirit to the conqueror of the Scots. "Thou makest, me sad and makest me sin / In envy," the king confides to Westmoreland,

> ... that my Lord Northumberland
> Should be the father to so blest a son,
> A son who is the theme of honour's tongue,

while the king sees "riot and dishonour stain the brow" of young Harry (1.1.78-85). On the eve of Shrewsbury, the king charges his son with betraying the "greatness" of his blood, by being a prey of "fear, / Base inclination," while expressing again admiration for Hotspur, whom he sees as "Mars in swathling clothes." Thus, he shames his son, reminding him that Hotspur, though young, "leads ancient lords and reverend bishops on / To bloody battles and to bruising arms." Harry promises redemption, "I will wear a garment all of blood, / And stain my favours in a bloody mask, / Which, washed away, shall scour my shame with it" (3.2.16-137).

Has Harry proved his courage by fighting and killing Hotspur at Shrewsbury? Critics think so, but Falstaff doubts it. He impugns the valor of the future king, reflecting in *Henry IV,* that he is like his father, of "cold blood" and would have been fated to suffer "male greensickness," had he not "manured" his "lean, sterile, bare" body with sherris-sack. Without it, the Lancasters blood would have remained "cold and settled" and left the liver "white and pale," a sure sign of cowardice. The Lancasters' valor, Falstaff insists, "comes of sherris." "Hereof comes it that Prince Harry is valiant." By drinking "good and good store of fertile sherris," he has managed to become "very hot and valiant" (4.3.92-135). At Shrewsbury, Harry has found the courage to set aside for good the dark legend of the Lancasters' congenital cowardice, but only as the son. He must prove it as a king. This is another reason why the reputation for valor plays a central role in Henry V's decision to go to war with France. Henry's youthful recklessness harmed his reputation. He now listens to the voice of heroism and decides to go to war to undo the damage.

Not only can a war be started in order to build or uphold a vaunted reputation for valor, but an ongoing one can be kept alive to confirm and publicize the valor of the warriors who are engaged in it. In *Troilus and Cressida,* an unworthy cause, such as the Trojans' "mad idolatry" implicit in their resolve to keep Helen, supports the Trojan War. Returning Helen would be reason enough to stop warring, but the reputation for valor among the warriors, and the resolve to protect and enhance that reputation was overpowering. It overrides any other consideration that might put an end to it (2.2.22, 61, 125). Troilus, Hector, Achilles, and Ajax measure themselves and their moves in terms of their respective reputations and disregard military or moral issues. These heroes have complicated personalities, and their deeds and thinking are indecisive or reckless. Some have allowed their reputation to go to their head, undermining the very virtue that has made them famous. Ulysses notes that Ajax and Achilles have become corrupt and lead a frowsy life. He charges them with subverting authority in their camp and jeopardizing the success of the military enterprise. Valiant exploits, Ulysses explains, have spoiled Achilles, "Having his ear full of his airy fame, / Grows dainty of his worth" (1.3.148-149). As a result, he has become unruly and arrogant, ignores the plans of the leadership, and refuses to fight. He has grown indifferent to duty, even charging his own comrades with "cowardice." He lives withdrawn from them and spends his time with Patroclus, lying "upon a lazy bed" (1.3.148-49, 201). Not only does his legendary reputation for valor stand divorced from military endeavors and success at Troy, but it has also undermined his mind. "Possessed he is with greatness," Ulysses judges:

> And speaks not to himself but with a pride
> That quarrels at self-breath. Imagined worth
> Holds in his blood such swollen and hot discourse

That 'twixt his mental and his active parts
Kingdome Achilles in commotion rages
And batters down himself (2.3.173-179).

As for Ajax, an enormous vigor and a cranky temper have combined to yield a martial virtue streaked with lunacy. Ajax has already a reputation for valor when he appears on the scene, and he feels that he no longer needs to exert himself on behalf of the Greek cause. The military requirements of the enterprise leave him indifferent and, shielded by his reputation, he acts like a spoiled brat. "He is valiant as the lion, churlish as the bear, slow as the elephant: a man into whom nature hath so crowded humors that his valor is crushed into folly" (1.2.25-28). His mad valor generates the same arrogance that governs Achilles, and like him, Ajax sabotages the war effort. Given the failure of warriors like Ajax and Achilles, it is no wonder that victory has so far eluded the Greeks. Nevertheless, it is imperative for them to renew the fight to show the world that they have courage. Seven years of fruitless warring have been a real misfortune, Nestor notes. But this is valor's moment, for "valour's show and valour's worth divide / In storms of fortune." When adversity strikes, "the thing of courage" ought to come alive and oppose it. Adversity is the grand occasion for the proud warrior to show real courage, "In the reproof of chance / Lies the true proof of man" (1.3.33-54). The Greek warriors must now perform fresh deeds of valor if their reputation has to mean something.

On the side of the Trojans, there is more enthusiasm for carrying on the war. They believe that valor creates fame and reputation, and their desire for fame is strong. For the Trojans, the war has no rationale other than the "potential for fame in time to come." [27] Troilus makes a point that what renders the war "good" is not the cause, but the opportunity to establish and preserve their reputation for valor. The war "hath our several honours all engaged," and it must go on to preserve and enhance their reputation, he declares. Troilus's stance is opposed by his own brother, Hector, who deems it reasonable to release Helen and end the war. Hector appeals to reason and the appeal infuriates Troilus, who sees reason as the enemy of valor. He rejects the role of his reason in the name of valor. "If we talk of reason," Troilus declares, "let's shut our gates and sleep. Manhood and honor / Should have hare hearts." Reason repudiates "manhood"[28] and robs the warrior of his reputation. The demand for "worth" and "honour" turns reason into "spans and inches so diminutive" that reason must not be heeded. Besides, reason hides "fears" and shows cowardice. The fear of showing fear induces Troilus to turn an acknowledged wrong, the kidnapping of Helen, into the springboard for valiant deeds.[29] "O, theft most base," Troilus proclaims, "that we have stolen what we do fear to keep!" (2.2.27-54, 98-99, 133). Once reason is repudiated, wrongdoing is defended in the name of valor and manhood legitimized as the tool of vice.

Hector attempts to deflect the arguments in favor of fighting for valor's sake and, upset by Cassandra's wailing, he charges Troilus with obeying the impulses of his madly hot temper and blames him again for ignoring the "discourse of reason." In the face of Troilus's insistence on keeping Helen, Hector launches into a panegyric of those "moral laws / Of nature and of nations" that protect the sanctity of marriage, and he concludes that all civilized nations enforce these laws to curb the appetites of those guilty of disjoining wife from husband (2.2. 22, 61-62, 123-125, 179, 190-196). Forgetful of his reputation for valor, Hector at this point emerges as the champion of reason and peace.

But no sooner has he finished with his defense of reason against the demands of valor, then he inexplicably declares to Troilus: "I propend to you / In resolution to keep Helen still." Why does Hector choose "against reason and against himself"?[30] Right after he abandons the cause of reason, he declares that keeping Helen "tis a cause that hath no mean dependence / Upon our joint and several dignities" (2.2.200203). "Dignities," having the meaning of "honor" and "worth," come from "soldiering bravely in war,"[31] that is, from valor. Hector falls in line with the warriors who wage war to protect and enhance their standing as heroes; he now believes that soldiering bravely counts more than reason. Valor must be displayed even though its use requires the lengthening of a senseless war. Hector's earlier arguments in favor of reason and justice are followed by an abrupt and inexplicable reversal that magnifies his need to preserve and reinforce a reputation for valor over justice and reason.

In the end, Hector is unable to stave off the call of heroism. The right and wrong surrounding Helen, vanish, and the display of Trojan valor becomes the incentive to continue the battle. When it is clear that the Trojans intend to keep Helen and keep on fighting, the "fame" gained by valiant deeds, Troilus confidently asserts, will "canonize us." So brave Hector declares his allegiance to Troilus and to a "band of brothers" whose valor sets them apart from their matrix, the "great" but inept Priam: "I am yours," Hector pledges, "you valiant offspring of great Priam." And Helen, who in Diomedes's view is a "contaminated carrion" full of "bawdy veins," becomes the defender of valor, "A spur to valiant and magnanimous deeds" and an inspiration for the "courage" necessary to beat the Greeks (2.2. 209-211, 217-218; 4.1.77, 79). The code of valor among these warriors is unforgiving. Their reputation firmly rules them. When at the end of the play, despite the pleas of his wife, of Cassandra, and of Priam, Hector gets ready for the showdown with the enemy. He reveals to them, "I do stand engaged to many Greeks, / Even in the faith of valor, to appear / This morning to them." (5.3.80-82).

Fighting for one's reputation while ignoring causes and the military implications may satisfy the ego of the warrior, but it can produce lethal results. A concern for reputation may become an obsession. Montaigne warned about violating the limits of reason. Valor has its limits, like the other virtues, and once transgressed, we find ourselves on the path of vice. Unless we know its limits well, we will pass through valor to temerity, obstinacy, and madness."[32]

One who did ignore the limits was Mark Antony. He was one of Rome's great generals, a legend in his lifetime, "the hero" of fantastic exploits.[33] Shakespeare brings to *Antony and Cleopatra* Antony's reputation for martial prowess. But at the end of his career, he embraces irrationality and faces self-destruction. In Egypt, he rejoices in his love affair with Cleopatra and proclaims his indifference for the majesty of the Roman empire, "Let Rome in Tiber melt, and the wide arch / Of the ranged empire fall! Here is my space!" (1.1.34-35). However, he is unable to forget his heroic past and his ties to Rome. He is unable to adapt to a lifestyle wholly different from that of a Roman hero. In Caesar's view, Antony's affair with Cleopatra is a catastrophe. The great general "hath given his empire / Up to a whore." Members of his entourage see that the general's heart, "in the scuffles of great fights hath burst / The buckles on his breast," is now soft and weak. It has become "the bellows and the fan / To cool a gypsy's lust." The result is that "the triple pillar of the world" has been transformed "into a strumpet's fool." Antony himself, caught in the web of Egyptian politics and in Cleopatra's snares, senses that he is compromising his warrior self. At one point, he appears resolved to free himself of the passion that enslaves him in order to preserve his strength and standing: "These strong Egyptian fetters I must break," he tells himself, feeling that if he remained bound to Cleopatra, he would be lost "in dotage" (1.1.1-13, 34-35, 120-121; 3.6.65).

In his first encounter with the Caesar's forces, his dotage shows up when "like a doting mallard," he flees from the enemy and follows Cleopatra's retreating fleet. "I never saw an action of such shame," Scarus in disbelief registers Antony's performance, "Experience, manhood, honour, never before / Did violate so itself" (3.10.22-24). Antony realizes the meaning of his action. "I have fled," he admits afterward, and in doing so, (I have) "instructed cowards / To run and show their shoulders." Worse yet, he knows that his flight and defeat are a deadly blow to his standing as a valiant warrior: "I have offended reputation, / A most unnoble swerving." He is ashamed of himself, knowing that his behavior on the battlefield has dishonored him: "What I have left behind / 'Stroyed in dishonour" (3.11.8-9, 48-54).

Antony at first displaces the cause of his cowardice on Cleopatra. He assails her womanhood as an object of sexual desire, which has captivated his will and reason, and undermined his prowess. "You were half blasted ere I knew you," Antony bluntly tells her. "You have been a boggler ever." He hammers her relentlessly, shifting onto her the cause of his failure as a warrior, "I found you as a morsel cold upon / Dead Caesar's trencher; nay, you were a fragment / Of Gnaeus Pompey's." But she ensnares him again, and he decides to fight.

Before the battle at Actium, he worries anew about his reputation, and resolves to redeem himself. His rage against Cleopatra dissolves, "Where hast thou been, my heart?" (3.13.106, 110, 117-19, 173) Antony asks, surprised by the resurgence of his martial spirit.[34] And he describes his future deeds, predicting a performance on the battlefield that will immortalize both him and Cleopatra, "I will appear in blood, / I and my sword will earn our chronicle." His words elicit from Cleopatra the response he likes to get, "That's my brave lord!" She says. The response strengthens his resolve to display prowess: "I will be treble-sinewed, hearted, breathed, / And fight maliciously." In the rebirth of his courage, Antony has found again his martial identity. His euphoria makes him her ally and strengthens the bond of love, "Since my lord / Is Antony again, I will be Cleopatra." She believes he can be the hero of old, as she sees him go "forth gallantly." Enobarbus catches Antony's words. He thinks his reborn valor is an illusion hatched by an enfeebled mind bent on self-destruction, "A diminution in our captain's brain," Enobarbus speaks aside, "restores his heart: when valor preys on reason, / It eats the sword it fights with" (3.13.175-180, 186-187, 200-205; 4.4.36).

Antony's end is decreed the moment he decides to prove his valor, a decision that reflects the "diminution" of a mind held hostage by his obsession with a virtue he no longer possesses. The impairment of his mind does not prevent him to fight on the battlefield and to think that he deserved victory. Yet his valor was inadequate, and yielded defeat. He gradually convinces himself that Cleopatra is responsible for his loss of valor and depicts her as a "triple-turned whore. She has robbed me of my sword."

> I, that with my sword
> Quartered the world and o'er green Neptune's back
> With ships made cities, condemn myself to lack
> The courage of a woman (4.12.13; 4.14.24, 58-61).

Critics agree that after the second defeat Antony changes. The soldier becomes a lover and the opportunist a meditative poet.[35] He changes because his struggle against the force of a passion that undercut his martial spirit throughout the play has ended. He has yielded to his love of life, and no longer struggles against it. For a while he is at peace. He no longer has to squabble with Cleopatra about military affairs; no longer is his reputation for valor in question; no longer has he to live with the guilt of having "given his empire / Up to a whore," because the whore is now his true love. He abandons himself to the emotion of love, to that same emotion that all along in the play has ruined his reputation as a Roman hero. But in the end, the burden of dishonor becomes too heavy for him to bear.

Around the same time Shakespeare was detailing Antony's resolve to fight valiantly against the dictates of reason, in Spain, a famous personage was living the same drama, allowing valor to prey on reason to the point of schizophrenia. Don Quixote, acting out his impossible dream of heroism, wants to give himself the chance to show valor in battle, a virtue he does not have. His desire is similar to Antony's useless resolve to recapture the heroic temper that he no longer possesses. Cervantes echoes Montaigne's warning: "Valor when it turns to temerity has in it more of madness than of bravery."[36]

Don Quixote decides to put "his valor and the might of his arm" in the service of justice and in wooing "the weaker sex," Dulcinea. His decision to put valor to good use is firm, and he would take up any cause in order to become famous. However, he has no real courage. His thoughts of serving justice, women, and the weak are only pretexts for gaining recognition as a man of valor. The cause is irrelevant; his cause is to show valor. He is not driven to change the world for the better, only to change himself into a hero and be recognized as such. Nonetheless, in his diminished mind his decision to perform courageous deeds turns him into a man of destiny, "I am he for whom are reserved the perils, the great exploits, the valiant deeds."[37] Both Antony and Don Quixote fail in doing deeds of valor, and in securing the love of their lovers and heroic fame for themselves. Their resolve to show valor and gain a reputation is the result of the "diminution" of their minds, and for both of them the consequence is self-destruction.

Don Quixote violates his reason every time he acts with what he thinks is valor. Having unhorsed the gallant Biscayan with a lucky stroke of the sword, Don Quixote asks Sancho if he has "ever seen a more valorous knight than I on all the face of the earth." Sancho's reply serves to feed his master's illusion, "I have never served a more courageous master than your Grace." The knight even invents enemies in order to live the illusion that he is acting with valor. He transmutes windmills into "lawless giants" so he can do battle with them in "righteous warfare." He announces that this is the day when there "shall be displayed the valor of my good right arm," and he proceeds to spear with "much courage and boldness" a herd of sheep, which he imagines to be the evil Ali Fanfaron's soldiers.[38] When the knight becomes dissatisfied with himself and reaches the point where he begins to doubt his prowess, his resolve intensifies. The sharp sound of six falling hammers awakens his courage, convincing him that even though he fought no battle, he displayed "the requisite courage for undertaking and carrying" the adventure through.[39]

The adventure of the lion is the centerpiece of Cervantes's novel.[40] It is where Don Quixote's "unimaginable courage reaches its highest point. As he stands defiantly before the open door of the lion's cage, the lion simply turns around and lays down. For Don Quixote, the encounter is decisive and "leaves nothing more to be said on the score of valor. Some critics are fascinated by the adventure of the lion, precisely because it displays valor for its own sake. "What marvelous courage," the philosopher De Unamuno commented, "what uncompelled valour, this of Don Quixote! Without motive, without object, it was courage pure and simple."[41] The knight himself eventually becomes fed up with his courage—pure, simple, and fake. Stunned and battered as a result of his adventure with Sansón Carrasco, Don Quixote rejects the cornerstone of his valor, madness. Valor stops preying on his reason, and reason resumes a legitimate role in his life. In the end, he restores the value of reason by repudiating all deeds done in the name of valor, indicting the books of chivalry that were his source of inspiration for living the heroic life, which he now recognizes as being full of nonsense and a fraud. Having jettisoned valor, he dies in a manner that does not leave the impression that he would be remembered as a madman.[42] The recovery of reason redeems a life that had been the prisoner of valor thriving on madness.

In the plays of Shakespeare not one protagonist recovers the reason which was lost to the cause of valor. The obsession with valor and his own reputation drive Coriolanus, the legendary Roman general to unreason, and keeps him prisoner till death. Coriolanus enters the first scene fully arrayed with a hero's reputation. Conversely, Mark Antony has fallen in disgrace and desperately wants to recapture a lost reputation through new valorous deeds. Antony needs to prove himself a hero in order to validate his manly existence. Coriolanus, on the other hand, does not have to prove anything. His reputation for valor was well established when he first appears. The poet Auden was right in noting that Coriolanus has two flaws, his passion to excel and his passion for approval.[43] But approval for what and excellence in what? He wants to excel on the battlefield as a valiant warrior, and he craves approval of his heroic performance from the plebians. He succeeds in realizing the first wish, but he fails in the second. For Don Quixote, it was a new game, and capturing fame and reputation takes up most of the narrative. But both Antony and Don Quixote are driven to validate their lives by showing martial virtue.

Both history and literary criticism are unanimous in defining Coriolanus as an exceptionally heroic warrior. He "is clearly and consciously made by Shakespeare to appear heroic," one critic notes; he "is brave."[44] His "valour," which "exceeds all tales of it," is "extraordinary" and "incredible," and marks him out as a singular Roman.[45] It is the basis of the reader's "esteem," an esteem that grows "as his prowess and manliness have met all tests."[46]

Rome's ethos explains to an extent his enormous reputation. "Valiantness was honoured in Rome" above all other virtues, and was considered the virtue par excellence, Plutarch explained.[47] In Rome, valor was "not only a cult, but also a condition of survival," and Coriolanus cultivated martial virtue so intensely that he lived "to give continual fresh instances of his prowess."[48] Cominius, the Roman general, confirms the exceptional place held by valor in both Rome and in Coriolanus's life, "It is held," he declaims on the Capitol, "that valour is the chief virtue and / Most dignifies the haver." Coriolanus' virtue has rewarded him with "good success" on the battlefield, inflating his reputation and his arrogance. He even "disdains the shadow / Which he treads on at noon." His valor is so eminent that he "cannot in the world / Be singly counterpoised" (1.1. 260; 2.2.99-100). He battled Aufidius five times and, as the Volscian himself admits, "so often has thou beat me" that "my valor's / Poisoned." Coriolanus perceives Aufidius, not just as a rival, but as a competitor in the exercise of valor. He is a warrior whom Coriolanus needs to challenge on the battlefield to prove his own superiority. "Were I anything but what I am, / I would wish me only he," Coriolanus confesses his bias for the Volscian. For a warrior like Coriolanus, wars are made, not for political ends, but to afford heroes like himself the occasion to show their valor and to grow in public standing. He stresses his preference for fighting Aufidius, "To make / Only my wars with him. He is a lion / That I am proud to hunt" (1.10.7-8, 257-258, 261-264). More than Rome's enemy, Aufidius is the measuring stick for him to assess his own prowess.

He is angry toward his fellow citizens who refuse to grant him the recognition his reputation deserves, namely, a seat in the Senate. His status on the battlefield entitles him to the consulship, but the plebians have grievances against the ruling classes, and he is resented by association. The Senators would not release enough corn to feed the people, and Coriolanus frames the crisis that the lack of corn has generated in Rome in the context of his obsession for valor. "Where there is no valour, there can be no desert—no right to eat, let alone to govern." Unfortunately, he believes that his reputation for valor gives him the right to discard the rules of the political game in Rome. He refuses to show his wounds in public to the plebians, "those measles," he declares before Cominius, Agrippa, and the other senators, "I have shed my blood, / Not fearing outward force," he tells them. It is enough.

The plebians' lack of martial valor is to Coriolanus such an ugly sin that they must be punished, not redeemed. The plebians were cowards on the battlefield and forfeited their right to food, "Being i'th'war, / Their mutinies and revolts, wherein they show'd / Most valour, spoke not for them (3.1.161-163). His only political notion, if such it can be called, is that if you refuse to fight on the battlefield, you are a coward, and you have no right to live in the Roman commonwealth. Brutus is struck by Coriolanus's judgment: "You speak of the people / As if you were a god to punish" (3.1.100-106). Coriolanus is indeed the god of heroism, and he intends to punish Rome and her people according to the heroic code. Brutus traces the root of the widespread aversion for Coriolanus precisely to his heroism and arrogance, "The present wars devour him! He is grown / Too proud to be so valiant," (1.1.7-8, 27-28, 297-298).

It is not Coriolanus's physical or moral being that have been devoured by war; it is his reason and his judgment. To the Roman people, his overweening pride demeans any good that his martial virtue might bring to the commonwealth. The Romans are uncomfortable with this warrior. His reputation feeds an extraordinary disdain for the plebians, a disdain that soon turns into open hostility.

The conflict between the plebeians and Coriolanus plays a central role in the tragedy. The cause has more to do with an irrational emphasis on martial valor over the essential requirements of the ordinary people's life, than with some kind of "psychological function," such as an automatic opposition to what others stand for,[49] or with an arcane "conception and moral value of history."[50]

Obsession with valor implies disdain for cowardice, and Coriolanus's hatred of cowardice runs deep. When he first appears on the scene, he speaks to express it, reviling the plebians as curs and weaklings, fearful in war and arrogant in peace. In war they are bold in mutiny, and in peace brave in opposing the Senate's authority. In their mutiny and opposition, "your valor puts well forth," Coriolanus tells the people (1.1.231-232, 287-288). Their cowardice is confirmed in his mind when at Corioli, the Romans are repulsed by the Volsces. He brands them "shames of Rome," accusing them of having run "from slaves that apes would beat." What can I say, he asks Menenius Agrippa who is urging him to go through with the formalities for appointment to the consulship, that I was wounded fighting valiantly while "some certain of your brethren roared and ran / from the noise of our own drums"? (1.4.42-47; 2.3.53-55). The hero has no choice but to refuse to show his wounds to cowards. He cannot tolerate a people incapable or unwilling to live by the heroic code. He insults them at the unfinished ceremony for his appointment to the consulship when he refuses to show his twenty-seven wounds, and declares that his "own desert," his fame as a warrior, not the protocol that brought him to the Forum, even though Agrippa reminds him that even the worthiest men in Rome have displayed their war wounds to get appointed to political office. The real reason why he refuses to show his wounds is that he cannot comply with something that is desired by a people he despises on account of their cowardice. He believes that his fame as a valiant warrior alone gives him the right to public office, "Better it is to die, better to starve, /Than crave the hire which first we deserve" (2.3.50, 70, 72, 116-117). If pride in his exceptional valor keeps Coriolanus from complying with the protocol for appointment to the Senate, the destruction of his pride, which means the destruction of his reputation, will change his mind. This is his mother's calculation. When she urges him to show his wounds, she takes from him any merit for being valiant and lowers his pride. Volumnia has great influence on her son precisely because she mothered his valor. From childhood, she destined him for a life of fighting and heroism, turning the child into a precocious warrior. "To a cruel war I sent him," Volumnia says proudly of her son's early trial, "from whence he returned his brows bound with oak," proving "himself a man" (1.3.2-18). Because he was indebted to her, he performed his deeds of valor "to please his mother." When she bluntly tells him: "Thy valiantness was mine, thou suck'est it from me" (1.1.35-38; 3.2.155), she strips him of his martial virtue, which is the basis of his reputation and the source of his arrogance and hostility for the plebeians. When this occurs, Coriolanus regains for a brief time the use of his reason. But the loss of his reputation that comes with the knowledge that his mother is the source of his valor unhinges him.

"There is a world elsewhere" (3.3.165), Coriolanus says on leaving Rome when he is accused of harboring tyrannical designs, a world where he can be his old valiant self. In Antium he tells Aufidius that he defected because his heroism was ignored:

> The painful service,
> The extreme dangers, and the drops of blood
> Shed for my thankless country, are requited
> But with that surname (4.5.75-78).

Rome's enemies would give him the opportunity to fight and be recognized as a hero. Finally free of his mother's prop, Coriolanus tells Aufidius that he will fight and "stand / As if a man were author of himself / And knew no other kin" (5.3.3739).

But in the end, Volumnia destroys the hero she created by inducing him to hold in check the rage he is ready to unleash on Rome. When, under the Volscian banner, he wavers in his resolve to attack, Aufidius sneers, "Thou boy of tears" (5.6.118).

What hurts Coriolanus most is the impugning of his "manhood," his "heroic virtus." He resents "boy" more than "traitor."[51] Aufidius has degraded Coriolanus from hero to wimp, an insult that destroys his very self. His reputation gone; Coriolanus has nothing left to live for. His murder by Volscian conspirators, "a deed whereat valor will weep" (5.6.157), is premeditated and executed in such a way as to deny him the possibility of displaying in this last violent event, the virtue that gave him his enormous reputation and turned him into a legend.

VIOLENCE

Valor is inextricably tied to the use of violence, and heroes have often justified its use while pursuing ends that cast on valor itself a dark cloud. The intensity of violence stands out in those works and events where the religious spirit drives the warriors to fight and to kill. Religious faith can justify all kinds of atrocities, but they are not called atrocities; they are called valiant deeds. In the *Song of Roland*, the protagonist loses the battle but triumphs as a valiant warrior on account of his ability to shed an enormous amount of enemy blood. Roland rides through the battlefield and bears all over himself the signs of valor:

> Would you had seen him, dead man on dead man piling,
> Seen the bright blood about the pathway lying!
> Bloody his hauberk and both his arms with fighting,
> His good horse bloody from crest to withers likewise (1.105).

Midway through the battle "by scores and thousands lie Paymin corpses spread." Thus, Archbishop Turpin judges the French to "have fought with valour and success." The archbishop witnesses and admires Christian courage, "Right valiant are our men, the like of these hath no lord under Heaven" (1.111).[52]

Jerusalem Delivered (1575) by Tasso offers a striking spectacle of battlefield violence eulogized as valor. The shedding of Pagan blood, artistically refined, emotionally charged, and restated throughout the poem, makes bloodshed the highest value of the whole Christian enterprise and at once a distinctive sign of the Crusaders' valor. After a month's siege, the Crusaders stormed the walls of Jerusalem, and on the morning of July 15, 1099, they broke into the city. They killed all they met, men, women, and children, and continued the slaughter throughout the afternoon and the evening.[53] Led by Godfrey of Boulogne, the Crusaders in the last battle renew the assault on the left wing of the enemy force. Each warrior "comes dyed with the enemy's blood, each adorned with the spoils of triumph." When there is no one left to kill, Godfrey and his entourage go to the Church of the Holy Sepulcher where they pay homage to God and worship him. "Not yet having laid aside his bloody mantle, the commander in chief goes to the temple with the others, and there hangs up his arms. He devoutly adores the great Sepulcher and discharges his vow," showing that he used well the martial valor that his God had granted him. It was indeed God himself who had willed the war and who had given the Crusaders the means to win it. "Not hope of praise, nor thirst of worldly good, / Enticed us to follow this emprise," Godfrey reveals to the Saracen emissaries Aletes and Argantes as they met early at Emmaus:

> Our courage, hence our hope, our valor springs,
> Not from the trust we have in shield or spear;
> Not from the succors France or Grecia brings.

Courage is a gift of God, and it will never let the Crusaders down; it springs from "his [God's] grace, his mercy, and his powerful hand."[54] Religious faith is not the only motive that justifies violence as valor.

In Italy, the burning faith stoked by the Christian religion enabled Tasso to call the Crusaders' savage killing at Jerusalem valor. In England it was the national spirit and the imperialistic drive that sent her soldiers into the battlefield to be valiant and kill. England placed her military virtues at the service of overseas expansion and empire building. Valor was a vital virtue. To Francis Bacon, who regarded war as the key to national power and glory, courage was more valuable than weapons and horses. Although a people may have sufficient tools of war but were "of weak courage," their country would be nothing but "a sheep in a lion's skin." To be a real lion, England needed "good and valiant" soldiers. To foster bravery, it was necessary to boost the morale of the people, the army's source of manpower. To this end, Bacon counseled, the noblemen should be kept from oppressing the people, and their tax burden should be lightened. The lighter the taxes the more "valiant and martial" the people would be. He endorsed the revival of some Roman customs— building trophies and monuments for the war dead, honoring soldiers and generals in victory—to "inflame all men's courage."[55]

As a political essayist and philosopher, Bacon voiced views held by many influential Englishmen about the value of martial valor. Clergymen promoted it not only as a military virtue, but as a moral and political asset. "All people of understanding," one of them wrote, despise a coward and "respect a man of valor." Because valor elicits the respect of the citizenry, public offices should go to "men of courage."[56] Other military writers used religious arguments to praise valor and justify war. When the Lord intends to make a people and a nation famous, Geoffrey Gates wrote, he "stirreth them up to high courage, and maketh their mindes and bodyes apt to the warre."[57] Thomas More alone held an opposite view. Not only did he imagine the citizens of Utopia celebrating bloodless victories as singular triumphs; he imagined them boasting "of having acted with valor and heroism whenever their victory [was] such as no animal except man could have won, that is, by strength of intellect." [58]More' s view was utopia and had no place in contemporary life, whereas the view of intellectuals and clergymen remained close to historical reality.

Shakespeare's imagination shares none of the enthusiasm for martial valor that his contemporaries' glowing eulogies reveal. In some of his dramas, valor plays a relevant but often sinister role, which distorts moral and civic values. This role of violence under the guise of valor is represented in *Henry V* as an expression of the royal will.

The terrifying speech about the cruelties of war that the king delivers before the walls of the besieged city of Harfleur in France intends to scare the inhabitants into submission. Shakespeare shows, a critic notes, an instinctive revulsion for bloodshed in his works dealing with the military and war,[59] but King Henry V on the battlefield shows a different sensibility. At Harfleur the king appeals to his soldiers' capacity for evildoing in an attempt to arouse their fighting spirit. He orders his soldiers to act with the ferocity of animals and to become brutes, "men of grosser blood," once the attack is unleashed on Harfleur:

> Then imitate the action of the tiger:
> Stiffen the sinews, summon up the blood,
> Disguise fair nature with hard favored rage;
> Then lend the eye a terrible aspect (3.1.7-10).

Two scenes later, Henry reveals to the inhabitants of Harfleur and their governor the plan he has made for his soldiers to bring about a bloody mass slaughter:

> And the gates of mercy shall be all shut up,
> And the fleshed soldier, rough and hard of heart,
> In liberty of bloody hand shall range
> With conscience wide as hell, mowing like grass
> Your fresh fair virgins and your flowering infants (3.3.10-14).

Henry regards his troops as evildoers and expects them to act as such. These "valiant soldiers" reveal themselves before the walls of Harfleur to be a gang of "ruffians and rapists."[60] And the king gladly takes responsibility for the violence they are to mete out:

> What is it then to me if impious war
> Arrayed in flames like to the prince of fiends,
> Do with his smirched complexion all fell feats
> Enlinkened to waste and desolation? (3.3.15-18)

These soldiers belong to the same army that fights at Agincourt. Many of them were tainted with crimes even before they enlisted. Their deeds on the battlefield will be a rough replica of their deeds in civil life. Knowing his men, the king felt that he could appeal to their baser instincts and get the results he expected, turning them into killers and heroes.

On the night before the battle at Agincourt the king, disguised as Thomas Erpingham, roams around the English camp. He may be "ripe for exploits and mighty enterprises" (1.2.125), but he is worried about the readiness of his troops and their courage in the face of the coming battle. He wants to assess firsthand their morale and to encourage them.[61] One of the soldiers he meets, Bates, says that he loathes the approach of the day because he and his comrade Williams fear that it will be their last one. The disguised Henry replies that the king, too, may be afraid, but that he shows courage in keeping his fears to himself to avoid disheartening his army. To Bates "outward courage" is false courage if there is fear hiding in his heart. As for himself, he would rather be "in the Thames up to the neck" than on French soil waiting for the morning to go to battle (4.1.96-121).

The soldiers are unprepared to fight with valor and are "frightened about dying."[62] Henry tries to instill courage in them and tells them they are fighting a good war, "his [Henry] cause being just and his quarrel honourable" (4.1.122-132). The good cause argument, however, fails to breathe courage in the soldiers. Williams supposes instead that the cause "be not good" and concludes that death will be grim and the king's responsibility heavy, for "blood" alone will be the soldiers' "argument." The king will have a heavy reckoning to make for leading his men to their death in a war without a just cause. Williams's reply irks Henry, and he sets forth a long counter argument intended to absolve himself from any responsibility for the eventual death and wounding of his soldiers and, implicitly, to spur them to fight with valor (4.1.138-160).

They must fight with courage, the king bluntly tells them, to make up for the crimes they committed in civil life. Their valor will spring from their lawlessness in civil life. Many of them had indeed joined the army to avoid punishment for acts of violence, including murder,[63] and their sacrifice on the battlefield of Agincourt will be their punishment. Some "gored the gentle bosom of peace with pillage and robbery," others have on their conscience "the guilt of premeditated and contrived murder." They have escaped the punishment of the law, the king notes, but will not escape God's wrath. They "have no wings to fly from God. War is his beadle; war is his vengeance" (4.1.165-181). Knowing that the men he leads are accustomed to practice violence in civilian life, Henry prods them to reenact on the battlefield the violent deeds they have done in civil life. By urging them to bring to bear their capacity for evildoing on the enemy, Henry is asking them to turn the vices of peace into the virtues of war.[64] Thus, unlawful violence in private life will be transmuted into valor on the battlefield. Their sacrifice on the battlefield will be both an act of courage and an act of redemption. Henry's arguments can be regarded as part and parcel of that royal hypocrisy, ruthlessness and bad faith, that some critics have recognized in the play.[65]

The English troops matched their king's expectations. The next day at Agincourt they killed many Frenchmen, among them the prisoners of war, and won the battle. In the process they turned the battlefield into "a story of slaughter-yard behavior and outright atrocity."[66] The story must have pleased Henry, for the bloodshed showed that his men fought the way he wanted, with a valor that enabled them to win.

At Agincourt Henry shed no blood; he came through without a scratch.[67] He was supposed to imitate the valor of his ancestors, the very reason he went to war, but he failed. The battle was conspicuous for the absence of the king.[68] Neither he nor his nobles showed any valor. Just before the Earl of Salisbury and the dukes of Exeter and Bedford ride into battle, they exchange words whose emptiness reduces valor to empty rhetoric. And this is all Shakespeare does with aristocratic valor in the play—writing about it inanely without showing it:

> Bedford: Farewell, good Salisbury, and good luck go with thee!
> Exeter: Farewell, kind lord. Fight valiantly today;
> And yet I do thee wrong to mind thee of it,
> For thou art framed of the firm truth of valor.
> Bedford: He is as full of valor as of kindness,
> Princely in both (4.3.13-18).

The heroes of Agincourt are the soldiers who as civilians had "gored the gentle bosom of peace with pillage and robbery." As a result, the St. Crispin declamation, which meant to underscore the heroic deeds of an aristocratic "band of brothers" on the battlefield, is highly misleading.

Henry's penchant for less than orthodox methods of warfare and for extravagant deeds of violence under the guise of valor is shown by the plan he had formulated for his soldiers in battle and in its aftermath. To the French herald Montjoy, who had come to the English camp to plead for peace just before Agincourt, Henry conjures up a uniquely ghoulish image in Shakespeare's theatre—that of putrefying English corpses as valor in action. The English soldiers, Henry tells Montjoy, will fight and show valor, twice. First, they will die and turn themselves into "valiant bones." Secondly, the "abounding valor in our English" will show again through their corpses' power to hurt the French by the pestilent scent of putrefaction,

> And draw their honors reeking up to heaven, Leaving their earthly parts to choke your clime, The smell thereof shall breed a plague in France (4.3.111-114).

Samuel Johnson noted that this low-grade mixture of valor and violence is an image that "does no great honor to the poet."[69] But it is really to Henry V that the image does no great honor.

Violence had ramification outside the military field. When exercised under the guise of valor, it was decreed a crime. "There are so many incivilities mingled with our manhood," Thomas Milles lamented the violence masked as valor that took place in civilian life at the beginning of the seventeenth century, "that they sympathize rather with wild Goats, or the heat of Bulles, than with the real excellencie of humaine nature, which being the Image of Divinitie, figures into us another kinde of strength and courage that which is proper to brute Beasts only."[70] The practice of violence disguised as valor struck the historical imagination of Walter Raleigh. "Valor" is nothing more than the "hardiness of thieves, ruffians, and mastiff dogs," unless it serves "good things" and "lawful enterprises." He judged Alexander the Great "as valiant as any man." However, his valor was of the same brand as that of "troublers of the world" in general, who caused "great destruction and effusion of blood."[71] Thomas Hobbes assigned to martial valor no noble feature and called it naked violence. As such, it posed a distinct peril to the welfare of the commonwealth, "Courage, (by which I mean the contempt of wounds and violent death)" predisposes men to do deeds that undermine the peace of the community.[72]

Alcibiades's unnamed friend in *Timon of Athens*, is one of those troublers of the world capable of subverting the peace of a community. Alcibiades appears before the Athenian senate to plead for the life of his friend, who is responsible for using his prowess to kill a civilian. At the beginning of the pleading session, Alcibiades casts on the accused criminal the mantle of valor. He tells the senators that, though he killed in hot blood, he did it "with a noble fury and fair spirit" and without any "cowardice" (3.5.11-18), a manner that should mitigate the crime. Alcibiades tries to pass the crime off as a sign of his friend's "great courage"[73] and to place him above the law. His defense rests on his friend's reputation for valor earned on the battlefield, which should exempt him from prosecution, especially because he committed the murder to defend that reputation, "Seeing his reputation touched to death," Alcibiades notes, "he did oppose his foe" (3.5.19-20). One of the senators perceives that Alcibiades is "striving to make an ugly deed look fair" by setting "quarrelling / Upon the head of valor," that is, justifying crime by valor.[74] The senator then strips valor of any virtue, defines it as violence, and condemns it. "Is valor misbegot," he says of the deed of the indicted soldier, "and came into the world / When sects and factions were newly born." He stresses the virtue of forbearance, "He is truly valiant that can wisely suffer / The worst that man can breathe," but "to revenge is no valour" (3.5.25-40). The senator's reply stuns Alcibiades, a man of arms himself, who looks on valor as the highest value. The senator's words undercut the very spring of bravery as Alcibiades conceives it. He feels compelled to defend the highest virtue of his profession by stressing the evil of restraint and peace: "Why," he asks in disbelief,

> Do fond men expose themselves to battle,
> And not endure all threats? Sleep upon it,
> And let the foes quietly cut their throat
> Without repugnancy? If there be
> Such valour in the bearing, what make we Abroad?
> Why then women are more valiant
> That stay at home (3.5.43-49).

Alcibiades's defense of valor's measure falls on deaf ears, but he does not desist from harping on it. He cites the defendant's intrepidity under fire in a recent war to try to elicit the senators' admiration and leniency, "How full of valour did he bear himself / In the last conflict and made plenteous wounds!" Another senator opines that the soldier's reputation cannot be used as a defense, because this very reputation for valor has led him to live like an outlaw. That senator redefines valor as brutal violence, "He is a sworn rioter; he has a sin / That often drowns him and takes his valour prisoner." His sin is a kind of "beastly fury" that has led him "to commit outrages / And cherish factions" (3.5.69-74). Not even the pledge by the defendant to die fighting courageously on the battlefield appeases the senators. "Let the war receive" his life "in valiant gore" (3.5.66-67, 85), Alcibiades vainly pleads. The senators reject the argument that future valor can redeem crime; they want the defendant executed.

Shakespeare composed *Timon of Athens* at about the same time as *Coriolanus*. In *Timon of Athens*, he articulated the same concept that he represented in *Coriolanus*—the influence of a soldier's battlefield reputation on his behavior in civil society. Although Coriolanus committed no murder, his warrior pride troubled the Roman community a great deal.

With Coriolanus, martial courage takes on the exclusive face of violence. Growing up, his mother did her best to educate her son to the ideal and practice of violence. She fancies his performance on the battlefield against the Volsces, and proudly describes it to her daughter-in-law:

> His bloody brow
> With his mailed hand then wiping, forth he goes
> Like to a harvestman that's tasked to mow
> Or all, or lose his hire (1.3.34-37)

Having cultivated assiduously her son's violent temper, she accordingly conceives his martial acts as naked violence. "Methinks I hear hither your husband's drum," she tells Virgilia, who fears for her husband's life, "See him pluck Aufidius down by the hair." By Volumnia's standard, Coriolanus's wife is a coward, but she reassures her, "He'll beat Aufidius's head below his knee / And tread upon his neck." Virgilia has nothing to do with her mother-in-law's ghoulish fantasies, and cringes, "His bloody brow? O Jupiter, no blood!" (1.3.29-30, 46-47). Volumnia counteracts this unwarlike utterance by extolling what horrifies Virgilia—the virtue of bloodshed and the fruit it bears:

> Away, you fool! It [blood] more becomes a man
> Than gilt his trophy. The breasts of Hecuba,
> When she did suckle Hector, looked not lovelier
> Than Hector's forehead when it spit forth blood
> At Grecian sword, contemning (1.3.38-43).

Sanctified by motherly approval and admired by friends and foes as the means of success in war, violence is raised to the virtue of valor and becomes Coriolanus's ruling principle. He has grown up, and lives like those soldiers who "nothing do but meditate on blood" (*Henry V*, 5.2.61-62).

Coriolanus fights for Rome but he ignores the politics and the war aims of his country. For him war is a sport and a personal challenge, and above all, it fulfills his highest purpose—living the heroic life. Of him can be said what Shakespeare wrote about another warrior, he "is trule dedicate to war"[75] for its own sake. The aristocracy, too, is aware of his limitations as a Roman citizen. "Worthy man!" is all that Menenius Agrippa says about Coriolanus's performance against the Volsces, underscoring in low key his valor but ignoring the benefits it might have brought to the commonwealth. On his part, Cominius frankly defines Coriolanus's heroism as an end to itself. He "rewards his deeds with doing them." Titus Lartius, another Roman general, evaluates Coriolanus's performance at Corioles, where he was a warrior "not fierce and terrible / only in strokes," but also capable of making the "enemy shake, as if the world / Were feverous and did tremble" (1.4.57-61; 2.2.127). Ruled by a "fundamental brutality," his natural element is "carnage."[76] Coriolanus has turned the politics of the Roman state into the politics of violence, "cracking ten thousand curbs" (1.1.7073). The killer instinct is so deeply entrenched in him that he brags about it even at the least opportune moment of his career when he switches over to Aufidius's side. "A goodly city is this Antium," Coriolanus broods smugly as he enters that "world elsewhere" after his break with Rome:

'Tis I that made thy widows: many an heir
Of these fair edifices fore my wars
Have I heard groan and drop (4.4.1-4).

Following on the path of Shakespeare's tragedies, Macbeth's tragedy, one critic notes, "is the tragedy of courage,"[77] when martial virtue leads its owner to criminal violence in civilian life. The courage that in battle distinguished the hero of the play is carried over into civil society and used as a virtue to commit a crime. Macbeth uses the reputation that has made him renowned in battle and admired by others to rationalize a murder and seizure of the crown. The King himself, destined to be a future victim of Macbeth's perverted courage, shows special admiration for Macbeth's valor in battle.

The decision to kill is apparently taken as a result of Lady Macbeth's urging. Some "weaknesses" keep Macbeth from reaching out boldly for the crown. Ambition spurs him, but the "milk of human kindness" (1.5.17) keeps him from evildoing. He alone cannot overcome his weaknesses. He lacks the "illness" needed to achieve the "ornament of life." Lady Macbeth instills in him the "illness" he needs to pursue the kingship with success. She sets out to "chastise with the valour of her tongue" his apathy, prefiguring the act that her verbal skill will awaken in him. When the time to kill approaches, Macbeth tries to dismiss the project with a curt "we will proceed no further in this business" (1.5.20; 7.34). But Lady Macbeth nails him with the argument that sparks the necessary "illness". She imposes her "notion of manhood as morally blind courage" on her husband and, as one critic notes, succeeds "in separating valor from justice."[78] But there is no separation. On the contrary, for the Macbeth couple, valor becomes justice as soon as the murder of Duncan is identified as an advantageous political move. Lady Macbeth appeals to the valor of her husband at the same time that she flashes before his eyes the specter of cowardice—the last thing in the world that a man of Macbeth's reputation would want to be tainted by.

She whips up his pride in valor, and removes the apathy and doubt that at the last moment, were holding him back:

> Art thou afeard
> To be the same in thine own act and valour
> As thou art in desire? Wouldst thou have that
> Which thou esteem'st the ornament of life,
> And live a coward in thine own esteem...? (1.7.43-47)

Lady Macbeth makes it clear to her husband that refusal to murder Duncan amounts to cowardice, and the "reproach of cowardice," Johnson noted in his discussion of the tragedy, "cannot be borne by any man from a woman, without great impatience."[79] Given Macbeth's status as a man of exceptional valor, he is less likely than any other man to bear his wife's taunt. His valor challenged, he responds with a reply which is both defensive and aggressive, confirming himself as a man of valor, "I dare do all that may become a man; / Who dares do more is none." Lady Macbeth appeals again to his manhood, "Be so much more the man." Her final appeal is decisive. It overcomes his last flicker of hesitation, "But screw your courage to the sticking-place," she goads him, "and we'll not fail" (1.7.47-48, 51, 70-71). In the end, she persuades her husband to commit the murder by urging on him "the excellence and dignity of courage."[80] Being a virtue, and one that has made Macbeth's reputation, courage justifies vice in Macbeth's imagination. Faith in his martial virtue propels him toward murder and kingship. The symbolic dagger dripping blood, the tool of valor and the maker of his reputation, appears to him in a dreamy vision and strengthens his resolve. "Thou marshall'st me the way that I was going," he acknowledges, "and such an instrument I was to use." The tool of valor in his hands makes him acutely aware of time wasted and delay; the urge to proceed seizes him, "While I threat, he lives, / Words to the heat of deeds too cold breath gives." Finally, the mere sound of a bell "invites" Macbeth into Duncan's room to do the deed (2.1.54-55, 7374). But Lady Macbeth, who has none of her husband's virtue, had to "unsex" herself in order to summon "the direst cruelty" and advocate murder (1.5.42-44).

What predisposes Macbeth to go along with his wife's incitement to commit murder is the knowledge that his valor entitles him to do what ordinary men refrain from doing. The prodding by his wife alone was probably inadequate to bring him to murder the King. Instead, the great value that Macbeth himself placed on valor is decisive in turning him into an assassin. His crime is so enormous, some critics who tried to figure out its cause argue, that its source is hard to identify. [81]On the contrary, it can be tied to his valiant performance on the battlefield and to his reputation as a hero. In the battle against the forces of Donwald, Macbeth displayed extraordinary valor, bathing in reeking wounds, making "strange images" of death, engaging his sword in "bloody execution" and finally cutting open the body of the rebel. The emphasis on the carnage, one critic suggests, prepares our minds for Macbeth's "later deeds of blood." The killing done on the battlefield will be carried on in the royal palace.[82] The link between the two spheres of action, the battlefield and political society, is established by the soldier's courage which, proven on the battlefield and universally recognized, has gained for him a sort of right to live and operate on a level other than the strictly military one. The prestige of valor has erased the difference between lawful and criminal killing, legitimating the latter.

On account of his military valor Macbeth was bound to be held in high esteem. The chosen darling of valor has become so proud as a result of his performance in the battle against the forces of Donwald, and Duncan's praise of it, that he overvalues the quality that enabled him to win. The King, on learning that "brave Macbeth" has fought "like valour's minion," is carried away in admiration, "O valiant cousin, worthy gentleman! Macbeth "is full so valiant," he tells Banquo (1.2.21, 26, 37-42, 63; 1.3.96). When he names him Thane of Cawdor, his extraordinary reputation for valor is established in the public eye. It is easy to imagine Macbeth seduced into feeling "that valor is the chiefest virtue and / most dignifies the haver."

Scottish society fostered valor and inflated its value. No one in the play talks about martial virtue serving some social or political purpose, such as the common good, the security of the state, or freedom. Almost everyone in the play is mesmerized by Macbeth's performance on the battlefield and sees him strictly as an exceptional man of arms. Since the Crown rewarded successful acts of violence in war, not as political or moral victories, Macbeth's self-esteem is on a par with his reputation as a superior practitioner of violence. He thus comes to eat on what Banquo enigmatically styles "the insane root / That takes the reason prisoner" (1.3.87-88). The "insane root"[83] has something to do with the pride derived from the successful practice of violence, rewarded and legitimized as martial virtue. It is the same reputation for valor that led Antony and Coriolanus, and now leads Macbeth, to eat up "the sword it fights with." The insane root is the headiness of exceptional heroism which, born out of victory, the hero has come to cherish and wants to renew. The seizure of the crown accomplished by bloodshed in the name of valor is the first step on a path the hero must walk to its bitter end. "I am in blood / Stepped in so far that, should I wade no more, / Returning were as tedious as go o'er," Macbeth reflects (3.4.168-170). These words are spoken in the third act, but they can also describe Macbeth's mind-set emerging from his earlier victory over the rebel Donwald.

Like the reports from the field and the King's admiration, Macbeth's encounter with the Weird Sisters builds up his trust in the value of martial valor. Why would one of the witches prophesize that Macbeth would be king? The prophecy must be seen as grounded on his performance on the battlefield. It was uttered soon after Macbeth had left the battlefield, and most certainly was based on his performance. He hears it while the memory is fresh in his mind and in those of the audience. The witch could not have made it unless Macbeth had wanted to fulfill it. The prowess he showed in war has to be regarded the desire that moved the witches to prophesy.[84] Indeed, he felt himself worthy of the Crown. The prophecy fixes Macbeth's reputation for valor and links it to the King's murder that will be committed in valor's name. "Two truths are told," Macbeth says, alluding both to the honor bestowed on him by Duncan and to the witches' prophecy, "as happy prologues to the swelling act / Of the imperial theme" (1.3.140-142).

Neither guilt nor failure disjoins Macbeth from his belief in the value of valor and in his right to use it without discrimination. He remains wedded to the quality that turned him into an exceptional criminal and "dies a courageous soldier."[85] Even though he learned that Macduff "was from his mother's womb / Untimely ripped," and that he has the edge in their duel, Macbeth puts up a spirited fight. He summons valor by damning cowardice, "Before my body / I throw my warlike shield: Lay on," he tells Macduff, "and damned be him that first cries 'Hold, enough!'" (5.8.37-39).

Prince Hamlet could achieve the ultimate end of his troubled life—if he were able to avenge his father's death. Taking revenge is imperative. Its legitimacy is supported by trustworthy evidence—the testimony of the Ghost, and the Ghost's explicit request to take revenge on the reigning king. However, neither the injunction, which Hamlet accepts, nor the demand for justice, which he feels strongly, can inspire valor in him. In one of three soliloquies he recognizes himself to be "three parts coward:"

> Now whether it be
> Bestial oblivion, or some craven scruple
> Of thinking too precisely on the event –
> A thought which, quartered, hath one part wisdom
> And ever three parts coward—I do not know
> Why yet I live to say this thing is to do,
> Sith I have cause, and will, and strength, and means
> To do't (4.4.39-46).

His reluctance, or inability, to summon valor and to kill seems odd, for other protagonists of Shakespeare's plays use valor for reasons less valid than Hamlet's. He will eventually kill Claudius, but the killing will not be the outcome of Hamlet's decision to make him pay for his crime. In the end he acts suddenly and impulsively, without thinking, and ends up killing Claudius almost accidentally. The deed has nothing to do with a conscious act to execute revenge. Nor does it have anything to do with courage in the service of justice.

Hamlet's various reasons for delaying to act "are evidently not the true reasons," a critic notes.[86] Then what can be the real reasons? One of them is because he lacks valor, and his mission is dependent on it. In the most famous of the soliloquies Hamlet explores the extent and meaning of his cowardice by defining valor. "To be, or not to be" signifies not simply to live or to die. "To be" means to live like a man of courage, and courage consists in taking up "arms against a sea of troubles / And by opposing, end them." It means that if you are brave, you are the master of your life. "Not to be" means yielding to "the slings and arrows of outrageous fortune"; it means to live like a coward, and that is a living death. "To be" articulates itself best in standing up to the oppressor's wrong; "not to be" in yielding to it (3.1.57-58, 71). What is really in Hamlet's mind is that "to be" coincides with killing Claudius, and "not to be" with the failure to do so. Had Hamlet deliberately acted with courage and carried out the revenge, he would have shown himself and the reader "to be," a man of valor—a seventeenth century hero, worthy of his inheritance as the future king of Denmark.

But he is a coward, and he recognizes himself as such. He had rather sleep or die to end the pain that living in a world out of joint causes him. Yet, even "The sleep of death," he warns …must give us pause… for "what dreams may come." Killing Claudius would be a deed of "great pitch and moment," but "the dread of something after death" stifles the courage necessary to undertake such enterprises in this world, since they entail risking life. The fear of death, spelled out in the soliloquy with unusual resonance, magnifies Hamlet's inaction. A good Christian, Hamlet is worried about whether he will be able to go before God clean of all sins, or whether he will be burdened by them and damned to hell. This is the uncertainty that "makes calamity of so long life." This fear cuts down manhood, inducing men to put up with the evils of this world. And this is cowardice, "Conscience does make cowards of us all" (3.1.66-86).

To go a little further into Hamlet's state of mind, the handling of Yorick's skull in the graveyard scene adds another dimension to his lack of action. The skull signifies death, a critic notes, in all its ramifications, and this literal fact of bodily disintegration increases his general melancholy. "Did these bones cost no more the breeding but to play at loggats with them? Mine ache to think on't" (5.1.90-91). The veil that covers the every-day world, ornamented and tasked with people's endeavors, is lifted, and he sees into the true nature of things, all ending as mere bones in the soil, and this insight gives him pause. Hamlet is paralyzed between his Christian dread of what may come after death, should he fail in his endeavor to kill, or to succeed and have sinned in the act. He ignores the good things that Yorick did when he was alive and the pleasures he gave to Hamlet himself. He is unable to accept the fate that befalls every human being, and to acknowledge the worth of a life that has born fruits. For Hamlet, death nullifies the value of life. This vision compounds his cowardice and makes it less likely for him to act.

If it were true that Hamlet is unable to kill his father's murderer because he doesn't want to follow the obligatory code for revenge, why does he explain his procrastination by accusing himself "of being a peasant, a coward, an unnatural and unfeeling son?"[87] Because he now thinks that he really is a coward. In the aftermath of the player's speech Hamlet feels, again, that he ought to take revenge, and being unable to proceed, he defines himself a vile coward:

> This is most brave,
> That I, the son of a dear father murdered,
> Prompted to my revenge by heaven and hell,
> Must like a whore unpack my heart with words (2.2.580-584).

He understands very well the meaning of courage and cowardice in the context of his personal problem. Nevertheless, he keeps himself from turning into one of those characters who have had recourse to violence in the name of valor, and as a result, cheapened both the virtue and themselves.

It would seem that by the time Shakespeare composed *Hamlet*, he had become prejudiced against valor and, as a result, refrained from imparting it to Hamlet, keeping him from reaching his goal and from a deserved victory. But would it have been a legitimate revenge and a victory for him, had he acted valiantly? Having portrayed martial valor in diverse contexts, without ascribing to it any particular moral or political value, but reducing it to a crime, Shakespeare has made it difficult to assign to valor a rightful role in the life of individuals and society. If Hamlet had been turned into a deliberate killer supported by valor, instead of an accidental one, he would have been placed on the same level as the other valiant protagonists who in the imaginary world of Shakespeare use their martial virtue to gain reputation, political advantages, or to commit crimes. He would have been endowed with a quality that Shakespeare regarded a vice. It would have degraded him as well as his cause.

Though he lacks the courage to kill Claudius, Hamlet still craves the virtue. But desiring what he cannot get solves none of his problems and causes a great deal of tension within himself. The tension created by the desire to be brave and the knowledge of being a coward, increases when he is confronted and implicitly exhorted to act with valor by Fortinbras and his soldiers marching to a war of conquest. Oblivious of the risks in going to war in a distant land and indifferent to the insignificance of the gains to be made, Fortinbras tells Hamlet, "We go to gain a little patch of ground / That hath in it no profit but the name." Fortinbras and his men are nevertheless resolved to go ahead. Faced by the singular courage of Fortinbras, Hamlet feels more than ever a coward, and the pressure on him to act mounts, "Why yet I live to say this thing is to do, / Sith I have cause, and will, and strength, and means/T' do't," but he does not do it (4.4.17-18, 44-46).

This military enterprise makes Hamlet well aware of the need for courage to perform extraordinary deeds, but it fails to give him the incentive to proceed against Claudius. In spite of the pressing need to overcome cowardice, Hamlet cannot act.

Fortinbras is a "tender" but very brave prince, known for his "unimproved mettle hot and full" (1.1. 96), a kind of barbarian with primitive vigor of body and mind. In the face of uncertainty, he shows extraordinary boldness as he:

> Makes mouths at the invisible event,
> Exposing what is mortal and unsure
> To all that fortune, death, and danger dare,
> Even for an eggshell (4.4. 50-53).

Fortinbras and his troops are formidable examples, exhorting Hamlet to take action. But they fail to inspire him. They are marching to a distant land and are defying death for a flimsy reason. But Hamlet, who has a compelling reason to act boldly and defy death, acts like a coward and feels sorry for himself:

> How stand I then,
> That have a father killed, a mother stained,
> Excitements of my reason and my blood
> And let all sleep (4.4. 56-59).

In the face of examples that should spur Hamlet to valiant action, he spurns them all. Why? One critic suggests that the example of Fortinbras is "humiliating."[88] On the contrary, it is illuminating. What Fortinbras's army shows is that valor is going to be used for a meaningless purpose, and that it should be shunned. Fortinbras is going to wage a war of conquest that will gain him nothing but an insignificant patch of soil. He and his men are moved by "a fantasy and trick of fame" and Fortinbras himself is one of those greats who find "quarrel in a straw" (4.4.55, 61) and who delights in the display of his courage. This is the lesson Hamlet learns without openly acknowledging it, and this is the reason why he cannot bring himself to imitate Fortinbras and kill Claudius. Fortinbras's martial valor is unjustified. Should I, Hamlet might have asked himself, use the same means that Fortinbras uses for questionable ends? The vice of the valor lies in the worthlessness of the cause it serves. This is what alarms him. He feels that he would demean himself if he used the same means to kill Claudius. In other words, the means has been tainted by the unworthiness of the cause that Fortinbras pursues. Fortinbras's mission has no value, and in Hamlet's eyes, his valor is reduced to mere violence.

It may very well be that Frederick Nietzsche has the final say on Hamlet's inability to act by defining Hamlet's "melancholy" as a state of suffering in which are "submerged all an individual's past experiences." In this state there is an ascetic, will-negating mood that he calls the "lethargic element." In perceiving his mother's weakness, his uncles' treachery, his father's murder, and finally in Fortinbras's unworthy enterprise, Hamlet has torn open the veil of any illusions he may have had about these people and events. He has penetrated into the true nature of things. He does not act because he knows that his action will change nothing. It cannot bring back his father, or make his mother into his former ideal, or himself, the son, he once was, because "Knowledge kills action."[89] Action requires the veil of illusion over all the structural elements that make up civilized society, such as codes, laws, and precepts, including the imperative for revenge, heroism and /or valor.

Shakespeare had given himself little room for the use of valor in the pursuit of a good cause. In his plays, he has been unable, or unwilling, to find a good enough cause to justify killing and to call it valor. He is reluctant to grant Hamlet a quality he has come to view as a vice, even though revenging the murder of the father is by all accounts a good cause and the killing of Claudius would be a valiant deed. Had

Hamlet been stirred by valor and had he proceeded with the murder, the event would not have been right by him. Had he killed, he would have turned himself into another pseudo hero of his times, a murderer hiding behind a facade of valor.

The origins of valor make it possible to see to some extent why it morphed into violence, and why violence was exercised as valor. Montaigne, an author whose work had some influence on Shakespeare, is the first writer to look at the blending of valor and violence and to trace it back to primitive societies. In those societies valor consisted in superior physical attributes. The strongest men had a superior capacity for violence, and this capacity rendered them exceptional. Their physical strength was considered valuable and was admired. Strength and capacity gave to these extraordinary men power and mastery over the less strong, both in the community and on the battlefield. "The first virtue that manifested itself among men and gave some the advantage over others was this one [valor], by which the strongest and most courageous made themselves masters of the weaker and acquired particular rank and reputation." Or else, Montaigne surmised, the strongest did not even have to impose themselves on the rest of the people. Since primitive nations were very warlike, they prized and highly rewarded the one quality that stood out in war and which was most familiar to them, valor. The passing of primitive ways changed many customs and ways of life, but in many societies, the value of force as valor remained intact. It was an unfortunate evolution, and Montaigne questioned its end results as he saw them at work in his own society. Valor as violence is a mark of degeneration, "It is the quality of the porter, not of valor, to have sturdier arms and legs; agility is a dead and corporeal quality; it is a stroke of luck to make our enemy stumble, or dazzle his eyes by the sunlight; it is a trick of art and technique, which may be found in a worthless coward, to be an able fencer."[90]

Montaigne's ideal of valor was inner strength, which is shown by his effort at keeping true valor separate from violence, repudiating the latter. He lived in a society that valued valor only as strength and skill in the handling of weapons, and he questioned this value, warning that a violent man is not necessarily a "valuable man or a worthy man" in an ethical or spiritual sense. He judged those men who in his society were regarded as valiant "for the most part men who have little care for the culture of the soul, and to whom one can suggest no other blessing than honor, and no other perfection than valor." In prowess alone there is no human excellence. The Civil wars helped Montaigne see the dubious value of valor as conceived by his contemporaries, "No other virtues are given little or no value nowadays; but valor has become common through our civil wars, and in this respect, there are among us souls firm to the point of perfection, and in great numbers." In the Civil wars, which Montaigne judged a "true school of treachery, inhumanity, and brigandage," there could be no ethical or spiritual values associated with valor.[91] War was useful to those Frenchmen who desired to gain aristocratic privileges. To gain them they needed first of all a reputation for valor; thus, they needed to fight in the wars. General François De La Noue, a friend of Montaigne and himself a protagonist of the Civil Wars, knew that many ambitious Frenchmen swore they "cannot live unless war breaks out here and there." In France, wealth and greatness ultimately came from what De La Noue termed "a readiness to vent one's spleen" and from "bravery." Without war, a French man's reputation for valor and standing in society would be imperiled. Some even sang about this desire, singing the praises of war: "War is my country, / My armor, my home / And in every season / To fight is my life." They must wage war, these gentlemen argued, so that "courage does not become spoiled by the rust of inactivity." As a result, many French gentlemen in the sixteenth century became so engrossed in the pursuit of valor and war that they disregarded elementary education. How far the quest carried them away from culture and reason is shown by their inability to sign their names.[92]

Montaigne identifies true valor with inner strength through the almost surreal story of the American Indians whose inner strength defied the terrible violence that was used against them. He focuses on the real thing, interior strength, which is measured by the Indians resistance to suffering. The native Americans fought neither for the conquest of new land nor political power. What fueled their wars was "Their rivalry in valor" and a desire to assert "in valor and virtue" the superiority of one tribe over another. Victory was not gained solely on the battlefield. After the battle, the winners terrified their prisoners in order to extract from their lips some weak or base word, or to make them want to flee, implicitly revealing their weakness. They wanted to break the enemies' spirit and turn them into cowards. Only if the victors were to succeed in this intent, did they believe they had truly won the battle. It is in the destruction of their inner strength "that true victory lies," Montaigne maintained. On the other hand, it may happen that the prisoners wrap themselves in "the grandeur of an invincible courage" and refuse to surrender, defying their captors and denying them real victory. It is in the behavior of the captured warriors to show whether or not "the worth and value of a man is in his heart and his will.... Valor is strength, not of legs and arms, but of heart and soul; it consists not in the worth of our horse or our weapons, but in our own."[93]

Unfortunately, Montaigne's vision brought no change to the idea and practice of valor. Valor continued to play out its role as violence in even more significant ways, reducing itself to pure violence, and confirming his view that violence was the basis of political and social authority in the commonwealths.

Both Giambattista Vico and Edward Gibbon represented valor as the dominant value of the societies they chose to investigate. In *The New Science* (1744), Vico envisioned the "age of the heroes," which is the middle stage of what he styled the "ideal eternal history." By making the heroes the protagonists of this stage, Vico revealed the ethos of the aristocratic class of his time, and assigned to them a central role in mankind's evolution. The heroes were both warriors and rulers. They established their leadership at the outset of the age, becoming more violent and bloody as their heroism grew. Their heroism sprang from the successful exercise of violence within their commonwealths, ruling absolutely the people, and fighting against external enemies.

The heroes bring to life the second stage of Vico's ideal eternal history and dominate the life of their cities. The dawn of the heroic age shows how a group of people, the "abandoned" and the "simpletons" conceived by Grotius, Pufendorf, and Hobbes, became heroes. They rebelled against their masters and oppressors, the "impious giants," and turned to "the strongest" men within the group to save themselves. The strong men slew the giants and took under their protection the less able among them. The performance against the giants, which displayed the superior strength and fighting skill of the strongest men, brought out and established the idea of "heroism." In the beginning of the heroic age, the heroes were both merciful and ruthless, "sparing the submissive and vanquishing the proud."[94] But eventually, they felt that their heroism deserved some reward. As a result, they asserted their superiority by stripping those less able (refugees) of their freedom and by oppressing them. Even so, the refugees continued to enhance the heroes' reputation by testifying to their martial virtue. In the end, the erstwhile victims of the giants, who are now named plebeians, became the slaves of the heroes "who had saved them by granting them asylum."[95]

Why did the heroes exercise harsh power over the plebeians and keep them as slaves? They did it because, one historian holds, at that early stage of human evolution the laws were cruel, and men could be governed only by force. If the heroes had not acted the way they did, they would have lacked the authority "to cause unruly savages to prostrate themselves" before them.[96] But the plebeians were not unruly and dangerous savages; they were dispirited and helpless creatures who looked upon the heroes as protectors, and who presumably craved the rule of law, since they had fled from the lawless giants among whom force alone prevailed. Besides, what good would it do to rebel against the heroes? None. The heroes were unassailable, and thus secure, because at the beginning of the heroic age tyrannizing entailed no risk or danger for them.

Tyrannical rule was one aspect of the heroes' violent way of life. The other was war with other peoples. The heroes possessed an enormous strength, which was spent fighting against internal and external enemies. Strength alone counted, because in the age of the heroes, war was eternal and widespread, and no one else but the heroes could wage it.[97] Not only were the defeated brought under the heel of the victors, but also war and victory enhanced the heroes' reputation and hardened their rule. Living by the "law of war," which prescribed robbery and plunder, was the most spectacular way for them to display and their heroism and confirm their privileges. Only the law of war regulated the relations among them, so the cult of violence was fostered with no restraint. The pillar of the law was "the inhospitality of the heroic peoples," which led them to regard alien neighbors as perpetual enemies and to fight them fiercely. All the heroic nations carried on "eternal wars with each other."[98] Of the inborn proclivity of the heroes, Alexander Pope wrote with magnificent intuition and humor:

> Heroes are much the same, the point's agreed,
> From Macedonia to the Swede;
> The whole strange purpose of their lives, to find
> Or make, an enemy of mankind![99]

In the absence of war, looting and raiding of one nation on another and indiscriminate pillaging prevailed. These activities served to establish and reinforce the heroes' power and reputation. Among the Germans in the heroic stage, robbery "was reckoned among the exercises of valor." The heroes had no choice but to kill or be killed, to vanquish or to be vanquished. There was no ideological or political motive behind their deeds; only naked enmity for alien peoples and pride in the use of violence. The heroes' destiny was to live and die by violence.[100] John Milton caught a glimpse of the heroes' place in the world. They were the giants of *Genesis,* as well as the belligerent and powerful aristocrats of his age, "men of high renown," identified as "great conquerors" and considered "gods, and sons of gods." They were admired for their might, which in their time was called "valor and heroic virtue" and was employed in oppressing the people.[101] And for the heroes of more recent history, Milton judged them "valiant indeed and prosperous to win a field, but to know the end and reason of winning, injudicious and unwise, in good or bad success alike unteachable."[102]

Violence being their way of life, the heroes cultivated it assiduously. The heroic education of the young was "severe, harsh, and cruel." The Lacedaemonians, whom Vico regarded as the heroes of Greece, taught their young sons to fear neither pain nor death and to make their exercise of violence fearless and proficient. The renowned Greek hero, Achilles, went strictly by the code of violence, and even made it a tool of desecration. When Hector proposed that the victor in their final fight should bury the vanquished, Achilles replied that lions make no pact with men, and told him that he would desecrate his body, "If I kill you, I shall drag you naked, bound to my chariot, three days around the walls of Troy (as indeed he did), and finally I shall give your body to my hunting dogs to eat." Achilles was "the hero of violence," and as such he disdained reason and referred "every right to the tip of his spear."[103]

Heroism went to the heads of the heroes. To underscore the prestige and power that the exercise of violence bestowed on them, the Roman heroes made themselves the sons of God or even God himself, and "took the name of gods over the plebeians of their cities, whom they called men." They promoted the belief that they had been created by Jove himself or engendered under his auspices. They identified themselves as "born of Jove, and "godlikeness" reinforced their absolute power over the plebeians. By claiming divine origin, they enabled themselves. Their so-called "Divinity" led them to further distance themselves from the plebeians, who ultimately came to be regarded, not as "men," but as "beasts."[104] Like Montaigne more than a century earlier, Vico sees valor as a force shorn of values useful to the pursuit of the common good, but he goes beyond Montaigne in revealing the consequences of its exercise.

Heroism enabled the strongest and fearless of men to dominate public life and to violate the laws of humanity. "Precisely because the nobles of the first peoples considered themselves heroes and of a nature superior to that of the plebeians, they were capable of misgovernment of the poor masses of the nations." The proof of the heroes' ungodly life lies in an emotional page that Vico writes about some personages in Roman history—a period he regards as the classic age of the heroes.[105] The Roman heroes abdicated their civic responsibility, revealing their capacity for social and civic evil. They became such a pain on Vico's mind that he loses his scientific objectivity, and lets his emotions take over. "What of the heroes of this time?" Vico asks in disbelief as he confronts their misdeeds. Brutus, who consecrated his house in the person of his two sons to the cause of liberty; Scaevola, who terrified and routed the Etruscan king Porsenna by plunging his own right hand into the flames, Manlius called the Imperious, who cut off the head of his own son for a breach of military discipline, Curtius, who threw himself into the abyss, the Decii, who sacrificed themselves to save their army, Attilius Regulus, who returned to a certain and cruel death at Carthage to preserve the sanctity of the Roman oath. The deeds of these personages were noble, but they persevered in acting like heroes and did nothing for the common man who lived in misery and oppression in their commonwealths. "What did any of them do for the poor and unhappy Roman plebs?" Vico asks. "Assuredly they did but increase their burden by war, plunge them deeper in the sea of usury, in order to bury them to a greater depth in the private prisons of the nobles, where they were beaten with rods on their bare backs like abject slaves." The heroes' tempers, fired by their arrogance, kept them from behaving with justice and humanity. "The nature of the strong is to surrender as little as possible of what they have acquired by valor, and only so much as is necessary to preserve their acquisition," and since whatever was earned by valor had equal value, "Hence we read so often in Roman history of the heroic disdain of the strong who will not suffer an ignominious surrender of what was won by valor." Irresponsibility and misrule render the heroes infamous. "For certainly Roman history will puzzle any intelligent reader who tries to find in it any evidence of Roman virtue, mercy and justice."[106]

The advent of the "age of men" spelled out the end of the age of the heroes. The plebeians became suspicious of the "pretensions of heroism" and understood themselves to be of an equal human nature with the nobles. The plebeians rebelled against the heroes and put an end to their power. The end of the heroic age heralds the coming of an age that sets aside valor and force as the basis of social and political life. The men in the new age are "human, intelligent, benign, and reasonable, recognizing for laws, conscience, reason, and duty." Human law replaced force. All are born free in their cities and are accounted equal under the laws.[107] Mankind enters the "age of men" and reaches the human stage by getting rid of the heroes who lived and ruled by violence alone. However, valor as a "barbarian" virtue remained alive in eighteenth-century thought. Carl von Clausewitz, who bestrode that century and the following one, will prescribe barbarian valor as the appropriate virtue for modern armies.

In the meantime, Edward Gibbon had no knowledge of *The New Science* when he wrote his own work. He recognized in barbarian valor one of the causes that brought about the demise of the Roman empire. The heroic cult toppled the people that conquered and ruled the ancient world, and in the *Decline and Fall of the Roman Empire*, Gibbon conceives, like Vico, of valor and power growing out of the heroic cult, and that the fading of the Roman heroes, did not signal an advancement into a more humane stage.[108] On the contrary, it was a regression to sheer savagery and a marked victory over civilization. The victory of the barbarians over the Romans simply replaced one breed of heroes with another. Roman prowess shriveled at the same time that the barbarians' martial valor emerged, a valor far less human and far more brutal than that of the erstwhile masters of the ancient world.[109]

The "exercise of military prowess" on the part of the Romans played a role in the breakdown of the Roman empire.[110] Although the arms of the Republic lost some battles, they were always victorious in war. Their rapid advance to the Euphrates, the Danube, the Rhine, and the Ocean[111] showed that their warriors were irresistible. However, their military prowess proved ultimately to be a disadvantage, for it gave them a false sense of security as it aroused the antagonism of the conquered people. Britain, for example, was conquered, but the Roman legions were unable to subdue the island, as the native Caledonians fiercely fought for their independence. Britain remained a festering wound on the body of the empire. Trajan, who was under the spell of Alexander the Great's legend, aspired to emulate his deeds, and went to war against the Dacians, and in five years subjugated them. This success rekindled the emperor's thirst for military glory and fame. He made an expedition against the eastern nations, vanquished the Parthians and turned Armenia, Mesopotamia, and Assyria into Roman provinces. However, Trajan's triumphs, far from making Rome more powerful and feared, aroused the antagonism of the peoples he had defeated, who turned against Rome, especially after his death.[112] Just when the barbarians were putting pressure on the borders of the empire, Roman military manpower was weakening. Valor no longer matched the standard that in earlier ages distinguished the legions. In those ages, public acknowledgment gave them the incentive to wage war in order to preserve and enhance the free government of which they were members. And the Romans believed that the glory of the company, of the legion, and of the army depended on "the prowess of a private soldier." The soldier's persuasion that his rank and reputation would depend on his own valor gave the legions of the republic the martial courage that made them "almost invincible." Cowardice was not tolerated; the centurions punished it with blows and the generals with death. "From such laudable arts did the valour of the Imperial troops" grow. But now, in less pure ages, pay and ambition alone spurred men to enroll in the legions. The "new" soldiers' interest lay in serving under generals who paid them well, and as mercenary servants of a despotic prince, they caused war to be degraded into a trade. The conquered men of Spain, Gaul, Britain, and Illyricum now supplied the legions with "brave and robust" soldiers who possessed "personal valour," but no sense of belonging to, and serving, a country and a government of which they were members. As a result, their personal valor turned out to be useless, and the true "military spirit" of the Roman military forces evaporated.[113]

The mercenary spirit turned valor into an exercise of violence at the service of partisan power politics and personal gain. The prowess that once helped build and defend the empire, now came to serve corruption and the violence of despotism. No group better than the Praetorian guards reflected the decline of Roman valor and its results. The Praetorians were selected on the basis of their prowess and were given the duty to protect the emperor. But they betrayed this mission and used their prowess to enhance their own power and to protect the despots who bribed them. By the end of the second century, they wielded power over the senate, the public treasury, and the emperor himself. They provided an infamous example for the legions; some of whom emulated their lawlessness and defended their behavior with the same obstinacy as that of the Praetorians.[114]

As valor became corrupt among the Romans, it grew strong among the barbarians, emboldening them and sending them on the path of conquest. Gibbon projects barbarian valor in all its primitive, irresistible force at the same time that violence and self-interest gradually extinguish the Roman valor of purer ages. If it is true that Gibbon "admired only a rational heroism,"[115] he must have been overwhelmed by the brutality of barbarian valor. He may not have admired it, but he acknowledged it, writing of the "well known valour of the barbarians of Europe," of the valor of the Germans, of that of the Scythians and Tartars, "renowned for their invincible courage and their conquests," and of that of the Bulgarians and Hungarians. For the latter, especially, "the merit and fame of military prowess" counted above all else, to the extent that all other qualities valued by mankind appeared vile and contemptible. Gibbon places special value on barbarian valor because it dared challenge Roman might. "When we recollect the complete armour of the Roman soldier, their discipline, exercises, evolutions, fortified camps, and military engines, it appears a matter of surprise how the naked and unassisted valour of the barbarians could dare to encounter in the field the strength of the legions."[116]

The harsh life of the barbarian helped develop their valor: "Cold, poverty, and a life of danger and fatigue, fortify the strength and courage of barbarians." Naturally, they wanted to eliminate their discomforts and this desire contributed to the skill that enabled them to achieve it. For, they believed that the improvement in their standard of living, must come, not from their own toil, but from the use of force. To the Germans, for instance, "to solicit by labour what might be ravished by arms" was considered below their dignity. Poor, voracious, and turbulent, the barbarians stood, "bold in arms," ready and impatient to plunder the fruits of the civilized world. The Franks, "bold and valiant to the verge of temerity," needed a plentiful supply of wine and food to carry on their warlike enterprises, and their "high and intrepid spirit" enabled them to get it.[117] Driven by a powerful impulse to satisfy life's basic needs, the barbarians lived to fight, and to be successful they needed to fight with valor. The "glory" of the Franks consisted in war and rapine; proud of their prowess, they derided the lifestyle of the Italians who had degenerated from the "liberty and valour" of the ancient Lombards. The Alani, too, looked on war and rapine as "the glory of mankind." War and plunder invigorated the character of the Germans, breeding the virtues that distinguished barbarians in general—faith and valor. The German chiefs did their best to gather the greatest number of "valiant companions," who in the hour of danger were expected to show exemplary courage. "It was shameful for the chief to be surpassed in valour by his companions, and shameful for the companions not to equal the valour of their chief." For the Germans it was impossible to forgive cowardice, and the brave man was the favorite of their martial deities; he was destined to enjoy immortality: "All agreed that a life spent in arms and a glorious death in battle were the best preparation for a happy futurity" in this and in the other world.[118]

Intense exertion helped the Germans to become valiant. Endowed with large and masculine bodies, they were adapted to violent exertions which "inspired them with constitutional bravery." When free from the cares of shepherding, the Tartars devoted their time and energy to the "violent and sanguinary exercise of the chase." Nowhere else in his work does Gibbon establish the relationship between violent exertion, on the one hand, and valor in war on the other, better than in his portrayal of the Scythians. The Scythians avoided chasing and killing harmless animals. They were only interested in showing their courage, and to this end they boldly faced the angry wild boar, especially when it turned against them. They even provoked the fury of the tiger. "Where there is danger, there may be glory, and the mode of hunting which opens the fairest field to the exercise of valour may justly be considered the image and school of war." The barbarians relied entirely on the operation of instinct, and for this reason, they were "nearer to the condition of animals," a state of being that enhanced their valor. The valor of the Germans was proportionate to their lack of civilization: "Their climate, their want of learning, of the arts and of laws, their notions of honour, of gallantry, and of religion, and their sense of freedom, impatience of peace, and thirst of enterprise contributed to form a people of military heroes." Their "naked and unassisted valor" enabled them to face the strength of the Roman legions and the various troops of the auxiliaries. They "poured forth their whole souls" in the first attack and would never retreat or surrender. And "by the effort of native valour" the barbarians prevailed over the controlled and "artificial bravery" of the Roman mercenaries.[119] Contrary to Tacitus first, and Machiavelli later, both of whom saw in the simple and rude life of the Germans the virtues of probity and innocence,[120] Gibbon sees the Germans as "a herd of savages," and their life ruled by the brutishness that bred valor and led to military triumphs.[121] His view left no room for approval or admiration for what Tacitus, Machiavelli, and the French historiographers, Montesquieu and Mably, whom Gibbon had read attentively, considered virtues.[122] Gibbon only acknowledged the meaning and power of the brutish qualities that enabled the barbarians to bring down the Roman empire.

If martial valor, essentially primitive violence, is a product of barbarism, one might think its existence would be impossible in a civilized age which, having discarded barbarism, can no longer produce that kind of valor. But this is only speculation, for valor as primitive violence has remained alive and well, both as a concept and as a military virtue. Aptly, it has survived as the result of "degeneration," that is, a reversion of civilized man back to barbarism. It has survived as a vice but also as a legitimate and respected value since it is useful to military organizations and enterprises.

Gibbon studied barbarism as "a problem of degeneration."[123] In a different context, Carl von Clausewitz, too, will study martial valor as the fruit of degeneration, deliberately willed and cultivated by the leadership. Degeneration will emerge as a valuable military asset, heralding a world where civilized man has to summon the strength and cruelty of the barbarian to be considered a hero.

DEGRADATION

Beowulf knew that he was valiant; he had boundless confidence in his valor, and he sought out enemies to demonstrate his heroic temper. Roland was equally confident of his valor, and the battle at Roncesvalles gave him the occasion to display it in a grand manner. These warriors were tightly bound to the heroic code for heroism's sake. They ignored danger, death, defeat, and common sense, enabling themselves to live and die by the code. Except for Hamlet who, suspicious of its ultimate value, refused to resort to valor to carry out revenge, Shakespeare's heroes were resolved to play their role even when the value and use of valor were questionable. No fear or scruple could halt the impetuous heroes envisaged by Vico and Gibbon.

All of the above were exceptional men, and there were few of them. But in the modern age, military requirements called for many men like them, for heroes who could fight and win the battles and wars that were becoming more and more numerous. In the eighteenth century, national armies needed many good soldiers, and valor was needed for fighting on a large scale. Because the military prowess of the members of the upper classes was insufficient to fight successfully, valor had to be created and spread among ordinary people. National armies required vast numbers of men, and many had to be recruited from all over Europe by impressment or bounty. These men were trained by brutal non-commissioned officers who lashed and drilled them until they could perform like automata on the battlefield and impassively face enemy fire.[124] This method was rudimentary and only partially effective, since only external force prompted these men to fight with courage. For training to be effective it was necessary to bring about a change in the soldier's identity so that he would be prompted by a new kind of instinct, a spontaneous impulse. To achieve this, it was necessary to bring men back to savagery, to the time when blood lust and violence were natural and instinctual properties, and instill in them the kind of violence that amounts to courage. This was the plan for creating valor by the first theoretician of modern war, Carl von Clausewitz.

It is noteworthy that Vico's and Gibbon's thinking on barbarism as the foundation of martial virtue lives again in a Prussian mind predisposed to regard barbarism as a military virtue. Clausewitz unconsciously turned the historical findings of Vico and Gibbon, into a doctrine affirming that modern man needs barbarism to act with courage on the battlefield. Civilization has separated man from his darker instincts, whereas the demands of modern warfare need to accommodate them. In order to fight with bravery, men should be forced by discipline and training to restore and nourish a taste for blood with the result that human degradation is raised to the rank of a military virtue.

Clausewitz's thinking came primarily from his experience on the battlefield. In 1793, he served with the Prussian army as a twelve-year-old lance corporal, and afterward he opted for a military education and career. In 1803, he graduated from the Berlin War College at the head of his class. He fought against the French and was taken prisoner when Napoleon defeated Prussia. In 1812, he became a colonel in the Russian army, took part in the battles of Smolensk and Borodino, and witnessed the retreat and destruction of Napoleon's Grand Army. The Russian campaigns made an impression on Clausewitz and left indelible marks on both body and mind. Frostbite disfigured his face and arthritic pain afflicted his body. He turned to opium to alleviate the effects of violence on his own being.[125]

The French method of warfare and the tactics of Napoleon led Clausewitz to realize that war stepped forth "in all its raw violence," showing that its sole aim was not just to weaken the enemy and to force him to give up, but to completely destroy him.[126] In war the single battle is the central event, and its purpose is "simply the destruction" of the enemy's forces, whether by death, injury, or any other means. Having thus given intensity of violence and destruction the chief role in warfare, Clausewitz derides the idea of victory with little bloodshed, the concept governing the conduct and outcome of many past wars and calls it a "spurious philosophy." Bloodshed, the by-product of intense violence, holds the key to military success. "We are not interested in generals who win victories without bloodshed," he writes with scorn; slaughter may be an unpleasant spectacle, but it should not provide an excuse for "blunting our swords in the name of humanity." The military organization must endow its soldiers with the virtue that enables them to cause and to endure intense violence, and this is courage. Soldiers must possess "courage" and "morale," and military theory should propose only rules that give ample scope to these "finest and least dispensable of military virtues."[127]

Clausewitz believed that "what is most needed in the lower ranks is courage," since "the courage and morale of an army have always increased its physical strength, and always will." In order to create courage, the soldiers must be trained in such a way as to turn them into lower beings. In any primitive and warlike race, Clausewitz argues, "the warrior spirit is far more common than among civilized peoples." Among primitives, this spirit "is possessed by almost every warrior." That is why wars between savages are far more "cruel and destructive" than wars between civilized nations. The concept of "boldness," is an important virtue. It is the capacity to rise above the "most menacing dangers," and Clausewitz preached the necessity to develop the martial spirit that civilization has put in abeyance. War itself is the main tool for creating this spirit. "Today practically no means other than war will educate a people in this spirit of boldness, and it has to be a war waged under daring leadership. Nothing else will counteract the softness and desire for ease which debase a people in times of growing prosperity and increasing trade. A people and a nation can hope for a strong position in the world only if national character and familiarity with war fortify each other by continual interaction."[128]

Civilization and a higher intellectual level inhibit military virtue, since they thwart passion, the very basis of aggressive behavior and bravery. One reason that the warrior spirit lives among the savages is that they "are ruled by passion." But passion is missing among civilized peoples, Clausewitz says, because they are ruled by the mind and have learned to control their passions. Whereas, unhindered by the mind and impelled by passion, the savage has bred within himself "hostile feelings and hostile intentions." These two driving forces are very powerful incentives to "make men fight one another." Among savages, hostile feelings and hostile intentions are fueled by the "passion of hatred," but among civilized men the passion of hatred is absent. To enable civilized men to fight with courage, the passion of hatred must be reignited, and Clausewitz confidently writes that even the most civilized of peoples "can be fired with passionate hatred for each other."[129]

He believed that it is possible to arouse in civilized man the passions he admired in the primitives. It is merely dormant. The trick is to bring it back to life. Although it seems that civilized peoples have improved over their primitive past because they abstain from putting their prisoners to death or from devastating cities or countries. It is so only apparently. The soldiers of civilized nations refrain from killing helpless peoples and from ravaging towns only because intelligence plays a larger part in their methods of warfare and has taught them more effective ways of using force than those dictated by raw instinct. There is hope, Clausewitz says, for restoring barbarism together with martial virtue. The crude expressions of the instinct may have disappeared from the landscape of modern warfare, but the instinct that generated them still lives in modern man. For instance, the invention of gunpowder, the constant improvement of firearms, and the increasing volume of casualties on the battlefields testify to this instinct's latent, but powerful life. Firearms and the destructive ends they serve "are enough to show that the advance of civilization has done nothing practical to alter or deflect the impulse to destroy,"[130] which is valor in action. The military must exploit the impulse to destroy to create valor.

To revitalize the instinct, Clausewitz simply prescribes war. War itself creates courage. The battlefield, where soldiers are under stress and tested, holds the secret for bringing out hatred, savagery, and a valiant temper. Even where there is no national hatred and no animosity to start with, fighting alone is enough to stir up hostile feelings. The battlefield is courage's birthplace, "The seed [of the military spirit] will grow only in the soil of constant activity and exertion, warmed by the sun of victory... This spirit can be created only in war." Victory in particular yields a special effect. While draining the strength of the loser, it raises the vigor and the energy of the victor, helping him to "increase the scope of his courage."[131]

To become a brave soldier, civilized man must undergo "exertion" and "suffering," which require both privation and effort. Exertion and suffering encompass training and action on the battlefield. The soldier must be subjected to frequent exertions to the utmost limits of his strength. Trained in privation and effort, he becomes steeled against the dangers and fear that war arouses. This strength confers on him "indifference," a savage-like state that preserves his courage. Clausewitz calls indifference "a certain strength of body and soul," a quality that "primitive and semi civilized peoples usually possess." This strength of body and soul is "a permanent condition," meaning that, "having become second nature, it will never fail." Once an army has gained the qualities that primitive and semi-civilized peoples possess, it can keep its cohesion under the most murderous fire. It can suppress imaginary fears and can oppose real danger and fear with all its might. An army that is animated by the "indifference" of the savage is an army "imbued with the true military spirit."[132] Pushed to the edge of endurance by exertion and suffering, the soldier responds to the challenge by summoning an energy that gives him a power which is less than human but greater than that of an ordinary man.

This man will have a price to pay, but Clausewitz is oblivious of it. The consequence of his teaching on valor and degradation was perceived, and denied, by Clausewitz's apologists. Philosopher Raymond Aron, for instance, asserts that the conscript trained according to Clausewitz's doctrine "is not dehumanized by this apprenticeship."[133] But how can he avoid being dehumanized, if the kind of training Clausewitz has prescribed aims precisely at breeding in the soldier those qualities that are foreign to civilized men but proper to primitive and semi-civilized peoples?

Tolstoy, who had firsthand knowledge of the military and extensive experience, judged Clausewitz's doctrine quite differently. He knew that it was applied in training the Russian troops, and he denounced it. The common soldiers are instructed "to kill men," Tolstoy writes, and the best way to get them to do the killing is to subject them to the same experience as that of their future victims, violence of the worst kind. To get them to kill, these men are tortured by the same means—hunger, the whip, and the hot iron—used to train animals. They are taught to act "mechanically," without any reflection, in an animal-like manner in order to prepare them to kill. They will inflict on their enemies the same type of violence that has been practiced against them. The difference between men and animals is that training cannot compel animals to kill other animals, but men can be. Another difference is that animals suffer no degradation, but men do. The military training prescribed by Clausewitz and identified by Tolstoy realizes the purpose of bringing the recruit to a level where "the man has been destroyed,"[134] and the martial spirit has been created.

Tolstoy's opinion of Clausewitz's doctrine is relevant since his military experience allowed him to make a competent judgment. Along with his observations on Clausewitz, he elaborated his own view of valor in the context of the events that touched him and his country—Russian colonialism in the Caucasus where he fought as an officer, and Napoleon's invasion of Russia, which was heroically opposed by the Russian people in the pages of *War and Peace*.

In Tolstoy's early works, there is no martial spirit on the part of the Russian officers. They are conscious of danger and fear it. They want to act with courage, but cannot, and they are diminished by their impotence. To make up for their weaknesses they instinctively flirt with degradation. The Russian novelist represents both the passion and the hostility for valor as these feelings torment the officers. He knew well the Russian class that produced the officers' corps and saw in them something never before revealed by the literature on valor—the reason they wanted to show heroism, and why they were unable to be truly valiant. This is the conflict that will gain a new dimension in the Yankee soldier who is the protagonist of Stephen Crane's *The Red Badge of Courage*.

In "The Raid," the first of the *Tales of Army Life*, Tolstoy declares that war always interested him, specifically "the reality of war, the actual killing"—the event that, either carried out or suffered, reveals either courage or cowardice. But "what is courage," he asks at the beginning of the tale, "that quality respected in all ages and among all nations?" And "why is this a good quality, contrary to all others, sometimes met in vicious men?"[135] Because, Tolstoy answers, valor is a commodity that can purchase political or economic advantages, and because a reputation for valor carries prestige and recognition.

In the Caucasus, he had a firsthand knowledge of his comrades' lives and conduct. A few officers managed to behave valiantly on the battlefield, many others less so, and those underwent a painful interior struggle. The presence or absence of valor defined their moral and intellectual character. Captain Kraft has become obsessed with his imaginary deeds of valor. He narrates them time and again to the same audience, emphasizing his fighting spirit and stressing that once he led his soldiers in "a hell of fire" to capture fifteen enemy barricades. It is a lie, but the captain needs to have others believe what he says in order to feed his illusion of being the hero he will never be.[136] Most soldiers in the *Tales* are ruled by fear and ambition. They do not intend to be really heroic. They only want to be recognized as such to enhance their military and social career. One of the Russian traditions was for the men of the middle class to go to the Caucasus to fight the rebel hill men, and return "laden with rewards," to take their rightful place in society as a result of their valiant deeds. Since most of them want recognition without the necessary courage to earn it, they cheat and lie to reach their goal. Commander Bolkhov, who had volunteered for the Caucasus "to show his courage" and to garner rewards, stubbornly sticks around to earn the Anna and Vladimir orders, but without any success. His yearning for recognition is so strong that envy and frustration upset him every time an officer in his outfit gets a reward. But he has no ability to be brave. Upon receiving orders to participate in the raid that is the centerpiece of "The Wood-Felling," Bolkhov turns white as a sheet, and during the night before the action, he agonizes as if "one [were] condemned to death." He places his fist on his chest, twists it, and explains to Tolstoy, "This is what goes on inside!... I can't stand running risks. The fact of the matter is simply that I am not brave." He knows he is unable to act with real courage, and he suffers for his cowardice. "I feel that I am sinking, morally, lower and lower every day."[137]

Major Kirsanov, too, takes it for granted that officers wish to distinguish themselves, and then return home. But things have not worked out as he expected. He earned the Anna and Vladimir orders, traveled home, but then came back, and is still soldiering. His fellow Russians doubted his bravery and believed that the rewards he earned were a fraud. After ten years, Kirsanov is now approaching the time when an officer stationed in the Caucasus either takes to drink or marries a loose woman, a "curious creature," who no longer speaks or behaves the Russian way.[138] There were some soldiers who displayed courage in unusual ways, like the Spanish officer attached to a Russian battalion, who used to ride in front of the troops and stand where the firing was most intense, making a deliberate show of fearlessness. However, his performance could not be regarded as heroic, Tolstoy writes, for it showed only "physical" heroism prompted by vanity or curiosity. In a way it was a mockery of heroism, and this officer could not "be called brave."[139] A soldier shows real courage if his deed is "prompted by a noble feeling."

Sevastopol reenacts and expands the torments, hopes and delusions of the soldiers in the Caucasus. Combatants are torn between their desire to be brave and their inability to realize it. In the besieged city, danger never subsides, fear rules, and the quest for valor, or surrender to cowardice, are daily happenings. The aristocracy of birth and ambition press on the Russian officers to perform with bravery, but blood alone cannot produce it. Some, unable to act with courage, fabricate it to deceive others as well as themselves. Prince Galtsin sets foot in the Fourth Bastion, Sevastopol's hottest spot, witnesses the explosion of a bomb twenty yards away, and as a result, considers himself "no less courageous" than Servyagin, "a well-known brave" naval officer. Baron Pesth becomes "a hero in his own estimation" merely because he has been inside the Fifth Bastion's bomb-proof shelter. Other officers find it equally hard to act with bravery. Adjutant Kalugin's rush to the Fourth Bastion while it is under both artillery fire and an infantry attack turns into a nightmarish journey of a self, torn by fear and a desperate desire to show courage. Under the barrage, he is afraid and hurries along a trench "almost on all fours." The fear of showing fear forces him to regain control of himself, and he walks about the gun emplacements of the bastion, exposing himself to the sight of the enemy. He intends to create the illusion of being "ten times braver" than the battery commander. Back in his quarters, Kalugin tells Prince Galtsin of his ordeal, stressing the details that show him to be "a capable and brave officer."[140]

Those officers who are resolved to live up to a heroic image of themselves without cheating, have to fight fear as well as the enemy. Lieutenant Vladimir Kozeltsov is scared and regards Sevastopol a living "hell." He is resolved to be valiant, and imagines himself doing deeds of valor, fantasizing about French troops suddenly falling upon him and his brother as they stand on the bastions of Sevastopol. His imagination slides into a whirl of valiant deeds leading to a heroic death. "I shall fire and fire. I shall kill quite a lot of them, but they will still keep coming straight at me... there is no escape for me." He fantasizes that in defense of his brother, he runs forward, I "kill one Frenchman, then another to save my brother. I am wounded in the arm; I seize the gun in the other hand and still run on."

In reality, he cannot muster the courage needed to fight, and the duel between imaginary heroism and real cowardice continues. He suspects himself to be a coward, and he suffers: "Am I really a vile, miserable coward," he tells himself, "a miserable, wretched being!" When he reports to the commanding officer of his battery, he feels as if his cowardice has been detected. Alone in his quarters, he is merciless toward himself. "What a wretch I am—a coward, a despicable coward." Imaginary danger and real fear lead him to visualize a bomb piercing the roof of his lodging, causing wounds and blood and splinters flying into the room. Unable to get hold of himself, he turns to God asking for the virtue he yearns for, "If courage is needed and firmness, which I lack, grant them to me! Deliver me from the shame and disgrace which are more than I can bear." Eventually, Kozeltsov's fear of danger and of his own cowardice diminishes, only because fear "cannot long continue with the same intensity." He even finds the courage to stand for three hours on the threshold of the bomb-proof shelter, feeling "a kind of pleasure in tempting fate and watching the flying bombs." The following day, he is in ecstasy as he discovers that "not only was he no coward but that he was even quite brave." He has done nothing valiant, but the troops watching him while he discharges his duty around the battery "made him [feel] quite valiant." He becomes "vain of his courage" and shows off, walking about with an unbuttoned coat, conspicuous, and defiant of the enemy. He wants to be brave, for bravery's sake. But when he needs it the most, he is unable to summon it. As the French launch the decisive assault on Sevastopol, he stands petrified, unable to believe what he sees—an enemy that advances implacably and kills him.[141]

The older Kozeltsov fights well, marching into death's arms without any fear. On the point of death, an "inexpressible delight at the consciousness of having performed a heroic deed" comforts him. The delight comes from his awareness of having overcome cowardice and having reached the end of the same kind of agony that his younger brother went through. "For the first time in the whole of his service," he muses as he lies on a stretcher waiting for death, "he had acted as well as it was possible to act." What enabled him to overcome cowardice was resignation to death. When the first Frenchmen appeared on the breastworks waving their caps and shouting, he "felt sure he would be killed, and this increased his courage."[142] How could the certainty of death increase Kozeltsov's courage? Because death has become for Kozeltsov, as well as for many soldiers in Sevastopol, a way out of the brutish life they were forced to live there. "Our soldiers are brave," Tolstoy wrote in a memorandum compiled while serving in Sevastopol, "because death for them is a blessing."[143] For those soldiers who cling to life while they face death, heroic behavior is impossible because they are engaged in a silent duel between fear of fear and a vain wish for courage. On sighting the shell that reaches its apogee and then plummets toward earth, Captain Praskukhin and Captain Mikhaylov hug the ground. The shell crashes less than a yard from the two of them, and on hearing no explosion, Praskukhin is at first afraid of having "played the coward for nothing." But following the explosion, he gives "way more and more to fear" of death. Mikhaylov places himself in the hands of God, and repudiates the martial virtue that duty imposes on him and the profession that demands the sacrifice of his life, "Why did I enter the army?" His repudiation strips him of martial fortitude, a loss that he regrets as soon as he recovers from a slight head wound.[144]

Tolstoy's protagonists suffer because they are unable to act with courage, and as a result they die, or remain cowards, or become indifferent. Henry Fleming, the protagonist of *The Red Badge of Courage*, a novel influenced by Tolstoy's work,[145] also suffers, and he decides to do something decisive to overcome his fear. Shorn of courage at the beginning of his service, he is afraid and runs from the battle, after which he undergoes an intense crisis. The problem of wanting to be a man of courage, yet lacking the inner resources to become one, is the same kind of problem that beset many protagonists of Tolstoy's works. For Henry, however, it is an existential problem, which will grow to encompass his entire life, making his war experience essential to his identity. He is resolved to eliminate the cause of his suffering. Unlike the Russian officers who prized martial valor as a commodity that could purchase political or economic advantages, for Henry it was a matter of life and death. His resolve to be brave is so passionate that in the end, he is able to summon the beast, earn the "red badge of courage," and obliterate his cowardice.

Henry enlisted with enthusiasm. He dreamed of battles of old that "had thrilled him with their sweep and fire," but he has a "problem."[146] Since the beginning of the narrative he is tormented by his lack of courage. Martial valor becomes an extraordinary concern for him, partly because he has great difficulty in finding it. The fear that he might not be brave is such that at the beginning of his service, he seeks to counter it by resolving to do something that is impossible, "to mathematically prove to himself that he would not run from a battle." His fear and uncertainty are confirmed when he realizes that none of his comrades are tormented by "such a terrific personal problem" as he is. Nevertheless, he chooses to believe that they "were all privately wondering and quaking," comforting himself with the thought that they, too, suffered from the same fear. As the torment becomes unbearable, Henry feels he is in "a moving box" that he and his comrades "we're all going to be sacrificed" as victims of a phantomatic state machinery that forced them to enlist. A resignation that promises no heroic performance overtakes him. As for himself, he thinks that the government was "taking him out to be slaughtered!"[147]

Despite his misgivings and his unrealistic idea about war, at the beginning of the first engagement Henry faces the enemy with little fear and fights well. As the enemy launches the first attack, a "red rage" seizes him. He wants to rush forward "and strangle with his fingers" the enemies. The Northerners withstand the first onslaught of the Confederates, and Henry thinks that he has tested himself and passed the trial. He feels good about himself, and he goes into "an ecstasy of self-satisfaction." However, the second attack by the Southern forces reignites his fear, and he begins to retreat, then runs like a rabbit, his panic "wondrously magnified." Overwhelmed by fear, he leaves the battlefield and heads for a thick wood, resolved to bury his shame in the darkness of its recesses. He knows that he has behaved like a coward. He is now about to undergo a crisis, which will help him find the mettle to rejoin the fight and to find the courage he needs. Shortly before Henry's comrades launch a counterattack, he rejoins the troops. He is now back on the field, feeling a "wild hate" for the same foe and army that the day before had terrorized him. He is now possessed by a rage that turns quickly into a "dark and stormy specter," leading him to "dream of abominable cruelties." He takes up a position behind a little tree, resolved "to hold it against the world." When the enemy retreats, Henry goes instantly forward, lunging ahead to attack them. He and his comrades "launch themselves at the throats of those who stood resisting." He goes after the flag, relishing his strikes and the bloodshed he is causing in an attempt to snatch it. "He plunged like a mad horse at it," resolved to get it and struggles valiantly with the standard-bearer and snatches it from him.[148] With the pursuit and capture of the enemy flag, Henry reaches the zenith of bravery.

How could he become a hero in the same battlefield where he had been a coward, and in such a short stretch of time? How was he able to change himself into one of those mythical war figures he had imagined at home? On the battlefield, he found an extraordinary strength, what he calls the "throat-grappling instinct," which turned him into a valiant combatant. At home, before he enlisted, he was convinced that modern men no longer knew how to engage themselves in "Greek-like" battles. They lacked the throat-grappling instinct that enabled warriors of old to display a bravery that is nowadays lost.; the softness of civilization has suppressed the savage instinct. "Secular and religious education had effaced the throat-grappling instinct, or else, firm finance held in check the passions." To fight with courage, Henry discovers, men must jettison the effects that civilization has had upon them, or perhaps civilization itself. It is the same discovery and the same prescription for building valiant soldiers made by Clausewitz. Freedom from civilization will give them back that throat-grappling instinct which was the privilege of heroic warriors. Henry dreams of recapturing the barbarous instinct. But to regain it, something radical must be done. He recalls that he "had been taught that a man became another thing in a battle." This change into another thing, he thinks, will be the acquisition of bravery, and "He saw his salvation in such a change."[149] Once he has changed, he will redeem himself from cowardice by means of a spectacular display of bravery.

Crane deploys a rich animal imagery to show Henry's change into another thing. The animal imagery that represents war, soldiers, and Henry in particular, is relentless, varied, and unsettling. One critic, struck by the peculiarly unheroic quality of the imagery, dismisses it as "stereotype."[150] Another critic blandly notes that most references to animals function to establish the similarity between humans and animals, ignoring Crane's purpose in establishing this similarity.[151] *The Red Badge of Courage* holds over seventy comparisons of men to animals, and the most significant metaphors are those that represent a change in Henry, in his manner of fighting, and in his vision of war.[152]

In the grip of his crisis, he finds a metaphor for war, "the red animal, the blood-swollen god." If war is an animal, the combatant is an intimate part of it. When Henry rejoins the troops, he is primed to face the enemy and to fight. He perceives its advance as "ruthless hunting," His "rage" reappears, and he responds as a cornered prey of the hunters. "He was not going to be badgered" like a cat hunted by boys. He does not yield to fear. "A wild hate" for the enemy prepares him to "develop teeth and claws" to counterattack successfully. The enemy presses the attack, and the Northern troops are pushed back. But Henry is fearless, cries out "savagely," crouches behind a tree with "teeth set in a curl-like snarl," and makes ready to stand and fight. He now imagines his comrades to be like himself— "Animals tossed for a death-struggle into a dark pit." Even as the enemy retreats, Henry's courage shines as he goes "instantly forward, like a dog who seeing his foe lagging," intensifies the pursuit. The picture of Henry as a dog has taken deep roots in Crane's imagination by the use of the personal possessive "his" rather than the impersonal "its,"[153] the dog is explicitly identified with Henry.

Inspired by Henry's bravery, his comrades fight and advance, oblivious of danger and death. Henry seems unconscious of his deeds while performing them, but in the aftermath of the engagement, he is kind of shaken out of his trance, wakes up, and finds "himself a knight," a hero of old. His bravery in the final battle is so extraordinarily intertwined with animal-like brutality that some comrades talk about his performance with disbelief, look at him in amazement, and regard him a "war devil." Even the company lieutenant is impressed. He praises Henry's performance, defining his newly found identity, "If I had ten thousand wild cats like you, I could tear th' stomach outa this war in less'n a week." The observation sounded so pleasing to Henry that he takes it as a "little coronation." To his comrades, he now appears to be "another thing," so much so that they no longer recognize him, and they question him in disbelief, "Are yeh all right, Fleming? Do yeh feel all right? There ain't nothin' th'matter with yeh, Henry, is there?" The comrades confirm that he has become unrecognizable from his former self. They see Henry as a being who acted under the power of forces that were more, and at once, less than human. On the second day of the battle when they rest behind some trees, "they were become men again,"[154] for their animal-like performance is temporarily suspended.

The animal imagery used to represent heroic behavior troubles some critics, and rightly so. They point out that Henry's performance on the battlefield changes the value of courage from that of a virtue to a vice. It seems to support the critical view that Crane's intention is to denigrate "the highest expression of man's duty, courage." What is implied in Henry's "change from cowardice to wild courage"[155] is that in his degradation, he found the courage he had yearned for from the time he became a soldier. After the battle, "it was revealed to him that he had been a barbarian, a beast." Nevertheless, he pretends that his degradation had not occurred, for he had acquired the throat-grappling instinct, which guaranteed his "salvation." Barbarism enabled him to solve his problems. They had fallen like paper peaks, and he was now what he called a hero,"[156] a hero by virtue of his degradation.

The idea of finding salvation in becoming "another thing" in battle goes back to Clausewitz. *On War* might have caught Crane's attention, for it deals specifically with organized masses of modern men in battle, like those engaged in combat at Chancellorsville in *The Red Badge of Courage*. It deals, among other things, with ways to generate and support the martial spirit in soldiers and officers. It raises degradation to the rank of a military virtue and reduces civilization to a vice, since civilized cultures are a hindrance to arousing the spirit to successfully fight wars. Unhindered by the mindset and the restraints that civilization places on modern man, the savage has been able to breed within himself the warrior spirit that Henry was desperately looking for. By Clausewitz's standards, Henry succeeded in counteracting the "softness" that spreads around in times of growing trade and prosperity. This is the weakness that Clausewitz identified as the enemy of the "spirit of boldness," and that Henry himself had decried as an obstacle to military courage in modern times, the weakness that had suppressed his throat-grappling instinct. Henry regained this instinct, and he fought with the courage that he sorely missed at the beginning of his military adventure, confirming Clausewitz's belief that bravery is born when the soldier repudiates all civilized restraints.[157]

Henry's change and his "salvation" also depend on his experience with death. While in the thick wood where he suffered for his shame, he came across some dead soldiers and meditates on death. The sight of one dead soldier with black ants running over his face in a chapel-like enclosure at first horrifies him. He shrieks, places a hand on a tree to support himself and cautiously retreats. But two significant responses follow. First, he imagines that the body might spring up and pursue him, and then he feels "a subtle suggestion to touch the corpse." Both responses bridge the distance that his instinctive horror had placed between him and the corpse, establishing a bond between the living and the dead. As he walks away, the spell that the corpse cast on him persists, and he imagines the ants swarming over the gray face to feed themselves. He hears "some strange voice," telling him the meaning of the ants feeding on the corpse, "all life existing upon death."[158] The experience with the corpse suggests to Henry, that death holds more value than life. In death he discovers a secret vitality and brings his crisis to a resolution. This helps him fight without any fear when he rejoins his comrades for the last battle.

The idea of death engendering life expands with Henry's vision of the battlefield as the "grinding of an immense and terrible machine," a machine whose grim work fascinates him. He wishes he were in the midst of battle, close to death. He wants to see it produce corpses, and as he approaches the battlefield, he spots what he was looking for, several corpses. He joins the retreating column of wounded soldiers. The sight of the wounds at first intensifies his desire for a wound of his own, but he soon abandons the idea of taking a "red badge" as a mark of courage.[159] By now Henry has probably understood that a red badge as a mark of courage is an inherently phony idea, for one can be courageous and be without a wound, or one can show a bleeding wound without having been brave. A red badge is now irrelevant to Henry. He wants more than a red badge. He wants the real thing, the courage to attack and kill the enemy.

Henry believes that the wounded soldiers he is now among to have been unafraid of death. He projects onto them what he wants for himself, courage and happiness in confronting death, and he conceives them to be peculiarly happy. Both the tattered man, with two red badges of courage, one on the head and the other on one arm, and Jim Conklin, with a hidden one on his side, walk toward their death, and Henry tags along beside them. Conklin, who moves "like one who goes to choose a grave," is unconsciously playing the theatrics of annihilation for Henry's benefit, who will soon find the courage he needs to face the enemy. Suddenly Conklin becomes grim, leaves the road, and by now completely absorbed in the business of dying, heads for a cluster of bushes. His wild movements give him the resemblance of "a devotee of a mad religion, blood-sucking." Far from regarding himself a victim, he delivers himself into the hands of death with religious-like fervor, setting an example for Henry and stirring in him the need to discover for himself this mad religion and to become its devotee. In Conklin, Henry observes the demands of the red animal, which, true to form, is there, "an animal" within Conklin's, body kicking and tumbling furiously. The side of his body looked as if it had been chewed by wolves.

Next, the tattered man's approaching demise reveals the existence of the red animal when Henry notices that he was beginning to act dumb and animal-like. This last spectacle of impending death awakens in Henry an urgent desire to rejoin the fighting, so much so that he abandons his comrade who, in agony, begs for help. With the experience of death gained by the proximity to the dying and wounded soldiers, Henry has now found a reason to repudiate life. He wishes for death: "He now thought that he wished he were dead. He believed that he envied those men whose bodies lay strewn over the grass of the fields and on the fallen leaves of the forest."[160]

The sight of the dead and the dying soldiers leads Henry to work out a concept of war, death, and nature, which will strengthen his resolve to sacrifice himself in battle. Crane styles this concept "the theory of the greased pig," a theory that enables him to tie death to glory in war and fulfill Clausewitz's prescription for winning wars—rejecting civilization in favor of the primitivism that generates heroism. The theory goes that the progress of civilization has made humanity more and more comfortable, to love life and live long. As a result, the living far outnumber the dead, and nature has to intervene to reestablish the balance. War marks nature's intervention. Henry can now rationalize both war and valor and embrace them both. War is nature's chief way to right the balance. War "was a make-shift remedy created because ordinary processes could not furnish deaths enough." However, since war by itself may not be enough to entice men to die, the concept of glory was embedded in war-making to provide men with a powerful incentive to sacrifice their life. To have the necessary number of dead, "nature had to formulate a beautiful excuse. She made glory. This made men willing, anxious, in haste, to come and be killed."[161]

Henry embraces death, brings his fear under control, and finds the fortitude needed to fight with bravery. Life is devalued by the destruction of those sentiments that form the cement of humanity. In its cunning, nature knows that men "must be inspired by some sentiment that they could call sacred," like martial virtue, "and enshrine in their hearts, something that would cause them to regard slaughter as a fine endeavor and go at it cheerfully—something that could destroy all the bindings of love and places that tie men's hearts." This philosophizing helps Henry to devalue life and guide him toward violent death. He can now throw his life away recklessly, fearlessly, and become a hero in the process. The theory of the greased pig decrees that for death and glory to triumph, the essential things in life must be despised and destroyed. Having digested nature's secret plan for promising men glory and getting them killed, Henry, too, is ready to die. He succumbs to the call of death, submitting himself with an apocalyptic flair to what he judges to be mankind's death wish—for mankind "not only worshipped the gods of the ashes but that the gods of the ashes were worshipped because they were the gods of the ashes."[162]

The thought of his own death exalts him. He pictures himself "getting calmly killed" and imagines the "magnificent pathos of his dead body." His thoughts uplift him, and he feels "the quiver of war-desire." As a result, "he himself felt the daring spirit of a savage, religion mad." When his bravery reaches its highest intensity with the capture of the enemy flag, courage and death meet. Death will spare him, but he accepts it as he declares himself capable of "a tremendous death,"[163] yielding to its ecstasy in the frenzy of his last fight.

CAUSE

The desire to fight with courage coupled with the inability to do so caught Henry Fleming in a dramatic conflict. Crane resolved it by changing him into another thing, giving him the means to be fearless. One wonders whether degradation is the only way out of cowardice for the soldier who wants to be brave. The protagonists of *The Song of Roland and Jerusalem Delivered* show how a religious belief can drive combatants to fight with a willingness to die. But history has shown that religious fervor, has often arisen for less than a noble end. Outside of the religious field, cause begins to play a role only in the nineteenth century with Tolstoy. He is the first writer to recognize the value of cause and to ascribe to it a vital role in the combatant's performance.

Clausewitz placed no weight on a cause, and Crane abstained from giving Henry Fleming a cause for which to fight. Clausewitz conceded that soldiers may draw their martial spirit from enthusiasm for a cause, but the cause is irrelevant to courage, he declared. He believed that the absence of a cause can provide superior advantages to the combatant. Freedom from political and ethical worries enables the soldier to become absorbed by the appointed task and steeped in the spirit of the activity that generates courage. This is the first step in distancing the soldier from his human self and transforming him into another thing, savage and brave. This transformation, not the cause, is essential to the life of the martial spirit. Henry Fleming ignored the motive for which he fought. He had no notion about the cause or the aim of the Civil War; slavery, and freedom had no place in his mental space. His heroic ideal and resolve took shape at home where he lived war intensely in books and in his imagination. The battles he read about thrilled him with their sweep and fire. Envisioned wars and deeds of valor gained a mystical hold on him. He could see himself displaying "eagle-eyed prowess." But for all this, war failed to stir his moral and intellectual self; only superficial feelings stirred him. The church bell, tolling in the middle of the night to announce a great battle, sent him into shivers of "a prolonged ecstasy of excitement." The enthusiastic welcome of the crowds given his regiment during its trip to Washington, confirmed him in his belief that "he must be a hero."[164]

It is not by chance alone that Henry went to war without a belief in a cause, a thing so much more astounding in so far as the Civil war was fought for a good cause, human freedom. Rather, it is Crane's narrative strategy to show how the harrowing experience of the battlefield can produce heroism through degradation. The belief in a cause might have led him to fight gallantly. Instead, degradation turned out to be his means to valiant behavior. Had he made freedom his cause for fighting, degradation would have had no place in his being and his conduct. Had he understood the moral and political reasons for fighting, he would not have degraded himself in order to give himself courage. In the context of the novel, only the absence of his belief in the cause made his degradation possible.

A soldier without a cause is diminished on both moral and military counts. Tolstoy knew well the officers' corps and the social class that produced it, and he saw their desire to show valor, and at once, their inability to be truly valiant. He is the first writer to represent the combatants' fear, especially the officers who show both passion and hostility for valor. They want to act with courage, but are unable to do so, and they are dejected by their impotence. The officers in the *Tales* are ruled by fear and ambition but want to be recognized as brave to enhance their military and social career. Since most of them want recognition without the courage necessary to earn it, they cheat and lie to reach their goal.[165]

In *War and Peace*, the Russian army fights the French invaders. But the officers on the battlefield acknowledge no noble impulse and show no willingness to make sacrifices. They have no belief in the cause and show no courage in battle. Still, they try to convince their superiors that they are brave. At the battle of Schöngraben, a not better identified "thin, weak looking" colonel rides up to General Bagration to announce that his regiment withstood a French cavalry charge and lost more than half of its men. The report is a lie, but the colonel speaks of heroism and sacrifice to elicit Bagration's admiration for himself and his unit. When Bagration's adjutant, Zherkov, was sent by the general to the weakening left flank with the order to withdraw, panic prevented him from carrying out the order. In the meantime, the leaders who held the left flank do no fighting and squabble among themselves, mutually challenging "their courage." They all "believed themselves heroes" and were "anxious to display their pluck" before the general. True to form, General Bagration accepts his officers' deceptive claim of heroism and even praises them without any reservation. "I thank you all, gentlemen," Bagration addresses them in the aftermath of the engagement, "all branches of the service behaved heroically—infantry, cavalry, and artillery." Fake heroism works well as a tool for keeping the loyalty of the officers and their morale up. At Krasnoe during the retreat of the French some Russian generals were "burning to distinguish themselves," and to this end they fought some "sickening and meaningless" battles. They "believed themselves heroes and imagined that what they were doing was the noblest and most honourable achievement." After the battle, they even disputed among themselves who had gained the most distinction.[166]

One officer, the pipe-smoking Captain Tushin, stands out for his valor. However, his type of courage has to do more with the character of the man than with the cause he fights for or with his feelings about the war. Tolstoy considers him the hero of Schöngraben. Tushin is cool and efficient under fire, solicitous in helping the wounded, and fearless. He acts in such a way as to show "how heroic actions... are performed in battle by most ordinary" men. At the village of Schöngraben, he keeps four cannons constantly firing, protects the withdrawal of the Russians from the village, sets it on fire, and delays the advance of the French. His qualities reflect the "spirit" of the Russian soldier, which has to do with "modesty, simplicity, and a capacity for seeing in peril something quite else than the danger." The success of the day belongs to "the heroic steadiness of Captain Tushin and his men." His heroism was stoked by his sense of duty, his competence, and his honesty.[167]

In Tolstoy's vision, the cause is a belief that springs from moral or ideological values that the combatant spontaneously embraces, a belief that leads him to fight with a conviction and a resolve stronger than his love of life. The cause generates heroism, the tool of both military and ideological victory. Where there is no cause, or where there is an objectionable one, heroism is out of the question. In *War and Peace,* Tolstoy attempts to "deglamorize" military valor and the martial virtues in general, one critic believes.[168] He is right, but the martial valor that Tolstoy devalues is of a special kind. He denies heroism to Napoleon, and his denial is significant in that the French emperor and his army represented the most powerful and successful military organism of their time. Tolstoy attacks Napoleon's ideal of "glory and greatness," which was fed by his wars of conquest with the purpose of dominating other countries. To create his own heroic model, Tolstoy discards that of Napoleon by assailing his ideal of glory and his cult of heroism, which he cultivated with unparalleled skill.[169] That ideal thrives on wars made to kill people, to conquer countries, and to enhance Napoleonic power. It is no cause for warring and must be devalued, and the ideals destroyed. For Tolstoy, fighting Napoleon meant opposing death and destruction; it meant to defend life.

Tolstoy had already become aware of the life-denying power of conventional valor in the Sevastopol sketches where he had detected it among the reward-starved officers. They harbored, he noted, a little Napoleon in their hearts, "a petty monster ready to start a battle and kill a hundred men" just for the sake of building their reputation for heroism. This spurious idea and practice of valor contrasts with the valor that affirms life, which was shown by the Russian soldiers in the Sevastopol hospital. Tolstoy bestows on these men the honorific name of "defenders of Sevastopol," because they had fought and lived through the phases of "real" war, "blood, suffering, and death." Yet, none of them spoke of their fighting, their wounds, or of their misery, trying to cast themselves as heroes. Their cause was the defense of life, which was done by means of an inner strength that defied pain and fear, a strength very similar to that of the American natives imagined by Montaigne. The "grandeur and firmness of spirit" of these men enabled them to rise above pain and suffering. It allowed even older soldiers to sit up firmly, defying the burden of their ravaged bodies. Here in the hospital, a war between life and death is waged continuously especially in that section where the wounded wait for surgery. None of them laments his fate, nor does one make any attempt to cast one's injuries as the result of any heroic deed made for the love of country. These soldiers could take the misery that the battlefield had inflicted on them, because their martial spirit enabled them to keep their bodies alive and active. In the hospital, they now fight a battle without any weapon, or better, with the most powerful weapon of all, the strength of their spirit. Not only are they the defenders of Sevastopol. They are its heroes, as they defy pain, death, and hunger. The sight of "the heroism of the defenders of Sevastopol" gives Tolstoy "a joyous conviction of the strength of the Russian people."[170] Their cause is life itself, aided by that firmness of spirit that enabled them to stand up to suffering and death. Their heroism consists in defying the destructive effect of the battlefield.

Conventional martial valor is the enemy of life, and life defeats it. Tolstoy's vision is shown from a different perspective in Count Nikolay Rostov's encounter with a French officer at Ostrovna. Rostov pursues on horseback the dragoon, overtakes him, wounds him, and captures him. The officer was scared and running away, and there was no danger for Rostov and no risk. His exploit had little military significance.

However, the Russian commander cites him for performing a "gallant action" and recommends him for a decoration and a promotion. Rostov gains a reputation for "fearless gallantry" and is recognized as "an officer of dauntless courage." On his way back from the pursuit and capture, Rostov had already felt "some disagreeable sensation, a kind of ache at his heart." After the citation, he becomes silent and preoccupied and later suffers from an "unpleasant vague feeling of moral nausea." He realizes that the meaning of his performance has been falsified. He cannot believe that he acted with valor and is amazed at receiving the reward. "I can't make it out," he tells himself. He recalls that at one point of his supposed deed of valor, he had a distinctly unbelligerent feeling. The instant he struck the French dragoon, Rostov's martial eagerness "suddenly vanished." He looked at his foe to make out what sort of enemy he had vanquished, and discerned on his face, at first, terror, and then beauty and youth. The Frenchman's face, with a dimple on the chin and clear blue eyes, "was the most unwarlike, most good-natured face, more in place by a quiet fireside than on the field of battle." "Why," Rostov asks himself, "is this all that's meant by heroism? And was he to blame with his dimple and his blue eyes?" He recalls how frightened the dragoon was when he bore down on him and restrained himself from striking and killing him. Rostov sees himself as a distinctly unheroic soldier and his reward absurd, "My hand trembled. And they have given me the St. George Cross."[171] Rostov saw in the French dragoon, not the enemy, but a human face, beautiful, and vibrant with life, not the substance and purpose of valor—violence and death. He knows that the reward acknowledged something he had repudiated the moment he faced the French soldier, the moment Rostov refused to transmute life and beauty into death. He chose life over death and in the process, he repudiated conventional valor.

The scene representing the wounded Prince Andrey on the field in the aftermath of the battle at the Czech village of Austerlitz is perhaps the most meaningful repudiation of conventional valor and of the ideal of glory and greatness. Prince Andrey, lying on the ground with a head wound, discovers the truth about his own life and that of Napoleon, who believed himself to be another Alexander the Great. Andrey opens his eyes, sees the sky above him, and discovers the poetry of peace, "How quietly, peacefully, and triumphantly, and not like us running, shouting, and fighting. "How differently are those clouds creeping over that lofty, limitless sky. How was it I did not see that lofty sky before?" The sky becomes a symbol of the kind of life he had never known, a life in a peace divorced from the military virtues, "And how happy I am to have found it at last. Yes! All is vanity, all is cheat, except that infinite sky. There is nothing, nothing but that. But even that is not, there is nothing but peace and stillness."[172]

When death threatens the prince, life becomes an essential value, a value that he had never held before when his life was secure. He had believed in the military virtues and had made Napoleon, the highest representative of those virtues, his idol. But the prince knows now that if he had acted by military virtues alone, he would have never known the meaning of life and would have been an accomplice in its destruction. His enhanced sense of life enables him to see that the military virtues deny life, and he is now ready to repudiate them.

In the aftermath of the battle, Napoleon makes a tour of the field. He was fond of looking over the dead and wounded lying around on battlefields, thinking that in doing so he was showing "his dauntless spirit" and holding up his ideal of glory and greatness. Here the dead and the wounded frame the presence of Napoleon. "That's a fine death," he says as he looks at the Russian prince lying on the ground. "Fine men!" he again says of other soldiers on the ground, so praising the military virtue that forms the basis of his ideal, namely, death. For the emperor, the best in man comes out of death, and it must be acclaimed because it is part and parcel of the military virtues. Prince Andrey was an admirer of Napoleon and considered him "his hero." However, after his extraordinary inner experience, the admiration for his hero fades. The emperor is "a small, insignificant creature in comparison with what was passing now between his [Andrey's] soul and that lofty, limitless sky." Despite the halo of glory and greatness that still surrounds Napoleon, he appears to the wounded prince in a new, insignificant light. The emperor turns to him, who was thrust forward to complete the show of prisoners. "And you young man," the emperor asks, "how are you feeling?" Unlike his comrades, who reply to Napoleon's queries like brave soldiers ought to reply, Andrey remains silent, remembering "that lofty, righteous, and kindly sky which he had seen and comprehended." He refuses to embrace the rhetoric of valor and be drawn into the fraternity of the braves. Life gains new value as the value of glory and greatness is eclipsed. Andrey has now found a cause to carry on the fight in the future, the ugliness of the prevalent conception and practice of valor. He is called "mon brave" by Napoleon, and he reacts by remaining silent, stripping Napoleon of his shiny attributes. Napoleon is irrelevant. "So trivial seemed to him at that moment all the interests that were engrossing Napoleon. So petty seemed to him his hero, with his paltry vanity and glee of victory, in comparison with that lofty, righteous, and kindly sky which he had seen and comprehended, that he could not answer him. And all indeed seemed to him so trifling and unprofitable beside the stern and solemn train of thought aroused in him by weakness from loss of blood, and the nearness of death. Gazing into Napoleon's eyes, Prince Andrey mused on the nothingness of greatness."[173] A critic notes that wounded Andrey confronting Napoleon on the battlefield of Austerlitz regards "both glory and heroism as mere words."[174] Glory and heroism are words without meaning when set against the background of a life whose value and beauty Andrey has discovered. He "was only glad that people were standing over him, and his only desire was that these people should help him and bring him back to life, which seemed to him so good, because he saw it quite differently now."[175] The resurgence of the value of life coincides with the rejection of the ideal of glory and greatness.

In *War and Peace*, the attack on the life-denying power of valor gains relevance as the ideal of Napoleonic greatness emerges from the emperor's resolve to ennoble "every crime, and ascribe to it an incomprehensible, supernatural value." It was in Africa that he first transformed crimes against humanity into a military virtue. There a whole series of outrages was perpetrated on a helpless population, and those responsible persuaded themselves that performing atrocities "is noble, it is glory, that it is like Caesar and Alexander of Macedon, and that it is fine." In Africa it was revealed that "glory and greatness" were based on crimes hidden under the mantle of valor—on wars of conquest, on the tyrannizing of defeated peoples, and on indiscriminate violence. The mystique of Napoleonic glorification requires that military crimes be transformed into virtuous deeds. Bonaparte himself was so successful in redefining military values that his deeds on the battlefields bewitched most European countries. Europe's fear of, and complicity in Napoleon's crimes, transmuted them into glorious deeds, and fostered admiration for them, "There is no act, no crime, no petty deceit which he [Napoleon] would not commit, and which would not be at once represented on the lips of those about him as a great deed."[176] It is in the context of these crimes that Tolstoy's attempt at shattering the glamour of valor must be considered; no virtue can arise from criminal deeds. The other aspect of Tolstoy's deglamorization is the fight of the Russian people against Napoleon. Opposing Napoleon means more than simply seeking a military victory. It means destroying the military machine that embodies a code of heroism that requires death and destruction. The Russian cause is the destruction of the organism that upholds the ideal of glory and greatness, the very basis of Napoleonic valor.

The opposition to the invading army is worked out not as the enterprise of selected soldiers or generals, but as the endeavor of the Russian people as a whole. It is dictated not by metaphysical or ethical impulses as in the case of Prince Andrey, but by their instinctive reaction against an enemy bent on conquest and oppression. The Russian cause is the defense of their land and way of life. Napoleon's aggression generates in the people a spontaneous impulse to resist and to fight. Already, in "The Raid," Tolstoy had a kind of intuition about the value and role of cause in arousing courage. "In every danger there is a choice. Does it not depend on whether the choice is prompted by a noble feeling or a base one, whether it should be called courage or cowardice?"[177]

But in "The Raid," the role of a whole people in war is absent. It is only when Tolstoy starts to meditate and write about the French invasion and the spontaneous response of his people that he ascribes a central role to them. Theirs is a collective impulse that justifies the use of the martial virtues. This premise governs Tolstoy's artistic and military strategy. It shapes both the battle of Borodino and the Russians' pursuit of the retreating French across the steppe. The idea of animating the people with the spontaneous, untutored military spirit that would enable them to oppose and prevail over Napoleon's Grand Army and bring down the ideal of glory and greatness comes from some kind of unconventional force, which Tolstoy defines the Russian "spirit."[178]

The inspiration for Tolstoy's choice was born years before the struggle against Napoleon became the centerpiece of *War and Peace*. It was born in the Caucasus, not among Tolstoy's people, but among his enemies, the hill men fighting for their lives against the Russians. On his way to battle the rebels in the Caucasus, Tolstoy had an experience similar to Prince Andrey's at Austerlitz, a spiritual communion with nature, signaling a revelation. On a night march with the battalion that will attack and destroy the hill men's villages, the beauty and stillness of the night that breathed with "pacifying beauty and power" captures Tolstoy's imagination. The esthetic experience suddenly evokes the thing that denies both beauty and life—war. "Can it be possible," he broods, "that in the midst of this entrancing Nature, feelings of hatred, vengeance, or the desire to exterminate their fellows, can endure in the souls of men" and foster war? Hardly. But at the same time, another voice tells Tolstoy that war can be just and necessary. He questions both the Russians' and the mountain tribes' reasons for fighting each other, trying to discover on whose side "justice" resides. At first it seems to be on the side of the Russians, ostensibly fighting to keep their territories safe from the raids of the unruly tribes. But Tolstoy rejects the idea that territorial security justifies war. War is justified only if it is fought for the preservation of individual life. "On whose side is the feeling of self-preservation and consequently of justice?" he asks, "is it on the side of this ragamuffin—some Djemi or other—who hearing of the approach of the Russians snatches down his old gun from the wall, ... and on seeing that the Russians still advance, approaching the fields he has sown which they will tread down and his hut which they will burn, and the ravine where his mother, his wife, and his children have hidden themselves, shaking with fear—seeing that he will be deprived of all that constitutes his happiness—in impotent anger and with a cry of despair, tears off his tattered jacket, flings down his gun, and drawing his sheepskin cap over his eyes sings his death-song and flings himself headlong onto the Russian bayonets with only a dagger in his hand?" Or is justice on the side of this officer on the general's staff who is singing French chansonettes and who has come to the Caucasus "just by chance and to show his courage" and has become "the hills men's enemy" to enable himself to return to Russia and enjoy a comfortable position?[179] Justice is on the side of those ordinary people who defend, not privilege, but their right to exist, man's ultimate cause for resorting to violence. This defense enables them to oppose a ruthless enemy with a spontaneous, death-defying response.

A brief section of *Hadji Murat*, which also deals with warfare in the Caucasus, highlights the root of the tribesmen's response to the Russian attack on their life and property. It is vital for these people to respond, and in responding they show that a truly courageous act is valorous in the sense that it has a noble or worthy purpose. On returning to his hamlet raided by a Russian party, a Caucasian chieftain found his house destroyed and his young son dead, bayoneted in the back. Two other men lay dead on the street. The old grandfather sat on the ruins of the house staring blankly into space. The water in the fountain was polluted on purpose, and the food taken away. Women and children wailed, and hungry animals howled. The villagers felt an elementary emotion—rage. They refused to recognize these Russians "as men at all" and embraced an urge to destroy them. It was "an instinct as natural as that of self-preservation," like the "urge to destroy rats, venomous spiders or wolves."[180]

The passion that generated the energy in the hill people is the same that stirred the Russians threatened by the French invaders in *War and Peace*. The Russians suffered the same kind of onslaught that struck the hill men in the Caucasus, and the Russians defended themselves and their land with the same spirit that possessed the tribesmen. This unique spirit first shows up in the battle of Borodino. Tolstoy gives that battle an extraordinarily imaginative and, from the point of view of history, arbitrary interpretation. First, he inflates Russian losses, one-half of the army, whereas in fact the army actually had only 40,000 casualties, one-third of its effective force. And at the same time, he judges the battle a victory for the Russians. The Russian generals judged the battle a defeat for General Kutuzov, but Kutuzov judged it a victory, for the reason that the Russians suffered their losses "without being driven from their position."[181]

The battle could be defined as indecisive at best, as military historians do. Secondly, Tolstoy deliberately ignores the role of the military leadership. He seizes on the battle of Borodino as a grand opportunity to champion his view that historical events are divorced from those men commonly recognized as the movers of history, the leaders, including Napoleon. The outcome of the battle depended on the "millions of men," who fired the guns and transported provisions and cannons. They were the ones who held the power to determine the outcome. The leaders played only a minor role, while "an infinite number of varied and complicated causes" led those millions of men on the battlefield to follow their leaders' orders. The moving power of history and war rests with the mass of people, Tolstoy argues, "For the investigation of the laws of history, we must completely change the subject of our observations, let kings and ministers and generals alone, and study the homogeneous, infinitesimal elements by which the masses are led."[182]. The people in the field wield the weapons and have within themselves the will and spirit to win, or the resignation for defeat. Orders from above are significant only in the manner of their execution, but the strength of the execution depends on the spirit of the people fighting on the battlefield.

What enabled the Russian soldiers to withstand the French charges at Borodino was "the 'spirit' of the troops." Even though historians consider this spirit an indefinable and incalculable factor, nothing more than a concept derived from Joseph de Maistre's "general irrationalism," it nonetheless holds decisive power in *War and Peace*. Tolstoy calls Borodino a victory because he saw in the battle the "spirit of the army" in action.[183]

Some critics object to Tolstoy's glowing estimate of the battle, for it is hard to acknowledge the presence of virtue where slaughter prevails. "Why value courage," if it is shown by such action as the "senseless slaughter of Borodino?"[184]

Tolstoy ignored the senseless slaughter, because violence and bloodshed at Borodino had a special meaning for him. After witnessing the lackluster showing of so many aristocratic officers in the *Tales of Army Life*, Tolstoy couldn't help but admire a people who, prompted by the "spirit" burning within themselves, spontaneously faced the violence of the battlefield. The heroism of the Russians overshadowed other considerations.

At the height of the battle of Borodino, the Adjutant-general Woltzogen rides up to General Kutuzov's quarters and announces that the Russian troops "are completely routed." Kutuzov, almost choking with anger, cries out: "How dare you, sir, tell me that? You know nothing about it. Tell General Barclay from me that his information is incorrect, and that I, the commander-in-chief, knows more of the course of the battle than he does." What does Kutuzov know that the generals in the field do not? He knows almost nothing about the tactical victories or defeats taking place on the battlefield, and whatever he knows is insufficient to justify the sweeping denial of Woltzogen's report. Kutuzov knows that Murat was captured, but he gets bad news from a field commander reporting a weakness on the left flank, and he also learns that the town of Semyonovskoye is lost to the French. But he knows something that no one else knows, something that enables him to estimate the meaning and outcome of the battle in a way no one else can. Kutuzov knows what Napoleon at the end of the day feels in his bones, that after eight hours spent in a tense attack, the Russians "still held their ground." For Kutuzov, this meant a defeat for the French. He somehow also knows that Napoleon has read impending disaster in the faces of his staff. "All their faces were gloomy; all avoided each other's eyes." Napoleon's decision to hold back the Imperial Guard toward the end of the engagement reflected his sense of doom: Russian strength appeared to him great, and he knew that not even his elite troops would be able to turn the tide of the battle. "I am not going to let my Guard be destroyed," Napoleon replies to the general suggesting its deployment.[185]

Kutuzov also read the state of the battlefield in the faces of the officers reporting to him from the field. The old general detected something inexpressible, signs that "the spirit of the army" had come alive. Experience and wisdom taught Kutuzov that the fate of battles is decided not by the orders of the superior, nor the positions of the troops, nor by the number of cannons, but by "that intangible force called the spirit of the army." He casts Kutuzov in the role of the discoverer and interpreter of that spirit. Kutuzov "followed that force and led it as far as it lay in his power." He was so confident in the Russian spirit and in its power to overcome the enemy that at the end of the battle of Borodino, he issues the order to launch an offensive the next day. He tells his aides that the "enemy is defeated" and that tomorrow the Russians will drive the French out of Russia. The order for the offensive was transmitted to every officer and soldier in the field, and everyone "took comfort and courage again." The order reflected the strength of the spirit of the army along with the willingness to unleash it on the French.[186]

Historically, no such order was given, neither did the Russians attack the French on the day after the battle at Borodino. In the fall of 1812, the Russian army withdrew east of Moscow. The reason Tolstoy ascribed to Kutuzov the decision to renew the fight was to underscore the importance of the aggressive spirit in winning battles. The energy it produced came from an "outflow of a feeling that lay deep in the heart of the commander-in-chief, and deep in the heart of every Russian." Kutuzov's imaginary order to attack reflected his belief that the spirit of his troops was strong, that they wanted to fight, and that they knew they could win. In the end, having stood up to the French charges, the Russians not only reported a victory, but compelled "the enemy to recognize the moral superiority of its opponent." This is the victory that Kutuzov saw born out of the slaughter that was Borodino. Napoleon's subsequent flight from Russia meant the ruin of the invading army of five hundred thousand men, and the downfall of Napoleonic rule, on which, for the first time at Borodino, "was laid the hand of a foe of stronger spirit."[187]

The flight of Tolstoy's imagination away from the military and political facts fits his pattern of subjectivity. He is able to put an end to the Napoleonic hegemony in Europe and bestow on the Russian people the courage to fight and win. To this end, he even ignores Kutuzov's bungles. He never criticizes the general's conduct of the war. He transforms him from the aged sensualist and corrupt courtier of the early draft of *War and Peace* into an exemplary leader. Understandably, his purpose is designed to enhance the role of the military spirit in successful outcomes. He manipulates Kutuzov because he needs him as the "unforgettable symbol of the Russian people in all their simplicity and intuitive wisdom."[188]. Kutuzov's order to fight again the day after Borodino reflects, not military strategy, but Tolstoy's view that the leaders matter less than the inclination and will of the soldiers, that the "spirit," which consists in "the greater or less desire to fight and to face dangers on the part of all men composing the army," decides the outcome of war.[189]

Having discovered Russian valor in the spirit of the people, Tolstoy even resorts to arithmetic to show its role in battle along with the role of genius, maneuver, weaponry, and the number of troops. Suppose he writes in *War and Peace*, that a force of ten battalions wins a battle against a force of fifteen battalions by killing or capturing all the enemies while losing four of its battalions. The net loss is four battalions for the first force and fifteen for the second one. The result means that the sacrifice of four battalions yielded the destruction of fifteen battalions, or to put it another way, that four battalions wielded more power than fifteen. From the point of view of standard military science, which holds that the greater the number of combatants, the greater the strength of an army ("les gros bataillons ont toujours raison"), that hypothetical result makes no sense. So to explain how the loss of four battalions can lead to the destruction of fifteen enemy battalions, four must be multiplied by the X factor, which is the "spirit of the army" defined here as "the greater or less desire to fight and face danger," for "the spirit of the army is the factor which multiplied by the mass gives the product of the force."[190] Alarmed by both this attempt at translating intangible values into tangible ones, and by the claim implicit in Tolstoy's reasoning—that by mathematically manipulating military data one can discover "historical laws"—critics have branded the novelist's math in the fourteenth part of *War and Peace* a mystification. If the critics are right, then one must recognize that by ignoring military genius and weaponry to stress the superiority of the spirit, Tolstoy risked his credibility. In taking that risk he shows that he considered the role of the spirit in battle decisive.

What lends power to the spirit as a military tool is its root in the cause that the soldiers embrace. Tolstoy writes that between the battle of Borodino and the beginning of the French retreat, there was no relevant battle. After Borodino the French army no longer posed any threat to Russia and her people, and further action against the retreating army was unnecessary. Nevertheless, the Russians decided to go after the French, turning their retreat into the flight of a beast chased by a hunter. To highlight the role of the spirit, Tolstoy turns the Russian pursuit of the fleeing French across the steppe into a military epic. "The spirit of the men ran so high that individual men killed the French without orders and needed no compulsion to face hardships and dangers." Of course, Russian bravery had its limitations in so far as the Russians knew the French would be easy prey for the pursuing army. Why could there not have been more restraint now that Napoleon's army ceased to exist? Because Tolstoy had become wrapped up in his discovery of the "spirit of the army," and his imagination could not restrain the impulse even when it was no longer needed. It was the animating force of the Russians on the retreating French. He calls it a renewal of the spirit that had originally come to life at Borodino. In truth, what motivated the Russians was not the ease with which they could abolish the French, but the persuasion that they were destroying the enemies of life itself. Tolstoy narrates that "the cudgel of the people's war was raised in all its menacing and majestic power... till the whole invading army had been driven out." This simple but terrible weapon, the cudgel, caused "many thousands" of enemy soldiers to be slain by the Cossacks and common people alike, who killed the invaders "as instinctively as dogs set upon a stray mad dog."[191] The picture is ugly, but as a portrayal of the working of the Russian spirit, it is highly effective.

The hunting out of the retreating French was no longer a part of the Tsar's or Kutuzov's war. Overstepping the traditional rules of war was guided, not by the events of 1812 on the Russian steppe, but by Tolstoy's war experience in the Caucasus where the mountain men had fought a people's war against their would-be conquerors. It became a battle against an army bent on destroying the life of the tribesmen. Tolstoy's imagination is now guided by a vision of the spirit as the defender of life. Fighting was for the tribesmen "a question of life or death." They fought with the same terrifying abandon with which the Russians attacked the French on the steppe. Both the hill man and the Russian soldier attacking the retreating French go after the enemy as though he were a dangerous animal. In *War and Peace*, the enemy is a "stray mad dog." In *Hadji Murat*, the enemy is depicted as "rats, venomous spiders or wolves."[192] All are a danger to human life, and if life is to be preserved, they must be destroyed.

Tolstoy recorded in some detail an account of the Russians under attack while withdrawing from a village they had pillaged in the Caucasus. The withdrawing troops were helpless in dealing with the hill men's tactic. The soldiers of two Russian battalions on the march caught glimpses of the pursuers mounted and on foot, rifle in hand, running from one tree to another. Their boldness put fear in the bravest Russians who brought the cannons into action, but were unable to disengage, and even came under heavy fire from the hill men. Their daring action instilled fear in Tolstoy. "But why," he concluded, "should I describe the details of that terrible picture which I would myself give much to be able to forget!"[193]

The skirmish must have made an impression on him because he neither forgot that picture, nor did he intend to forget it, for it came back to haunt his imagination. He recreated it in the Russian pursuit of the retreating French. He must have wondered about the bravery and offensive power of the hill men, though they were fighting in apparently a disorganized and unmilitary fashion. They drew their fighting spirit from something more powerful than organization, training, and conventional strategy. None of the laws that compelled the Russian officers to serve, or the lure of a cushy career and a comfortable place in society, played a role in the tribesmen's decision to fight because the aim of their struggle was compelling, and belief in their cause transcended both life and death. The rebels in the Caucasus, like the Russians in pursuit of the French in 1812, "needed no compulsion to face hardships and dangers" because their "spirit... ran so high."[194] In those pages where Tolstoy writes about the Russian spirit rising against Napoleon's army, a sentence stands out: "Happy the people who, in the moment of trial... with ease and directness pick up the first cudgel that comes handy and deals blows with it, till resentment and revenge give way to contempt and pity."[195] The cause rests on a question of life and death and generates a heroism that exalts the warriors.

AGAINST DEATH

IN 1914 the great majority of men who marched to the frontline in the Great War had no choice between enjoying peace at home or fighting in the trenches. They were conscripted. New and grave perils challenged them—the degrading demands of trench life, the heavy artillery, the rapid firing machine guns, and gas. Just as the desire to act valiantly had put pressure on Henry Fleming in the *Red Badge of Courage*, so did the duty to serve and fight in the trenches pressure the combatants of the Great War to find the courage necessary to do their job. Some succeeded, others questioned the war and their role in it. But it is clear that Tolstoy's vision of the cause as a motive power capable of galvanizing masses of combatants into an irresistible fighting force finds no place in the imagination and history of the Great War.

In that war the combatants feared wounds and death more than in previous wars. Damage and death could be inflicted easily and rapidly, and at the end of the war, the number of dead and wounded would be enormous. The fear of death grew, and the number of desertions from all fronts was very high. The attachment to life had increased, and its preservation became for many combatants their only cause. Because the Great War was extraordinarily bloody, traditional valor was expensive for those who practiced it of their own will or who fought against it. It gradually lost its value, and in the face of the enormous losses in men on the Western and Italian fronts, valiant fighting came to be regarded as a waste. The Battle of Aubers Ridge in Artois in 1915, for instance, consisted of "a disastrous fifteen hours of squandered heroism" without any hope or sign of success. In one day, the British lost 458 officers and 11,161 men.[196] By the end of the first day of the offensive on the Somme, 60.000 soldiers of the British empire were dead. The large number of casualties on the Western front was alarming, especially to the troops. "We all know that there must be losses," an English combatant brooded, "you can't expect to take a trench without some casualties; but they [headquarters] seem to go on from saying that losses are unavoidable to thinking that they are necessary, and from that, to thinking that they don't matter."[197] However, headquarters insisted on launching attacks and sustaining losses, and not only on the Western front. By November 1915, the army on the Italian front had fought four of the so-called battles of the Isonzo River, losing nearly a quarter of a million men, wounded or dead, without achieving any strategic or territorial gain.

Why were so many soldiers sent to their death when their sacrifice produced no strategic gains? One reason was the prevailing strategy—the frontal attack. It was based on the belief that valor was the most valuable ingredient in battle, and that it counted more than the results of the fighting. Military leaders taught the recruits that "wars are won by the unconquerable spirit,"[198] the stuff of heroism, not by superior weapons and equipment. As a result, lives were sacrificed unsparingly. The troops were sent relentlessly on attacks and forced "out of one bloody misery into another," as one infantryman wrote.[199] Headquarters' demand for valiant behavior often sent soldiers on frontal attacks, in which they were easily decimated by the entrenched enemy. In spite of this, excessive casualties were not regarded as the symptom of a failed strategy and a waste of manpower, but as a sign of valor; or else it was the price that combatants needed to pay to forge a fighting spirit. For the first time in the history of organized warfare, valor became a vital virtue in the eyes of the leaders. At the same time, cowardice became a reprehensible vice, punishable by law. Military tribunals on the Western and Italian fronts punished the lack of valor, that is cowardice, occasionally by death.

Among officers, the fear of showing cowardice could be greater than the fear of being killed. On the Italian front, the pressure to show courage was high and the imperative to avoid cowardice intense. But the courage necessary to attack the enemy trenches, an officer who fought in the infantry recalled, was hard to muster even though one was resolved. As a result, he fell prey to the fear of showing fear. One was afraid of being afraid. This kind of fear "claws at the throat"; it was a common torment and an especially degrading one for officers. It was this "fear of fear" that the combatant wanted to overcome at all costs, even during the "flight forward," when the attack would become an act of desperation, a suicide, but could be regarded an act of courage. The combatant who rushed toward the enemy line was impelled by desperation; and ran, screaming, against the enemy and against his own fear. The rush marked the end of the spasmodic nightmare of being regarded a coward. "Thus, men through fear become heroes and win."[200] No one who has not known the Carso, the rocky plateau near Gorizia where the Italians fought many bloody but indecisive battles against the Austrians, can understand how fear gripped a man's throat and his struggle against it, another officer recalls. The assault was an opportunity to end the painful interior struggle with "the flight forward" toward death and away from cowardice. The run toward the enemy line ended the unbearable torment of uncontrollable fear.[201] On the other hand, a soldier might flee away from the enemy toward the rear of his own line showing more courage than he who attacks the enemy. He is more valiant because he will be under fire from both foes and friends, whose military police may capture and shoot him at any time. He, too, is brave since his flight will bring certain death.[202]

Robert Graves clearly saw the meaning and the results of the offensive strategy. Two days after England declared war on Germany, he enlisted in the Royal Welch Fusiliers, a regiment with a tradition rich in heroic exploits. He went to war resolved to play a heroic part in it. At the front, where he was sent as a nineteen-year-old officer, he learned that young officers gained respect by showing "personal courage."

He set out to prove that he had it and came to be regarded as having "more guts" than the other junior officers in his unit and was made a captain at the age of twenty.[203] At this point he had no misgivings about the war and no reluctance to risk his life. He was committed to "the values of courage and military efficiency."[204] Graves's comrade on the Western front and fellow poet, Siegfried Sassoon, was also inspired by a dream of heroism and glory. Some critics think that Sassoon went to war to celebrate a romantic idea of personal military courage. This is doubtful, for Sassoon was too proud to act by imitation alone. He wanted to experience war, but not to have the experience disturb his "heroic emotions."[205] He was hoping, mistakenly, that the war experience would allow him to go on soldiering and leave intact his desire to accomplish heroic deeds.

But soon enough both Graves's and Sassoon's ardor for heroic deeds cooled. They saw human losses mounting all around them, and soon became aware that the offensive was a strategy of sacrifice. They jettisoned militarism and turned against the heroic life. When orders for a "subsidiary attack" were given to Graves's unit just before the battle at Loos, the officers judged it nonsensical, a "funny scheme," knowing that they and their troops "will get killed whatever happens." The action resulted in "a glorious balls-up." Gas released by the English was blown back into their own trenches and the barbed wires remained uncut. When the main offensive started in September 1915, Graves watched from the fire-step of his trench the English troops being decimated by friendly fire. "My mouth went dry," he describes the sensation caused by the sight of the slaughter, "my eyes out of focus, and my legs quaking under me. I found a water bottle full of rum and drank about half a pint; it quieted me down, and my head remained clear." He called it murder. Loos crushed Graves's fighting spirit. When he returned to the trenches late in the fall, a black depression got hold of him. He felt neither excitement in patrolling nor "horror in the continual experience of death."[206] The excitement and the horror, which were once a source of his military machismo, now failed to provide him with courage. Having realized that headquarters' orders rendered bravery futile, indifference and resignation replaced spontaneous courage and military efficiency.

Graves' disappointment intensified. He charged both politicians and generals with "cursed incompetent blundering," which led to large losses and prevented soldiers like himself from performing heroically with a reasonable chance of survival. Death became unacceptable, and he turned against the war, condemning it as a war of aggression and conquest. Heroism became a deception. Two events revealed to him the true meaning of heroism and the unfairness in judging it. Two soldiers risked their lives to help their wounded comrades in no-man's-land and were proposed for the Victoria Cross to recognize their courage. The proposals were turned down solely for technical reasons. True valor, Graves is now persuaded, is ignored. Headquarters only values the behavior, no matter how heroic, that leads to the sacrifice of life, not to its preservation. Even though disenchanted, Graves continued to fight until he was wounded. In the aftermath of the war, he took no pride in his heroic deeds. He registered only the negative effects that the experience had on his body and soul. It took him ten years to recover from the trauma that the war inflicted on him. The spiritual loss was perhaps greater than the physical one. "Our youth," he wrote tersely of his inner loss in the poem "Recalling War," "became all-flesh and waived the mind."[207]

On the Somme, Sassoon witnessed the enormous losses in human life that the Allies were incurring, and he began to distance himself from the idea of heroism. Fighting was no longer the source of a heroic experience. Going over the top was now a "religious experience," which he defined as a "suicidal self-deceiving" escape from the evil of the frontline. War has become a problem. He realizes the "impermanence" of the "humanities" at the front, and he is shocked. His battalion, which had been part of his life, was almost completely destroyed, and the disappearance of close comrades becomes intolerable to him. He felt he had to escape the "bleak truth" that life at the front had become unbearable, and to do this, he resorted to making a parody of heroism. "Soldiers are citizens of death's grey land." He knew that self-inflicted wounds were common, that "brave men" had put bullets through their own brains, and that he too was now ready to do the same, but at the same time that he rejects war, he comes to fear and abhor death. Heroic action now becomes a cover-up for his lack of resolve to commit suicide. "The way out: I must play at being a hero in shining armor." He is now resolved to defy the forces of destruction as a pretext to seek death on the battlefield, and he discovers in himself "the invincible resistance of an animal or an insect, and an endurance" he could not believe he had.[208] After the death of his friend Dick, Sassoon sought revenge. He made reckless raids, displayed exceptional daring, and he became known as "Mad Jack." He knew that "animal excitement" enhances the capacity to kill, and he abandoned himself to the instinctive impulse. He was in fact acclaimed by comrades, by superiors in the field, and by citizens at home because of his apparent bravery.[209] Sassoon never thought about degradation, but now that his heroic ideal was dead, degradation became his motive power.

How hard it was to be a "pure" hero is shown by Private Bourne, the protagonist of *Her Privates We*. He was very serious about being a good soldier at the front. In the midst of the "heroic moment," that is, the assault on enemy lines, he found strength in his personal pride. "One must not break," he tells himself." But sticking it out cannot be produced by a simple act of will. In the course of several actions, Manning notes that "only the instinct of the beast survived in him," and clearly, he sees that the extreme of heroism is the same as despair. Despair generates a wave of ferocity, and by military standards, turns him into a hero. "A kind of maniacal rage filled him" after his friend Marlow is killed. Consuming hatred mixed with exultant cruelty takes hold of Bourne, and he goes on killing enemies with a ferocity that renders him unrecognizable. Manning explains this kind of behavior as a man's reversion "to the state primeval," a transformation that reveals an "extraordinary veracity in war."[210] War leaves men "naked" and forces them to act by instinct alone. They become "nocturnal beasts," hunting each other in packs. It is the "veracity" of war that enables soldiers to act with courage. In the course of his last attack, "pain and pleasure" coincide in Bourne. Exertion and rage shake him, while at the same time he feels "some strange intoxication of joy." He reaches "the limit of endurance," and is transformed into "the most abject and the most exalted of God's creatures,"[211] a being in whom heroism triumphs at the expense of the soul. Bourne confirms the view of an English officer on the Somme that letting loose the primitive passion for slaughter is what turns an ordinary soldier into a "good" one,[212] into a hero.

Sassoon's poetry testifies to his disenchantment with the heroic ideal. Among civilians the idea of heroism works on a conventional level. It hides the ghastly killings at the front, and enables a father sitting at home in safety to read about "dying heroes and their deathless deeds."[213] The military authorities betray the heroic ideal when they lead a mother to believe that her dead son had been "so brave" and "glorious" in the trenches, concealing the truth known to all around that son—that he was "useless," that he panicked at the sounds of explosions, and that he had tried to get sent home.[214] Similarly, British women falsified the meaning of heroism to please their vanity and fantasies, "You love us when we are heroes, home on leave," Sassoon charges, and you "worship decorations," believing that "chivalry redeems war's disgrace."[215] On the other hand, crafty officers take heroism as a game, and play "hero to the end" in order to garner rewards and decorations.[216]

Combatants who never wanted to be heroes, for instance, those portrayed by Henri Barbusse in *Under Fire*, respond differently to the demands of the battlefield. They are not surprised by the harshness of the environment nor by their leadership's orders. They were forced to go to the frontline, and to them the coercion was a prelude to the violence they are expected to withstand and to deal out. They are victims. At the outset of *Under Fire*, they are represented as living like troglodytes; their victimhood is confirmed. For these soldiers, the high-minded expectations of a Graves or a Sassoon at the start of their life in the trenches would be a cruel joke.

Barbusse's soldiers are anti-heroes, but they eventually become heroes of a sort in their effort to salvage their human identity in an environment designed to destroy it. They ignore fear, are free of the thoughts and feelings that tormented soldiers like Bourne and take no pride in their selves or their conduct at the front. They consider themselves victims of the military establishment's rules and decrees. Barbusse was perhaps the only combatant and writer to understand and describe the life of the combatants in the trenches. Trench life set them apart from the world of human beings. The trench that shelters Barbusse and his comrades is carpeted with a layer of slime, and each dugout smells of the night's excretions. "The holes themselves, as you stoop to peer in, are foul of breath." The soldiers that come and go from these pits are shadows, "huge and misshapen lumps, bear-like, that founder and growl... Faces appear, ruddy or laden, dirt-disfigured, pierced by little lamps of dull and heavy-lidded eyes, matted with uncut beards and foul with forgotten hair." No matter the difference in outward looks and behaviors, they all live the same kind of life. Under the same rough outlines, they "conceal and reveal the same ways and habits, the same simple nature of men who have reverted to the state primeval." These beings are so deeply changed that it is almost impossible to recognize them as men. They live like animals in a world where for more than fifteen months the rifles and the big guns have been firing from morning to night and from night to morning. They "are buried deep in an everlasting battlefield"[217] where the business of dying and killing rules their life. Their fight has not been against the German enemy, but against a kind of life that is comparable, if not worse than death.

Jean Norton Cru's opinion is that Barbusse is unable to portray the soul of the poilu (French infantry), and that he sees only their "material" life.[218] It is possible, however, to identify in the poilu two states of inner being that suggest otherwise. These states reveal that the soldiers are resolved to fight against the death that life in the trenches threatens and against the spiritual death that threatens when they are attacking the enemy. As his unit gets ready to go over the top for the last assault, Barbusse observes his comrades. He is struck by their dignity. Their posture is the sign of a peculiar heroism which is unexpected in these men who are immersed in the harsh life of the trenches and the battlefield. "They are not soldiers, they are men. They are not adventurers, or warriors, or animals made for human slaughter. They are civilians uprooted, and they are ready. They await the signal for death or murder; but you may see, looking at their faces between the vertical gleams of their bayonets, that they are simply men... In their silence, their stillness, in the mask of tranquility which unnaturally grips their faces, one knows the thought and the fear and the farewell. They are not the kind of hero one thinks of, but their sacrifice has greater worth than they who have not seen them will ever be able to understand."[219] Their heroism consists in the triumph of their humanity over the death and destruction decreed by the perpetrators of war. They are resigned to fight and die, but their inner strength enables them to defy the forces that condemn them to be killers or to be killed. The crucial event of their war experience, is the attack. It brings out the humanity whose task is to oppose the forces that aim to destroy it. Herein lies the worth of their sacrifice.

But once the troops start their advance through no-man's-land and toward the fearsome international trench, their state of being changes. They become real soldiers. "Fever" burns in their eyes, their faces become blood red, and their breathing turns into snorting. A more than human strength seizes them, hurling them in an irresistible race toward the enemy. "Driven as by the wind," they overrun the German trench. The French stop for a moment, as if to try to understand the origin and property of the superhuman force that, almost against their will, hurls them forward. It is "a frenzied excitement" that has driven "them all out of themselves" and to victory. They continue their race toward another objective, "elated, immensely confident, ferocious," conquering another trench, and destroying the enemy.[220] What these soldiers are doing is certainly heroic from the military point of view, but they are heroes not because they are driven by love of the country or by duty, but because they have been transformed into another being that is more, and at the same time, less than human.

The heroism of Barbusse's soldiers is rendered irrelevant by the awareness that they have been killers. A compliment from superiors or civilians such as, "my friend, you have been a wonderful hero," is unacceptable to these men. Their deeds, which have accomplished an important victory, merely allow them to identify themselves as "murderers," and to realize that the "soldier's glory is a lie," because there is no military virtue in killing. Ironically, this turning against their achievement on the battlefield, is what makes them heroes. After the attack, when there are no more Germans in sight and no more killing to be done, the frenzy subsides, and they realize they have won because of what they had become in the course of the attack. They feel they have become murderers as a result of a change that occurred in them. "We were all like beasts when we got here!" Corporal Bertrand describes their state of being. They realize that the action has turned them into heroes by conventional standards and, at once, into "domestic beasts."[221] They rebel against themselves as heroes and victors, cursing the organism that deprived them of their souls. Heroism and degradation coincide, but in a manner unlike Henry Fleming and Private Bourne, who were relieved that degradation helped them to act heroically. Barbusse's men are hurt by the loss of self-respect it has cost them to be considered heroes. The soldiers in *Under Fire* found themselves in the trenches almost without knowing how they ended there, and their behavior underscored how foreign the war environment was to them. In their minds and hearts, they still lived in the cities and their homes.

On the other hand, the soldiers of *All Quiet on the Western Front* are fully adjusted to life at the front. They have been trained for it. True to the teaching of Clausewitz that to be brave the soldier must shed his civilized habits, the military organization in ten weeks of training cured Paul Baumer, the protagonist of Remarque's novel, of his civilized habits. The battlefield will complete his reeducation, but in the meantime, he learned that what mattered most in the army was not "the mind but the boot brush, not intelligence but the system, not freedom but drill." He also learned that "a bright button is weightier than four volumes of *Schopenauer.*" In the end, he understood the meaning of what was being done to him. He was "trained for heroism" like circus-ponies for the circus. His mental and cultural frame having been reshaped, Baumer came to understand that an officer has more authority over him than his parents, his teachers, and even more than the values of Western culture, "from Plato to Goethe."[222] Training for heroism implies the replacement of those intellectual and moral values that are fundamental to civilized life with what Rudolf Binding called "a classic reversion to the primitive,"[223] and from this shift heroism is born.

The reversion progressed on the battlefield, culminating in the death of the soul. "We," Baumer reveals, "went courageously into every action." But to enable themselves to fight with courage, he and his comrades had first to become "hard, suspicious, pitiless, vicious, and tough." In the novel's most violent scene, they are carried forward by a wave that fills them with "a mad anger" that drives them to kill. A "frenzy of excitement" supports the action,[224] revealing extraordinary courage. But it is the kind of courage that has nothing to do with duty or patriotism. The state of being in which Baumer and his comrades find themselves in the midst of these actions is that of "unthinking animals" and of "wild creatures." Their "ferocity" turns them "into murderers" while fear and madness multiply their strength. This transformation enabled the German soldiers to fight valiantly. It also killed their humanity. Nowhere are they represented as heroic soldiers. Heroism cannot be attached to beings that are less than human.[225] Heroism has become the enemy of humanity in the sense that to become operative it first must kill the human self of the combatant. The only soldiers who in *All Quiet on the Western Front* show normal courage are the recruits new to the frontline. They have not been transformed yet and lack the instinct that leads and protects the veterans of the trenches. As a result, they fight willingly, but helplessly and get killed or wounded easily. They are so terrified that they only whimper softly for their mothers; their bravery keeps them from crying out loud. "The fine courage of these poor devils, the desperate charges and attacks made by the poor brave wretches" is shown by their battered chests, torn bellies, arms, and legs. Normal soldiers and men cannot be heroes and survive the ordeal of the battlefield.[226]

The cost of bravery to the combatants in *All Quiet on the Western Front* is high. The Germans, unlike the French, lose their souls. This is the price they pay for their supposed heroism. They resign themselves to the loss, and in the aftermath of the war, to a life that is death in life, that of the "lost generation." At the end of the conflict, Baumer and his comrades realize that for them to return to normal civil life will be impossible. For the sake of heroism, their humanity died on the battlefield, and they will be unable to live a normal life. "We will be weary, broken, burnt out, rootless, and without hope... We will be superfluous even to ourselves, we will grow older, a few will adapt themselves, some others will merely submit, and most will be bewildered; the years will pass by, and in the end, we shall fall into ruin." If you know nothing of life, as Baumer says, "but despair, death, [and] fear," then life itself cannot exist.[227]

In Italy the question of valor was a vital one. It transcended the battlefield. The country had an inferiority complex because it was unable to gain independence on its own in the nineteenth century; it lacked a warlike spirit. To martial valor was assigned the role of redeeming the country and its people. Military and political leaders alike believed that if Italy fought in the Great War, it would erase an unworthy past and gain the Italians a reputation for glory and heroism. The philosopher

Benedetto Croce thought that Italians had been cowards since the end of the fifteenth century when they did nothing to repulse the French invasions. But this war gave him hope; he saw the Italian army on the battlefield "definitely redeeming the Italian people" from the guilt of cowardice.[228] Croce's disciple, Adolfo Omodeo, believed too that war was a redemptive tool, a long "purgatory of our national faults."[229] The nationalist leader Enrico Corradini detected in cowardice the worst vice of the Italian people,[230] and so did another prominent nationalist, Alfredo Rocco, warning that unless it was suppressed, cowardice would eventually destroy Italy.[231] Today "the Italian soul is cowardly," proclaimed another philosopher, Giovanni Papini, adding that he was stating an irrefutable truth, "Italy is cowardly."[232] In order to cure the country of cowardice, it was necessary "to kill, to cut, to extirpate everything that was less than human in man." He saw in the coming of the war the salvation of the Italians. "The *dies irae* has come," he wrote with relief when it began. A purifying "warm bath of black blood" was needed, and finally the Italians were taking it. "It is a wholesale slaughter," he continued gleefully, predicting that it will rid Italy of its rabble and idiots.[233] And Filippo Marinetti, the leader of the Futurists, wished for war, because he believed that it had the power to call forth in lightning-like manner from every man just what the Italians needed: "Courage, energy, and intelligence."[234] Marinetti welcomed war in the name of heroism. Benito Mussolini welcomed war in the name of death, for death alone could reveal the courage of the soldiers, "A hundred thousand guns," he wrote from the front in 1916, "will not give us victory. Italy will win only if the soldier moves out to the offensive and shows the courage to come out of his defensive positions to face death."[235]

On the Italian front, the pressure on the combatants to fight heroically was high. The military leadership was devoted to cultivating the offensive believing that the frontal attack was the best tactic to fight and to win. Frontal attacks against the well-defended Austrian positions were widely ordered, and a high casualty count was regarded as a sign of heroism. During more than two years of war, up to the debacle of Caporetto, the Italian infantry took heavy losses and made no strategic gains. Nevertheless, headquarters held the offensive in great esteem. General Luigi Capello ascribed a "very great" value to the offensive in general and to the frontal attack in particular because it showed the heroism of the Italian soldier. He believed that the "Italian soul," not the heavy guns, was instrumental in the taking of Gorizia. Valor hatched by heart, mind, faith, and enthusiasm made its conquest possible. One should have seen our soldiers going over the top, the general wrote excitedly about their assault on Gorizia. They "threw themselves forward... in a compact mass, impetuous, confident." Having discovered that the role of valor had been paramount, the general ascribed "a moral value." to the victory at Gorizia. He regarded its moral value so highly that he urged the Italians to embrace that action to better themselves. "This, Italy needs! Steely souls able to carry the burden of present and future struggles."[236]

An officer described the attacks made in late 1915 on the Austrian positions as "human tides" thrown up the stony slopes of the Carso. It was impossible to make any breakthrough since Italian headquarters had no mortars or artillery to support the infantry. Nevertheless, the generals ordered the infantry to attack, again and again. The result was that thousands of soldiers got themselves killed, "heroically." Heroism means, not a spontaneous action done in the face of great danger, but submission to the superior order to go on an attack to gain insignificant patches of rocky soil. An attack like this, in which the majority of the attackers would be killed or wounded, showed a "courage" and a "resolution" that S. L. A. Marshall called a "repellent task." Repellent because courage was wasted, since headquarters knew that it was impossible for the attack to succeed. Courage was present, but it was useless, especially when confronted with the barbwire, which the Italian soldiers were unable to cut for lack of equipment: "The barbwire! Courage can do nothing against this miserable and terrible thing." But for headquarters, the sacrifice of lives counted more than the success of the attack. Heroism became the sign of the Supreme Command's folly. Headquarters kept pushing the troops up the rocky slopes of the Carso. "Attack! We can't! What does it matter? Forward just the same."[237] On the Carso, the combatants quickly found out that death was around the corner, for on that rocky area well defended by the Austrians, it was impossible to survive two or three offensive attacks, and the Italians attacked incessantly, showing outstanding heroism.[238] Still, the slaughter of the Italian troops was a signal achievement for the Supreme Command and for many commanders in the field because for them, death defined heroism.

For the Italian Supreme Command, the main aim of fighting was to sacrifice the troops in a show of valor. The Austrians say, Captain Giuseppe Prezzolini revealed in 1916, that the Italian troops "know how to die, but not how to fight."[239] Colonel Giulio Dohuet, a maverick in the Italian leadership, held headquarters responsible for a strategy demonstrating that the Italians "know how to die well," pointing out that, unfortunately, under the prodding of headquarters, that capacity was demonstrated once too often. That sacrificing lives was headquarters' chief aim is shown by their disdain for the Carnia zone, which produced only very few Italian dead. The Carso instead was admired, because on its slopes the Italians "were regularly butchered in great numbers."[240]

Given the enormous pressure on Italian soldiers to fight with valor and sacrifice their lives, it was nearly impossible for them to escape this fate. The strategy of sending troops on frontal attacks and branding them heroic actions worked well for headquarters because when pushed into no-man's-land, the degradation that occurred in the soldier diminished or canceled out the pain of knowing that his life was being squandered. A more spontaneous and useful form of degradation prevailed, however, and it is perhaps significant that it was first documented on the Italian front. In 1917, Agostino Gemelli, a chaplain and later a professor of psychology in Milan, identified and described the change that occurred in troops sent on frontal attacks. Gemelli was at first unable to see why the Italian soldiers, uncultured and ignorant of the cause they fought for, took great risks and performed heroic deeds on the battlefield. He soon realized that they acted with courage because during an action they "ceased to be men." When the action was over and they returned to their line, they broke into tears and collapsed. Another change had taken place. They regained the humanity they had lost during the action and "became men again."[241] No matter what happened to these men, he believed that headquarters could call their actions heroic.

However, the Alpine trooper and future novelist Emilio Gadda revealed one reason for the change described by Gemelli, and it is far from heroic. At the front, the combatant faced a choice: "To be or not to be." To be meant to be myself unchanged, a normal being unable to cope with stress, and to succumb to the terror of the battlefield. Not to be meant to undergo the change described by Gemelli, and maybe save my life. If the soldier wanted to be, he was doomed, but if he gave up his humanity, he would be able to fight bravely and perhaps survive. Degeneration went along with heroism. "The strong and the brave" ones were those combatants who had willfully shed their humanity ("della loro umanità si disumanarono").[242] Some combatants acknowledged that if officers and soldiers alike did not become indifferent, cynical, beasts, "there would be many suicides and only a few heroic acts."[243] Carlo Stuparich, Italian patriot and combatant from the Venetian region, declared that in becoming "more beastly than beasts," he and his comrades enabled themselves to be "so heroic."[244] However, it is doubtful that an action that depends on the death of the soul (self) can be defined truly heroic.

Often headquarters fostered "heroism" through the deliberate degradation of the troops. Alcohol, which caused "the appearance and feeling of courage,"[245] was used to manufacture courage. Alcohol produced such good results that its use became "institutionalized."[246] Headquarters liberally dispensed cognac to the troops before sending them on strategically important offensive actions. The troops, who knew the function of alcohol—that of making them do what their reason told them not to do—called cognac their "gasoline." But they also knew that, besides turning them into heroes, alcohol turned them into cannon fodder. When in Emilio Lussu's, *Un anno sull'altipiano* (One Year on the Upland), a company paymaster sends five men to the rear to fetch chocolate and cognac, the troops know that they will soon be thrown into another one of those deadly attacks that distinguished the Italian strategy. The soldiers acknowledge themselves to be animals marked for slaughter rather than men bound for heroic exploits. "They [headquarters] fatten the pig really well before killing it," the soldiers say.[247] For them, heroism was a tragic farce.

True courage was not missing on the Italian front, but it found no place and no recognition in headquarters' plans and operations. It came from the Alpini who as civilians were known to be fearless and endowed with extraordinary endurance. Those values conventionally regarded as sources of heroism— fatherland, family, duty—were meaningless to these men. They came from mountain villages and lived in the harsh environment of the mountains. They had to struggle to overcome adversity just to survive. At home they were brave for vital reasons, and they brought their bravery to the frontline. When the Austrians attacked, they were the first to counterattack, and their "cold courage" turned the battle into "a red, cheerful feast."[248]

The politics of heroism and death struck the imagination of Ernest Hemingway, who served on the Italian front. In *A Farewell to Arms,* as the Battle of Caporetto approached in the fall of 1917, the protagonist, Frederic Henry, is moved to respond to an Italian officer reciting the rhetoric of patriotism, glory, and sacrifice, "I had seen nothing sacred," he says, "and the things that were glorious had no glory, and the sacrifices were like the stockyards in Chicago if nothing was done with the meat except to bury it... Abstract words such as glory, honor, courage, and hallow were obscene beside the concrete names of villages, the number of roads, the names of rivers, the numbers of regiments and the dates."[249] The politics of heroism had transformed the inglorious death and burial of the soldiers into abstract words—glory, honor, and courage --- words that had nothing to do with reality, but only with the idea and plan of the leadership --- building the legend of heroism on the "inglorious" death of the soldiers. Death denies heroism, and heroism built on death is a lie. The rhetoric of heroism is designed to conceal what is central to war, the death of men. If heroism is bandied about in abstract and celebratory terms, then death and its meaning are concealed. On the other hand, to remember the places where the soldiers fought and died allows one to experience their deprivation and suffering. It indirectly underscores and stimulates a love of life, he believed. The context, places, times, and fighting units, are meaningful because they were witnesses to the struggle for the preservation of life, or its loss. Hemingway's vision implicitly rejects Henry Fleming's behavior in *The Red Badge of Courage* who, stirred by the death he saw around him, achieved the strength to return to the battlefield in a burst of raging energy to kill and become a hero. Fleming's embrace of death dealing is not an instrument of valor. What counts for Hemingway is that death as an irreparable loss. It renders heroism irrelevant. For Hemingway, valor is a blatant repudiation of life and must be rejected.

The First World War had indeed the power to change individuals in radical ways,[250] and the central cause for the change was heroism on the battlefield. Those combatants who embraced the idea of heroism became hostage to it, and later as veterans, they encouraged the politics of oppression and war, as they did in Italy. On the other hand, those veterans who rejected heroism and its rhetoric, withdrew from life and abandoned hope for a better future. This left those who embraced heroism to rule the politics of the world that followed the first war, a world that would again be beset by violence and death.

In Italy, the rhetoric of heroism triumphed, and following the end of the First World War, it became the main ingredient in the rise of fascism. The enormous sacrifice of lives the war had exacted, more than half a million dead, left the people disheartened and the economy in dire straits. The people became the prey of Mussolini's dictatorship.

It was inevitable that tyranny should follow that war, for tyranny's life blood is violence itself, and the legacy of the Great War in Italy was a culture of violence. Unbridled, it became the primary ingredient in the growth of fascism, which Mussolini in many instances likened to that practiced by the soldiers on the Italian front, and which he labeled heroism. Fascism wrapped the noble garment of heroism around violence, transforming it the same way that the military organization had transformed slaughter into heroism. A special effort was made to impress on the Italian people the idea that the sacrifices made on the battlefield were the essence of heroism and that heroism was necessary to strengthen Italy. Heroism became one of the tools in a political struggle in which the black-shirts became organized like military units.

The poet, Gabriele D'Annunzio became the standard bearer of heroism. In World War I, he had fought on land, on sea and in the air, and was recognized as the national hero. He called himself the "war's ascetic." After the war he did his utmost to keep the war alive in order to renew the heroism of the battlefield in an unquenchable search for glory.[251] He missed the heroic life and wanted to fight again because making war was his "only" reason for living. He believed that fighting established and maintained the "greatness" of his spirit.[252] Occasionally, he realized what his heroism was really about, and he was horrified, "My dreams are full of blood. Every thought of mine is weighted down by blood. Sometimes in my repulsive self, my past bleeds like a slaughterhouse filled with beasts quartered and hooked up." Nevertheless, it was impossible to quash his thirst for war. There is a kind of heroism that takes a man prisoner, he reflected (in the same vein as some Shakespearean heroes), and holds him forever, making it impossible for him "to live without a heroic reason for living."[253] D'Annunzio was one of them.

But with the armistice, the "straight heroic wills" were confronted by the "sinister gravediggers of heroism." It was vital that the heroic will should prevail over the gravediggers, and that the torch of heroism would be picked up and carried forward. "Let us accept our heroic necessity," the poet exhorted his followers, rejecting the twilight of the heroes. "Pain gives us life," he proclaimed in 1919 in Rome just before his march on Fiume; "sacrifice" creates us. So, D'Annunzio, in opposition to the terms of the Paris Peace Settlement that designated Fiume an independent state took the province for Italy. Let us trace through the rocky soil of the Carso another "sacred" path, the one that will lead from Ronchi to Fiume, D'Annunzio urged, and let us renew our sacrifice. After the conquest of Fiume, he felt at peace with himself. Heroism had finally reestablished itself. "Here," he will write gratified after taking possession of Fiume, "one breathes again the heroic wind."[254]

Ernst Jünger's experience on the battlefield was similar to D'Annunzio's. Danger gave him the "chance to show his manhood at its best." A divine frenzy seizes him as he gets ready to go over the top in the last German offensive. "Rage, alcohol, and the thirst for blood" push him where "the godlike and the bestial inextricably mingle." The animal imagery thickens as his heroism intensifies. He is a bird, whose "overpowering desire to kill winged" his feet. He is a werewolf, howling and hunting "on the track of blood," and he is a savage, who wants to take no prisoners because he is obeying the "primeval instinct."[255] After the war, Jünger intended to transfer "the fury of desperate animals" that held him on the battlefield to the struggle for nationalism. He warned his countrymen that he and veterans like him would tolerate no opposition. For four long years after the war, he proclaimed to the Germans, that they "have lived as beasts, not as men," and that they are fit and ready to bring to politics the same toughness that distinguished their lives in the trenches, "We veterans have become dour."[256] The essence of what was heroic on the battlefield would become the engine of German political life.

D'Annunzio lent ideological and political support to the young Mussolini, who had worked out the meaning and place of valor in politics while at the front in the Great War. Mussolini was aware of the carnage of Italians on the Isonzo front. He judged it according to the criteria of the Supreme Command, a mark of bravery on the part of the troops. He transformed the life of the combatants into a heroic saga, presaging the "religion" of sacrifice and heroism which would fuel the war he would decide to enter in 1940. The cult of heroism in fascist culture was one pretext to renew war. His experience at the front of the previous war showed Mussolini the possibility of availing himself of a people who, forced to sacrifice themselves by harsh disciplinary methods, knew how to endure. He surmised that it was possible to lead the Italians to their death in the interest of the fascist cause in the same way that in the Great War they had been sacrificed by the military leadership in the name of the heroic life. He became convinced that it was possible to get anything from the Italian soldier, including doing hard labor and above all making "the irresistible and deadly attack with the bayonet," an unmistakable expression of courage. Mussolini will proceed on the belief that modern war lends itself to the "prodigious exploitation of individual human qualities" of the Italians who, he believed, make war with "self-confidence and passion."[257] He was enthralled by their courage, as he liked to remember them going over the top on the Italian front. They were more than heroes, "I have seen these sons of Italy, and I can tell you that they have not been soldiers; they were saints and martyrs!"[258]

Heroic fighting at the front in World War I became for fascist veterans, the passport to using violence in peacetime. In the assault on the offices of the socialist daily Avanti! in Milan in 1922 and in their destruction by his henchmen, Mussolini detected an extension of the battles fought in the war that had ended in 1918. The blackshirts attacked the socialists in the building as if they were attacking an Austrian trench. They went over walls, broke through barbed wires and gates, defying the fire that was coming from the windows. "This is heroism," Mussolini reflected ecstatically, "This is the kind of violence I approve of, that I applaud." He defined the assault on the Avanti! "the most heroic" action done by fascism in the last four years. The Dottrina del fascismo (Doctrine of Fascism, 1932) was the official guide to sacrifice. It paved the road to war, exalting its value and the heroism implied in sacrifice. The doctrine holds that only war can bring human energies to their maximum tension, the point where heroism emerges. And war is necessary because only war places a mark of nobility on men. "Fascism believes now and always in purity and in heroism."[259] At the vigil of World War II, Mussolini dreamed of animating Italians with the "dedication of themselves" to the task of "never refusing to sacrifice, even the supreme sacrifice."[260] In 1942, he invented the concept of war as a "test" for the Italian people, a test of their courage and moral strength before danger and death, insisting that the test was for them an historical occasion to demonstrate their heroic temper.[261] Even at the vigil of his downfall, he still believed that the war must go on, because, he declared before the members of the great council, we are willing to live heroically.[262]

Many veterans who as soldiers had rejected heroism and its rhetoric, withdrew from public life. They became members of the "lost generation." What is it that "annihilates the past selves of young men" coming home from war that makes it impossible for them to "return to a past life"?[263] The men who formed the lost generation had repudiated heroism in World War I. They may have fought valiantly, but valor robbed them of their humanity. Baumer and his comrades, we have seen, formed the "lost" generation. They were unfit to go back to living a normal life. "We will be superfluous even to ourselves, ... the years will pass by and in the end, we shall fall into ruin."[264] After their extraordinary exploits on the battlefield, the men of Barbusse's squad, who have been heroic against their own will, recognized themselves to be stupid victims and ignoble brutes.[265] For victims and brutes, it is hard to live a normal life.

T. E. Lawrence was the hero of the Arab revolt. He achieved victory for the Arabs, but it was taken out of his hands by the British and French colonial powers who agreed in 1919 to carve up the former Ottoman territories. Feeling betrayed by his superiors, he rejected the accolades and became a significant representative of the lost generation.

Not only did he withdraw entirely from public life after the armistice, but he became so indifferent toward himself that he could not even take care of his most elementary needs. He could function only under military discipline. In July 1922, he joined the Royal Air Force as Private Ross. Expelled a few months later, he enlisted in the spring of 1923 in the Tank Corps, again in the ranks, under a new false name—Shaw. In 1925, he managed to get back into the Royal Air Force where he served anonymously until February 1935, three months before his death.

Lawrence's military performance caused him to become extremely introspective. Although he led the Arabs to victory, and was acclaimed their hero, his exploits in the desert drained him of "morality, of volition, of responsibility." He was troubled by guilt and shame, and powerless to regain a sense of his own worth. He became like a dead leaf in the wind, moved by "gusts of cruelty, perversion, lusts."[266] He saw himself leading "a Yahoo life," having handed over his soul to "a brute-master." His body moved around mechanically, and his mind left him with the result that he often felt that madness was about to overtake him.[267] He withdrew from the world and "immured himself" in the military,[268] becoming an outsider in a tragedy of waste. He struggled "to reclaim or re-create his soul," but failed.[269] He refused to play the hero, and in the aftermath of the war, he deliberately embraced degradation as a way to cancel from himself the stamp of heroism. He showed a "powerful need for penance through degradation and humiliation" and, among other things, the desire to be treated like a beast— "a compulsive wish to be whipped."[270] Lawrence had set out to punish himself for what the public viewed as exceptional heroism. He wrote a bitterly ironic account, of his "victories" in *The Seven Pillars of Wisdom. A Triumph.*

One of the reasons that caused the protagonist of *A Farewell to Arms* to turn against the war was the Italian headquarters' strategy of promoting heroism and courage knowing full well the soldiers were doomed in hopeless frontal attacks against the Austrians. As a volunteer corpsman whose job was to recover the wounded, Frederick Henry behaved bravely under fire. The rout of Caporetto ended his mission, and he narrowly escaped a firing squad when he was picked up from a crowd of fleeing soldiers. As one who had brought "so much courage to this world," and who was nearly killed for it, he testified to the truth about the conduct of war on the Italian front. The only type of courage that counted there was the gospel of death imposed by headquarters. Henry's courage was genuine, but this was the last thing the Italian military valued. Hemingway's intuition that the world "kills the very good and the very gentle and the very brave impartially"[271] reflects the Italian politics of heroism as he saw it.

But death does not always stifle heroism, and when it does not there is a valid reason. It is the belief in a deeply felt cause. Whereas the Italian soldiers in *A Farewell to Arms* do not know why they are on the battlefield or what they are fighting for, they easily tumble for the glory, honor, and courage that headquarters attached to the slaughter in order to justify what was essentially a war of attrition.

In a different category altogether, is Hemingway's novel, *For Whom the Bell Tolls*, in which death is no reason for repudiating heroism. The thought and reality of death do not turn Robert Jordan against his commitment to fight the fascists in Spain. Despite the incompetence and treachery of the loyalist leaders, Golz for instance, who could not even fix a date and time for blowing up the bridge, and political commissars like André Marty, a "crazy murderer,"[272] Jordon believes in the cause he fights for and is tolerant of his comrades. He tells Pilar that the only thing he feared was not doing his duty as he ought to. He will keep on fighting. He "fought now in this war because it had started in a country that he loved, and he believed in the Republic, and that if it were destroyed, life would be unbearable for all those people who believed in it." At times he thought that he was taking part in a crusade, and had "a feeling of consecration" to the duty of gaining freedom for the people of the world, a feeling that was like a "religious experience."[273] The strength of Jordan's belief in the Republican cause is shown by his often-quoted invective against the difficulties in getting his messages through to Republican headquarters. But no matter how vigorous and heartfelt the outburst, it leaves Jordan's faith intact, "Muck them to hell together, Largo, Prieto, Asensio, Miaja, Rojo, all of them. Muck every one of them to death to hell. Muck the whole treachery-ridden country. Muck their egotism and their selfishness and their egotism and their conceit and their treachery. Muck them to hell and always. Muck them before we die for them. Muck them after we die for them. Muck them to death and hell."[274] These are serious charges and distressing for Jordan who makes them. But they are insufficient to undermine his belief in the Republican cause because the cause is greater than himself, and heroic status is not consciously sought. His death seals his heroism. And so, it is with Jordan's comrade, Kashkin, whose belief in the cause must have been as strong as Jordan's since they risked their lives together. He "was very brave,"[275] even though he was afraid of death.

Killing has been taken as a sign of valor in *The Song of Roland*, *Jerusalem Delivered*, and *Coriolanus*. Amassing a large number of dead bodies conferred a heroic reputation on the killer. Hemingway reverses this position. He turns killing into a necessity at best, and a crime at worst. Heroes are those who die, accepting their own death as necessary and useful to the cause they fight for. Anselmo is no coward, and he has killed enemies, "but not with pleasure." Killing, he says, is a "a great sin." He kills a fascist guard and feels as though he "had struck [his] own brother." Whoever does the killing becomes "brutalized." Anselmo looks on it as a problem for the Spanish people as a whole, "I think that after the war, there will have to be a great penance done for the killing." He dreams of some form of civic penance organized so "that all may be cleansed from the killing." Jordan too rejects killing. "And you," he asks himself as his mission nears the end, "still believe absolutely that your cause is right?" He replies in the affirmative, warning himself that his belief is true only if he refuses to accept killing, "But you mustn't believe in killing. You must do it as a necessity, but you must not believe in it. If you believe in it the whole thing is wrong, he told himself."[276]

The story of the wholesale killing in the mountain village captured by Pablo's guerrillas, as told by Pilar, shows how killing can affect the killers, and why killing is the enemy of heroism. The tale of the slaughter of some twenty fascists places an enormous obstacle to accepting the Republican cause and fighting for it. How can one fight with courage for a cause which is represented by killers like Pablo and his men? The function of the tale is to define Pablo as a coward and to implicitly show Jordan's unshakable faith in the cause and his resolve to fight for it. This tale of slaughter coincides with Pablo's becoming ever more afraid of death. He "was brave" in the beginning of the Civil War, Pilar tells Jordan, but he is now "very flaccid." She reveals to Jordan that the night before she was awakened by Pablo who was crying as though there was an animal inside him, shaking him. "I am afraid to die, Pilar," he tells her. She throws him out of bed, declaring him "a ruin." The killing done by Pablo, who had the fascists in the village beaten to death with flails and thrown from the top of the cliff into the river, has undone him.[277]

Heroes are those who die, accepting their own death as necessary and useful to the cause. Their courage consists in giving up life while believing and defending its value. Trapped on the hilltop, El Sordo conducts a resistance against the attacking fascists, and then dies under the bombs of enemy planes while firing his weapon. El Sordo's heroism lies in his acceptance of death. Steadfast in the loyalist cause, death becomes a mere accident along the way, because life has a superior value, "If one must die, I can die. But I hate it. Dying was nothing, and he had no picture of it, or fear of it in his mind." He is ready to die, but he rejects death as a sign of heroism. His heroism consists in valuing life in the face of death. He loves life, and at the same time, he gives it up. He affirms the value of life in the moments before death when he sings the song of life just before fascist bombs rob him of it. "Living…was a field of grain blowing in the wind on the side of a hill. Living was a hawk in the sky. Living was an earthen jar of water in the dust of the threshing with the grain flailed out and the chaff blowing. Living was a horse between your legs."[278] He knows there is a price to pay for the life he has loved, but he also knows that his death may make it possible for the survivors to live the life he has enjoyed.

The last scene of the novel is taken up by the debate between Jordan's suicidal self, who wants to cut short his wait for death, and the stronger self who wants to face death at the hand of the enemy. "Suicide was a cowardly, unmanly act." Jordan's end recreates El Sordo's. Like him, Jordan is trapped, immobilized, and faces death at the hand of the enemy; he too sings the song of life. "He looked down the hill slope again, and he thought, I hate to leave it, is all. I hate to leave it very much... The world is a fine place and worth the fighting for, and I hate very much to leave it." His resolve to defend life is supported by the cause he chose to fight for, "I have fought for what I believed in for a year now. If we win here, we will win everywhere." He knows he is about to die, yet he believes that his death will help create a better life for the survivors. Here is the value of death, the renewal of another generation's earthly life. In the moments before the end, Jordan, like El Sordo, embraces life so strongly that he "could feel his heart beating against the pine needle floor of the forest."[279] Both El Sordo and Jordan die placing value on what they are about to lose; that is their heroism. They die without celebrating death, since they know that what matters is the future life their death will produce.

The point of view, that death is noble when fighting for a worthy cause, loses its validity for Hemingway in the context of the Second World War. His thinking holds that life is an enormous loss, and even a deeply felt cause does not justify heroism in the process of fighting for it. Even though fighting the Nazis was a noble cause, it was not enough to turn the individuals who fought against the Germans into heroes. For Hemingway, the value of earthly life is so high that its preservation overrides the sacrifice that may be defined heroic.

Hemingway places a lot more importance on the loss of life suffered by both Americans and their enemies than on their heroism. Death is a traumatic event; it obliterates the value of heroism if there is any, and celebratory rhetoric is rigorously excluded in Hemingway's work. His view on death indirectly celebrates life. The military tactical or strategic gains lose importance before the cost in human life. Death is a loss without any redeeming value. *Across the River and into the Trees* ignores deeds of valor. It represents wounds and death, which are no reason for pride; they are significant only in so far as they cause fear and loathing.[280] That the military strategy was responsible for rendering impossible deeds of courage on the battlefield, is the same view that Robert Graves held on the Western front. Colonel Richard Cantwell, like Hemingway himself, was a combatant in, and witness to, both the First and the Second World Wars, a kind of Frederic Henry grown into World War II. The conclusion of Cantwell's career redefines the novelist's thinking on valor that was born out of World War I. He is very conscious of his shrinking life, since he must live with a disabled hand and a damaged heart, and he recalls no heroic deeds. He is disenchanted with the American invasion of France and describes a terrific aerial bombardment of the enemy for the purpose of exhibiting the surrender of the Germans who are shaking with fear, as if they were ill with malaria. "They were brave boys" from a famed division, but the bombing was so brutal that it left them no room for bravery. Cantwell reduces the triumphant march on Paris to a meaningless military event that undercuts all possibilities of heroism. The taking of Paris was not even a military operation, for the French underground had taken the city before the Allies arrived. It was only an emotional experience. Asked if there was anything "noble" and "truly happy" about the event, Cantwell replies by stressing the preservation of life and property, "We had no dead and did as little damage as possible." The advancing Americans destroyed many "divisions on paper," which were "ghost divisions." Hemingway relishes the absence of heroic deeds done during the liberation of Paris. No violence or deaths are registered, and this was "noble." He was happy to be again on the streets he "knew and loved" and to know that none of his soldiers were killed, and no damage was done to the city.[281] Having eliminated violence and death from that event, the possibility of heroic deeds is precluded.

But even where violence and killing are prevalent, Hemingway is incapable, or unwilling, to extract any heroism from the events. Violence and killing only serve to underscore their inevitable results, death and destruction. The attack by the Colonel's regiment in the Hurtgen Forest is traumatic and devoid of positive results. The Americans marched against three towns that turned out to be fortresses, every second man in the regiment "was dead and the others nearly all were wounded. In the belly, the head, the feet or the hands, the neck, the back, the lucky buttocks, the unfortunate chest, and the other places." At any rate, "most of them got killed in those woods." Hemingway dwells on the unnecessary bloodshed caused by the victors and points to the bungling of the general in charge of the operation. Walter Bedell Smith was convinced that the attack would be easy, and his error turned the forest into a place where it "was extremely difficult for a man to stay alive," especially when attacking every day. Most of the soldiers who attacked were killed including three battalion commanders on the first day, and a General McNair was killed, by mistake. Finally, "the big kill day of all kill days" happened when several men from the academy at Gettysburg lost their lives.

Across the River and into the Trees underscores the waste of human life. Heroism is expressly repudiated. Hemingway gets rid of the signs that testified to his valor in World War I in the very same place where Cantwell repudiates the pension and decorations he earned while fighting on the Italian front at Fossalta del Piave. He travels from Venice to the Piave River, where he, like Lieutenant Frederick Henry in *A Farewell to Arms* and Hemingway himself, had been wounded about thirty years earlier. Here Cantwell searches for the spot along the riverbank where enemy fire hit him, and once he finds it, he performs a distinctly unmilitary and unheroic operation. He "relieved himself in the exact place where he had determined, by triangulation, that he had been badly wounded,"²⁸² and had earned recognition for bravery. One critic argues that by this gesture Hemingway confronted and acknowledged the climax of his life, after a pilgrimage which binds this book to his first one (*A Farewell to Arms*) with an iron band." The connection between the two novels holds, but in what way is the colonel's gesture the climax of Cantwell's life, if it is a climax at all? The critic's answer is that the scene reveals Cantwell's mingled disgust and reverence for his having been wounded. It is a revelation, not about the event, but about its meaning, because the event earned him the "Silver Medal for Martial Valor." The gesture is only the first part of the scene on the bank of the river Piave at Fossalta. The second part begins when Cantwell stands up. "Now I'll complete the monument," he tells himself, and with a pocket knife, he digs a hole into the moist ground and buries in it a ten thousand lire note. This represents roughly the amount of money he received over the past twenty years from the Italian government as a recipient of the medal for martial valor. "It's fine," Cantwell thinks, "it has merde, money, blood... It has everything—Fertility, money, blood, and iron. Sounds like a nation."²⁸³ The pronoun "it" stands for the "sacred" soil that in *A Farewell to Arms* demanded "glory, honor, courage." In these two symbolic gestures, Cantwell answers the demands of a nation at war, denying the conventional value of glory, honor, and courage and leaving those outworn emblems to rot in the great compost pile of the soil that robbed him of part of his life.²⁸⁴

Cantwell's hostility for the highest values of the military code comes from his experience in the army. A battered survivor of two wars, he has been marked both physically and mentally by its violence. By calling himself "an un-killed" character, Cantwell describes his life as a living death. Along with this rejection of military valor goes the trashing of the Italian warrior-poet and national hero Gabriel D'Annunzio. D'Annunzio worshipped heroism on the altar of death. Death appeared to him as nothing but the "shape" of his own "perfection." He admired the toil of the "indefatigable worker." On the day before Italy entered the war, D'Annunzio proclaimed before a gathering of followers his enthusiasm for sacrifice, "Our only value now consists in nothing else but our blood that will be shed."[285] He personified the ideals of heroism on the battlefield and celebrated death in the name of sacrifice for sacrifice's sake. He fought recklessly in the war and was wounded. In his book, *Notturno*, he turns suffering and death into an uplifting experience. Cantwell speaks of D'Annunzio as the high priest of death, recalling his saying, "Morire non è basta" (To die is not enough), and describes him, "Writer and national hero," "certified and true if you must have heroes, and the colonel did not believe in heroes." He turns the Italian national hero into a "phraser of the dialectic of Fascism, macabre egotist."[286] Nothing better than that attack expresses so well Hemingway's antagonism for heroic death and his support for earthly life.

The cause Americans fought for in World War II—ending Nazi and Fascist oppression in Europe and stopping the expansion of a treacherous enemy in the Pacific—was by ordinary standards noble enough to awaken a soldier's conscience and inspire him to fight with valor. But it did not. Destructive violence overrides heroism. Abhorrence of violence and fear spawned a distinctly anti-heroic literature whose extreme representative is perhaps *Catch-22*, Joseph Heller's vulgarly, bitterly funny novel about the men who flew bombing missions over Italy in the late stages of the war. Its shrill, relentless attack on valor is realized by raising cowardice to the rank of a virtue. The switch is prompted by superior officers' deliberate disregard of the safety of their men and by the latter's horror of violence. The victim of the catch-22 trickery is forced to keep on flying and to accept ever higher risks of wounds and death even though he is stressed by the number and danger of the missions already flown, and he qualifies for a period of rest. This imposition, which is one aspect of that "coercion" a military historian defines as one of the "inhuman" faces of modern war,[287] troubles the novel's protagonist, Yossarian. He responds to the imposition by doing his best to stay alive, fighting death with all his energy. His resolve to stay alive governs his life as a soldier. Death is to be avoided at all costs. Consequently, the enemy is not to be defeated; he is to be avoided. The enemy, Yossarian explains to a comrade bent on fighting and risking death, is anybody, friend or foe, who is going to get "you killed." Yossarian refuses to resign himself to death in battle. Each time he takes off on a flight over enemy territory, he is determined to come back "alive." One of the means he uses repeatedly to fulfill this is a fierce prodding of the plane's pilot to take evasive action as soon as the bombs are dropped. No standard procedure for taking evasive action exists, and Yossarian's resolve to keep alive dictates one. On each flight, the moment the bombs are released from his aircraft, he hollers to the pilot to steer away from the flight path to avoid enemy fire from the ground: "Hard, hard, hard, hard."[288]

The soldiers in Norman Mailer's novel, *The Naked and the Dead* live in a constant state of fear. Unlike those of *Her Privates We* in the Great War, who feared but tried hard to overcome their fear, the combatants in the American novel are oppressed by it. They make no attempt to hide or overcome it. None of them embrace fighting as their patriotic duty for country or their unit. No trace of heroism can be detected. About to land on a Japanese-held island, the knowledge that in a few hours some will be dead is in the mind of every man in the American unit. Having known the terror of combat before, Sergeant Martinez lay sweating on his bunk, "thinking with dread" about the coming morning, like Henry V's men at dawn break at Agincourt. The sound of shells swishing overhead makes him feel "naked." An explosion on the beach causes one soldier to suffer "an unreasonable panic," another one to sob and be shaken with trembling. Facing the jungle after the landing, Private Roth feels "a sick fear." He broods about sudden death, and his fear becomes "gnawing, guttish." A comrade dies, and his death "opened a secret fear" in Private Red. To him, the "idea of death was fresh and terrifying." As one who had been through much combat, he is far from inured to the spectacle of death on the battlefield. "He no longer had any illusion about the inviolability of his own flesh. He knew he could be killed," and feels he is doomed. "They ain't a thing you can do about it." And Private Stanley's "nameless" anxiety comes from "fearing death, really fearing it for the first time."[289] The prospect of death stifles the heroic impulse. Preserving life is the goal of these combatants.

The platoon's mission—marching thirty or forty miles through unexplored jungle, hills, and a mountain pass—was to scout the Japanese rear and to return to their base. The soldiers appear to be the least qualified to carry it out. The mission turns out to be an ordeal in which they exert themselves mightily, struggling against their physical and moral limitations. The uncharted territory instills in them "a new and subtler terror." "Unmanning fear" overtakes Lieutenant Hearn during a fire fight and "a cold charge of fear" seizes Private Wilson. As the patrol progresses, the men become "exhausted," moving forward like automatons. Toward the end of the ordeal, "the platoon dropped from one layer of fatigue to another," but the soldiers have now become used to exhaustion. The adjustment means that the extreme exertion has reshaped them, reducing them "to the lowest common denominator of their existence."[290]

The men of the reconnaissance platoon have overcome the harshness of the environment, the frailty of their selves, and their fear of death. Out of their struggle, the will to live was born, and though the mission turned out to be useless, it required an exertion that gave them a sense of accomplishment as they measured the endurance that enabled them to defeat death. In the end they feel they are heroes. As they leave the island, they point out the slopes of the mountain they crossed with "startled pride in themselves," arguing whether they had climbed each particular ridge, satisfied with their deeds: "We did okay."[291]

They are a special kind of heroes, for they have achieved no victory over the enemy, but only over themselves, over what scared them at the beginning of their mission, fear and the specter of death. Exertion on the battlefield toughened them and breathed into them the martial spirit. Unfortunately, the general in charge of the operation was not satisfied with the way the soldiers behaved and fought. They lacked courage, he surmises, and he decides to do something about it. "The only morality of the future," General Cummings lectured Lieutenant Hearn before sending him to his death on Mount Anaka, "is a power morality." And this power "can flow only from the top down." Patriotism is very fine, Cummings tells Hearn, echoing a fundamental Clausewitzian concept, "but fighting emotions are very undependable, and the longer a war lasts the less value they have." Soldiers must be forced to fight valiantly. On the battlefield, only two things count, "A superior material force and a poor standard of living." America as a whole has the highest standard of living in the world, and at the same time the worst fighting soldiers of any big power. They have an inflated idea about their "rights," but have no sense of duty. "What you have got to do is break them down." The general is angry. He realizes that in the course of the mission, the men resisted his authority. As he looks forward to another operation in the Pacific and to achieving better results, he figures that results can be achieved only by "molding" and "shaking up" his troops, first.[292] To make them truly valiant General Cummings will resort to "the breaking of men's spirit and the destruction of their wills.["][293]

Some critics believe that there are no heroes in Mailer's novel.[294]. There is at least one, hero, Sergeant Croft, the platoon leader.[295] But he is not against death; he does not care about it; he is not afraid of it. His heroism was born out of a violent temper and his experience in civil life. Unlike the soldiers who have built their military spirit through exertion and the experience of fear on the battlefield, Croft already had the qualities required to be a hero. He is a skillful killer. He ruthlessly and expertly leads the patrol across the island after the death of the ineffective Hearn. He stands as the instrument of General Cummings's aggressive ideas, assisting in "breaking down" the soldiers and helping them to reap the fruits of their inhuman exertion. He is supported by his violent instinct, not by the cause he fights for. Violence is the essence of his heroism. He craves killing and is unafraid of death. Death is his lodestar. On first arriving, as the landing craft approached the shore of the island, Croft felt "as though he were riding a horse at a gallop" before an action. He "hungered for the fast taut pulse he would feel in his throat after he killed a man." In action, Croft reveals himself an expert and a successful killer. He "fired and fired, switching targets with the quick reflexes of an athlete shifting for a ball." Having killed several Japanese, he attacked another group of them, successfully, forcing the line to break up and to retreat. Mailer tries to explain Croft's behavior. A "mean," hardy boy from Texas, Croft had hunted deer with a passion, defying the harsh environment, brawled with his age mates, and broke horses. While in the National Guard, he killed a man for the first time. Enraged by his wife's infidelity, he searched for her lovers to kill them. Some nights in his house on the Texas plains, an undefined rage would seize him, which "increased and increased." To him, the outside world, which is made up of "fuggin whores," a "bunch of dogs," and "deer to track," is the object of his hatred."[296] Life led him to exert himself beyond the limits of human endurance. What counts for Croft is the experience of killing, which will define his heroism on the battlefield. He is an uncivilized man who became so, not through battlefield exertion a la Clausewitz, but through the degradation that ruled his private life. He is absorbed by the business of killing and has no thought whatsoever about his own death. His heroism rests on a solid basis.

Croft is a hero because he is a good killer, but not all killers are heroes, and not all soldiers count on their killing prowess to become heroes. William Manchester who was a Marine sergeant in the Pacific War, writes in his memoir that the "boldness and audacity" of his comrades in the early 1940s is unquestionable. But whether the gains they made by using their boldness and audacity were worth the price paid in lives and degradation is another matter. He believes that the sacrifices in human lives diminished the value of boldness and audacity as military virtues. Manchester acknowledges that his generation is the last one that believed audacity in combat is a virtue, but he also defined its cost. He had walked "through the valley of the shadow of death," he recalls, and as a result, he had been "terribly frightened." He kept on fighting, without any heroic intent. "I became the least intrepid of warriors, a survivor, not a hero, more terrier than lion." However, officially he was recognized as a hero by the Secretary of the Navy. Still, he scoffs at valor and dismisses it as military rhetoric. 'Gallantry,' 'valor,' 'tenacity,' and 'extraordinary heroism'... didn't really apply to me. Indeed, at times it seemed to me that they applied to no one except the dead." He honors places like Tarawa and Mount Suribachi, units like the First Marine Division, and dates like December 7, 1941, but he dissociates himself from the official proclamations and extravagant praises of the sacrifices made in those places and on those dates. Like Hemingway, Manchester repudiates the military rhetoric that shrouds concrete, painful events. He sees heroism made real by the human cost that war entails, and he honors those places, units, and dates, "while hating the whole red and ragged business of war." Heroism is no longer the admirable side of the military enterprise. It embodies the cost in human lives, and is a cause for grief, not flashy rhetoric.[297]

Manchester's first kill of the war was far from heroic; it was a mortifying experience, showing the price he paid for an action that others judged to be heroic. Engaged in searching a hut holding a sniper, Manchester entered it and fell prey to a state of being far from heroic. "Various valves were opening and closing in my stomach. My mouth was dry, my legs quaking, and my eyes out of focus." He shot and killed the sniper who, entangled by the strap of his rifle, was unable to use it, while Manchester kept firing. No sense of heroism and victory came over him, only the ugliness of death and its loathsome presence. Having stopped firing, he sees "the dark, brown effluvium of the freshly slain, a sour, pervasive emanation which is different from anything you have known." Stupefied by the corpse that soon would swell, bloat, and then burst out of the uniform, Manchester recalls "a feeling of disgust and self-hatred." He vomited and urinated in his pants. When one of his comrades enters the hut, he does not congratulate Manchester for the deed that ensured the safety of many American soldiers outside. He approaches him, and then backs away in revulsion from his foul stench. Manchester was crying, trembling with his dirtied pants on. "I remember wondering dumbly," he notes in his memoir, "is that what they mean by 'conspicuous gallantry'?"[298]

Manchester is reluctant to portray himself doing deeds of valor. He demeans himself even when he has no real reason for doing so. At Tarawa, for instance, where he had just landed. He and his comrades lay down by a seawall and were waiting for the right moment to outflank the enemy and advance when an old acquaintance of Manchester, one Lieutenant Tubby, takes command of the Marine unit, with plans to take them over the top and make a frontal attack on the Japanese position. Manchester openly rejects the lieutenant's plan and is immediately attacked by him and called a coward in front of the troops. To support the charge, the lieutenant makes reference to Manchester's masturbating habits at officers' school. "I know your kind," he tells Manchester. "You think we could not hear you back in the squad bay, masturbating every night? Did you think they'd give a Marine Corps commission to a masturbator?" The lieutenant goes over the top and is cut down by enemy fire. He dies a heroic but useless death.[299] Now Manchester was no coward. He probably did not care about his reputation as a combatant. He regarded masturbation irrelevant when compared to the decision of incompetent officers to send their troops on frontal attacks. He knew better than his superiors and denounced the frontal attacks that the Americans launched once too often.[300] The tactic needed to be destroyed as a source of heroic behavior.

Manchester is aware that the Americans made notable sacrifices on the battlefield. He recognizes that "American valor" was necessary to defeat the fanaticism of the Japanese soldier, which for him was the highest form of heroism. "There were brave Marines" who knew the risk, saw the value of an objective, and decided to attack.[301] But the bravery displayed was not enough to compensate for the human losses. The price was too high, even though some soldiers paid it willingly. Manchester abstains from calling the Marines heroic, because by naming them heroes, he would be discarding– the value of the lives lost. The human cost of heroism kept him from glorifying it.

Manchester remembers that any unit that lost about 30 percent of its men in the Pacific theater usually lost its fighting spirit. However, the Marines at Tarawa lost 40 percent and more as they got closer to mainland Japan. Nevertheless, they kept on fighting hard. On Peleliu, the loss of the First Marines Corp was 56 percent; on Iwo Jima, the Twenty-sixth Marine Corp lost 76 percent; on Okinawa, the Twenty-ninth lost 81 percent. And it was not just the Marines to make big sacrifices. He also remembers that the pilots of the torpedo bombers that destroyed the Japanese warships at Midway knew they were flying to certain death, and similarly, the Air Corps pilots who flew over Ploesti knew they would not make it back. He refuses to call these acts of valor. He recalls the act of a major that by ordinary standards was valiant, but again no such recognition is forthcoming. The major asked the surviving men of his battalion to attack. He led the charge himself in the night, throwing grenades all the while inciting his troops to charge harder through shrapnel, small arms fire, and hand grenades. He was awarded the Congressional Medal of Honor posthumously. Manchester would like very much to find out why the major chose to attack. He could find no reason for it, and neither did the widow of the fallen major, who Manchester visited at their home in Oklahoma. "Apart from our shared grief," he writes of the encounter, "I was still trying to understand why he had done what he had done. I thought she might know. She didn't. She was as mystified as I was."[302] It certainly takes courage to do what the major did, but even so, Manchester would not define the behavior of this major as heroic. His deed is only memorable for its loss of life and the grief of the survivors.

Yet, the presence of valor dogs Manchester's brooding about the meaning of fighting. He remembers the Marines on Iwo Jima. "It takes courage to stay at the front on Iwo Jima. It takes something we can't tag or classify to push out ahead of those lines, against an unseen enemy who has survived two months of shell and shock... It takes courage to crawl ahead, one hundred yards a day, and get up the next morning, count losses, and do it again. But that is the only way it can be done." Courage consists in submitting to the necessities of the battlefield. The Marines appeared to be victims of circumstances that left them no choice. It was an enormous effort. There was not the spirit of "we came, we saw, we conquered." It was not only the fighting that tested them. It was the environment, too, like the mud in Okinawa. "In combat you fight in the mud, sleep in it, void in it, bleed in it, and sometimes die in it." What fighting does to the soldier is so dispiriting that it is impossible to attach to it a sense of heroism. In preparing his men for combat, he teaches them how to take advantage of the enemy's habits. He wants them to learn "a lesson in survival, not heroism."[303]

Death and suffering gain a significance that leaves no room for the image and concept of heroism as a virtue. The Marines who Manchester observed coming back from the line of fire, he recalls, were in such shape that it was impossible to see them as heroes or even themselves thinking they were heroes. The dull, sightless eyes of the young expressed "strain, misery shock, sleeplessness." The business of taking lives and fighting to preserve one's own has stunned them, wiping out their sentimental and intellectual sensibilities. The eyes of the veterans expressed utter indifference. They are men who have lost their youth and know that they will never recapture it. There is nothing in them that might hint at their success on the battlefield or satisfaction with their performance. They exhibit no heroic pride, even though they may have very well performed deeds that could be called heroic. "War is literally unreasonable."[304] One can be really heroic, but heroism destroys by taxing and damaging one's body and soul beyond repair. Danger, pain, fear, and death preclude thinking and speaking of valor. The cost is too high, and the cost is what lives inside the combatant. As Manchester wrote at the beginning of his memoir, he "honors" the places, the dates, and the units that distinguished themselves, "while hating the whole red and ragged business of war." To honor places, dates, and units might mean that the combatants are recognized as heroes. But hating war makes it clear that war, which has created the heroes, denies the very root and worthiness of heroism itself.

Soldiers in the field often did something that was truly noble and heroic, protecting one another at the risk of one's life. "Men, I now know, do not fight for flag or country, for the Marine Corps or glory or any other abstraction. They fight for one another. Any man in combat who lacks comrades who will die for him, or for whom he is willing to die, is not a man at all. He is truly damned." His comrades on the battlefield "were closer to me... than any friends had been or ever would be... I had to be with them, rather than let them die and me live with the knowledge that I might have saved them."[305] Knowing that death was reaping the life of too many soldiers, Manchester was drawn to his endangered comrades, to help them survive, and even share their fate. But this heroism has nothing to do with the heroism that the military leadership expects of men—to prevail over the enemy or to conquer territory, or both. If one fought for the survival of comrades, one might as well stay home. The country sends one to the battlefield to make war and to accomplish specific aims. The country does not make war to enable the combatants to find love and companionship in the ranks.

Manchester's inability to understand the reason why the combatants took big risks and made considerable sacrifices was the reason why he went back to the Pacific islands after the war. He wanted to exorcise his inner "darkness with the light of understanding." He had to take this journey back in time to understand his war experience, also because the darkness gave him nightmares. In 1978 on the beach of Tarawa, he thinks he has gained some understanding, but the understanding upsets him and makes him want to leave right away. The first things he notices are the signs of killing and destruction left from the fighting—rusting tanks, twisted artillery pieces, shattered landing crafts, concrete pillboxes. In other locations, he figures that hundreds of fortified positions still stand, many of them intact. He feels offended by the existence of these relics of war. They lead him to imagine the Marine assault on Tarawa. To gain a sense of the assault, he goes out in the surf a thousand yards to find the approximate point where they had left their landing boats and began advancing toward the Japanese. Retracing the path of the Marines, he walks back to the beach, and he realizes that their advance had been a frontal attack, the tactic made infamous by the Great War. "I feel anger roaring in my chest," Manchester writes as the realization strikes him, "and I think of the men who fell in the surf, sprawled like priests at high mass." What happened on that beach long ago leaves no room for reflection on heroism and sacrifice. What strikes him is the realization that the killing was the result of military orders that created a great many American victims; this realization unnerves him, "Suddenly the most important thing in the world for me is to leave." Here the "darkness" could not be exorcised. The sacrifice of the Marines was no heroic performance. The slaughter darkens Manchester's mind as he sees that the Marines were forced to endure "a bloody crime."[306] Of course, he could still have judged Tarawa a heroic performance, since the Marines fought well and prevailed. But the memory of the enormous number of dead on the beach created in the veteran a sense of "darkness" that American heroism could not outweigh.

Manchester and the members of his generation had been touched by the works of writers who gave young intellectuals "so much joy, ennobling sacrifice and bravery." But the war experience, far from ennobling them through heroism and sacrifice, left them disenchanted and "spiritually bankrupt."[307] They learned that they had to kill, a business hard on anyone's soul and mind, and to be killed. The lesson overrode their preconceived idea of valor and the way they intended to practice it in battle. They realized that it was too costly from the human point of view and unworthy of any idealization. They were like men condemned to death, obsessed not by a resolve to show their heroism, but by the thought of what would be the most likely conclusion to their life. "We moved on, each of us inching along the brink of his own extinction, never speaking of what we considered the unspeakable." They also knew the many sides of grief. Death on the battlefield was unsparing on the next of kin, and some relatives repressed their anguish at great cost to themselves. The combatants who lost comrades on the field suffered the same as their relatives did. While the case against the red and ragged business of war gains force in Manchester's mind, he has a veiled sense of guilt for having served in a way that the present-day generation has a hard time understanding. For the younger generation, it must be hard to see why the Americans faced "violent death" and acquiesced in "a monstrous conspiracy against our lives."[308] The older generation went to war not to ennoble itself through heroism, but to suffer death, the monstrosity against which Manchester has belatedly rebelled.

The classic narrative of E. B. Sledge, *With the Old Breed at Peleliu and Okinawa,* corroborates Manchester's estimate of the abhorrence of both death and heroism among combatants in the Pacific. The narrative traces their response to the events on the battlefield not as a triumph of their endurance and heroic temper, but as their consuming fight against pain and death. Landing on a beach and being under enemy fire caused Sledge to shudder and shake as though he were having "a mild convulsion." He sweated copiously, prayed, clenched his teeth, and cursed the Japanese. He was "terrified" by the shells flying over him. The artillery barrage was so intense that he had no way to keep contact with his comrades, and he felt he was on the battlefield all by himself, helpless in a tempest of violent explosions. In the midst of the tempest, he reflects on its virulence, "an invention of hell," the "essence of violence" and "of man's inhumanity to man." Shells not only tore up the body; they "tortured one's mind almost beyond the brink of sanity." At each shell explosion his vitality was diminished, his energy drained and he was left limp and exhausted. The battlefield experience left no room for heroic thought or action. The harm to his being was overwhelming. He recalls the shelling as "the most terrifying of combat experience." "I hated shells as much for their damage to the mind as to the body." Endurance of the barrage was no heroic deed; it was the occasion to underscore the shrinking of his physical and emotional resources. "Fear is many-faceted and has many subtle nuances, but the terror and desperation endured under heavy shelling are by far the most unbearable."[309]

For the combatants in the Pacific, the war was no field of valor. It was death in life, "a nether world of horror from which escape seemed less and less likely as casualties mounted and the fighting dragged on and on." Aside from the actual losses, a more subtle and destructive kind of loss devastated those who continued to fight. For them "time had no meaning; life had no meaning." They felt like being in a "meatgrinder," struggling not for victory, but for life itself. The real achievement was to stay alive and carry on in an environment that made living and fighting almost impossible. Heroism consisted in what the narrator is reluctant to say, and no superior would recognize, namely, continuing to fight despite fear of wounds and death. "Courage meant overcoming fear and doing one's duty in the presence of danger, not being unafraid."[310] Fear was enemy number one. The integrity of the soldier depended on defeating it. The sight of helpless comrades being slaughtered hit Sledge hard. The value that the leadership conferred on machines, tanks, aircrafts, trucks, and ships, which were carefully maintained since they were hard to replace way out in the Pacific, further demeaned human life, he thought, and gave the soldier the feeling that he was only a "thing," already bereft of life. For the infantry, who were expected to keep going beyond the limits of human endurance until they were killed, wounded, or dropped by exhaustion, the danger was even more real, and the strategy of unrestrained human sacrifice was hard to accept especially because the combatants were men who came from a country and culture that put value on individual life. The result of the leadership's callousness was evident to anyone who could look around. Healthy young men got hurt and killed day after day. Loss of life was a spectacle that sickened and revolted Sledge. He felt he "could not take it anymore... I was so terribly tired and so emotionally wrung out for being afraid for days on end that I seemed to have no reserve strength left." Preservation of life was the strongest wish. "Our minds thought only of personal survival." A million-dollar wound, the sure way to escape death, would fulfill the wish, but Sledge wanted to do his duty and save his life. He could have written about heroism, but he refrains from doing so because to write about heroism would make a mockery of the horror and pain of the battlefield. Horror and pain are what a soldier remembers, not as evidence of his heroism, but as proof of his having been able to preserve life. His comrades felt the same. They felt little pride in achieving the military objectives assigned to them, only great satisfaction in surviving the intense physical exertion of combat in the muggy heat of the Pacific. Okinawa turned out to be another zone of terror where fear and horror tortured Sledge and his comrades "like a cat tormenting a mouse." The same anxiety that held him in Peleliu seizes him again in Okinawa as a "greater and greater dread" overwhelmed him. What hurt him most though, was his comrades' "pain and suffering."[311]

KILLING HEROICS

Vietnam has changed the face of heroism, yanking it from a cause and confining it to destruction for destruction's sake and killing for killing's sake. Violence in its most complete form becomes the standard of valor.

Some descriptions and estimates of battles in Vietnam stress American heroism with a single-mindedness, uniformity of tone and style that are striking, and suspicious. There is a casual, almost brutal look at the result of skirmishes, which were part of the battle of the Ia Drang Valley in 1965, related in the popular *We Were Soldiers Once... and Young:* "My God, there has been a heavy battle here. Hell, there are bodies all over this valley down through here. For the last thirty minutes we have just been walking around and over and through bodies to get here. You guys have been playing combat for real here." Not one emotion or thought responding to the human cost of war, or an estimate of the war itself is aired. There is only wonder at, and a disguised complacency in, the killing and mayhem. The commander of the unit thanks the troops, telling them to be proud of what they have done for the country.

Another company holds its ground against the North Vietnamese, and it does it "in a stunning display of personal courage and unit discipline. The men held their positions and died fighting. Again, no thoughts are expressed on the inner toll taken, only the gruesome results interest the narrator, "It was incredible carnage. We went to areas where lots of artillery had come in during the night, and we saw our guys had been blown up [into] the trees. The bodies were already decomposed, and it had only happened the night before... The stench was unbelievable. We started hauling in whole bodies first; then we brought in the pieces and parts."

On being wounded a combatant feels fear. "Fear comes, and at once you recognize it and accept it. It passes just as fast as it comes, and you don't think about it anymore. You just do what you have to do." In sum, the veterans of *We Were Soldiers Once ... and Young* remember "many heroes but no cowards." Everyone lost friends, but what counts is that "the bravery they showed on the battlefield will live forever." Looking back on the deeds represented throughout the narrative, a veteran is enthralled and intones a nostalgic refrain, "Those were the days, my friend."[312] Those were the days spent in killing and dying with unmatched intensity.

Face to face with the killing, these soldiers showed no signs of distress. This is admirable; it enabled them to become heroes. General William Westmoreland, commander-in-chief of the American forces in Vietnam, would praise and reward the conduct of combatants such as these. He thought that Americans in Vietnam showed a lot of bravery and very little cowardice. "Acts of heroism [were] a daily occurrence," he said. Heroism, he further explained, was common because the war was hard, and "individual courage" was a "constant requirement."[313] However, because courage was required, does not mean that it was common. On the contrary, courage in the conventional sense, which is certainly what the general had in mind, was uncommon. The explanation is that the North Vietnamese fighting capability, inner strength, and willingness to sacrifice life, was superior to that of the Americans.

One reason why the combatants of *We Were Soldiers Once .. and Young,* fought and died with great resolve is that they accepted unreservedly the official line for the cause of the war. They went because their country asked them to go. The President ordered it, and therefore, it was their "duty to go."[314] For other soldiers, the cause was more problematic and their battlefield experience far more tortuous and far less glorious than that of the protagonists of *We Were Soldiers Once*. The Vietnam generation valued heroism but knew very little about its real face before stepping onto the battlefield. The dream of heroism intoxicated young Americans at home, but many would be disappointed in their expectations when they came face to face with a brutal, unorthodox, and difficult war. Ron Kovic, for example, "wanted to be a hero" since the time he was in high school. The recruiters from the Marine corps who spoke to his senior class made a profound impression on him. He felt as if his dream of becoming a hero was being realized right there and then. The recruiters told him that the Marine Corps built men by strengthening body, mind, and spirit,[315] just what an ordinary man needs to become a hero.

Kovic had an uncritical and shallow idea about heroism and embraced it with enthusiasm. At home, the celluloid heroes, like Audie Murphy of *To Hell and Back* and John Wayne of *The Sands of Iwo Jima*, kept his dream alive. He found Murphy "so brave" that when he saw him in action, chills went up and down young Kovic's spine. John Wayne was a true hero to Kovic. On the battlefield, Kovic will fight to keep faith in the belief that ruled his youth. Just before his last fight, he was still resolved in his faith, "I wanted to prove to myself that I was a brave man," he was telling himself while leading the assault on a village held by the Viet Cong, "no matter what happened out there, I thought to myself, I could never retreat. I had to be courageous." He was seriously wounded during the action, and the specter of death or mutilation caused him to lose his inner strength. "I couldn't even feel my body. I was frightened to death." In the end he repudiated the value of death, the would-be proof of his heroic endeavor. "All I could feel was the worthlessness of dying right here in this place at this moment for nothing."[316] The devastating wound will fill his life with pain and sorrow, while the ideal of heroism in general, and of his own in particular become the object of fierce contempt.

Philip Caputo, too, wanted the chance "to live heroically." When he saw a poster of an athletic Marine officer, and he read about the amazing deeds of the Marines, he knew that the "heroic experience" he sought was war. He needed to prove something— "my courage, my toughness, my manhood." While in training he diligently did his classroom work, but he was impatient for the romance of war, for the action, desperate charges and battles against impossible odds, the sort of things that movies like *Guadalcanal Diary* and *Retreat, Hell!* had shown him in the comfort of his home. However, the reality of war will gradually obliterate his notion of courage. Forces and feelings stronger than those that had induced him to seek a heroic life will kill his dream. Under fire he often faced the enemy with a lack of fear generated by an extraordinary state of being. Life intensifies, the senses quicken, and consciousness sharpens. "It was something like the elevated state of awareness induced by drugs." Under fire, Caputo recalls, "you seem to live more intensely." It was not the call of duty or a surge of patriotism that led him to act like a hero, but a headiness superior to what either alcohol or drugs could produce. A kind of extraterrestrial force enabled him to live the heroic life on the battlefield. But even though he distinguished himself, his knowledge of death made his experience a downer. It destroyed his youth in a few months and left him to live like an old man when he returned to civilian life. "[317] His heroic experience destroyed the remaining years of his life.

Lieutenant William Broyles was no naive recruit when he was sent to Vietnam in 1969. He went reluctantly. He was afraid of death, and he lacked the strength to set aside his fear. But on sighting Iwo Jima from the airplane that was flying him to Vietnam, he had a kind of revelation and found the resolve to go ahead and face combat. The sight of the famed island led him to think about the sacrifices made by the American Marines twenty-five years earlier, and he understood then the value that courage holds. The Marines died on Iwo Jima just to demonstrate their courage. "Never mind that all of them had died on Iwo so that a few pilots could have a place to land if they ran out of fuel.

It was not the result, but the courage, that mattered." After all, Broyles knew that to fight and to die with courage is the basis of the Marine mystique. To prove one's courage, not to gain victory, is what counts. A real Marine did not care if he might "fight and die for a fuck up."[318] What mattered to a real Marine was to behave by the code of the corps, uncannily, a throw-back to when heroism was a matter of personal pride and fighting to the death were ends in themselves regardless of the outcome, especially if invested with the recklessness and mystique that the Marines attach to the sacrifice of life in battle. At any rate, dying and fighting for a fuck up in Vietnam gave the Marines such a reputation for courage ("one Marine was better than ten Slopes"), that small units were sometimes sent against large contingents of North Vietnamese in the belief that the Marines would easily prevail. But most of the time, they failed, and the failure was one reason why the Marine Corps came to be defined as the "finest instrument ever devised for the killing of young Americans."[319] Fighting to the death willingly and without purpose was enough to create a distinctive reputation. If valor could be attributed to the Marines, it was proof of their fearlessness and contempt for death.

Despite the cockiness and swagger, the Marines were far from willing to sacrifice themselves for its own sake. They suffered from a lack of courage as much as the other combatants. On the battlefield, Broyles found that the Americans missed something that the North Vietnamese soldiers possessed, "a moral certainty so strong as to make the suffering of individuals invisible," a certainty that made them brave. Without such certainty, Americans were unable to defy death and fight valiantly. As a result, they "were afraid of death," while the Vietnamese were unafraid of it, and "were willing to keep on killing and dying, and we [Americans] were not." Moral certainty explains how it was possible for a people of tiny men, no bigger than boys, to succeed in driving out of their country a "race of giants." The North Vietnamese "saw death not primarily as tragedy but as part of a higher purpose. Like the Texans who fought to the death at the Alamo, they were ready to sacrifice themselves."[320] When there is a higher purpose in the hearts of soldiers, death becomes a mere accident along the way. The Americans, who on the whole were not engaged as deeply, had less courage.

Tim O'Brien, a veteran and writer who has made courage central to his work, found it very hard to define as well as to discover it among his comrades. "What's courage and how do you get it?"[321] is what he wanted to find out. Like many other combatants, he valued it highly and went to war to prove to himself and others that he had it. Courage was the means to prove his manhood. It was neither proof of his patriotism nor the means to success on the battlefield. He, and some of his comrades during their training at Fort Lewis were resolved to perform valiantly. If they did not, they believed, they would implicitly admit that they were "not brave, not heroes." One must be brave, or else he is a coward, so they thought; there is nothing in between. But soon, O'Brien began to question war and the meaning and value of courage. He questioned war because, he told the chaplain at the base, he felt that it produces pain and death. The chaplain shared none of O'Brien's gloom. He made it clear that war was a valuable experience, specifically because it offered every fighting man the chance to show his mettle. War can be questioned but not rejected, the chaplain argued, because it gives man the chance to raise himself above anonymity and to distinguish himself by showing valor on the battlefield. "Where the hell do you fit the guts and bravery into your intellectual scheme?" The chaplain replied with a question that turned war into a golden opportunity for anyone to become a real man. War is essential, he said, because only in war can a man show his best quality, courage. It is a hidden virtue, which only war can bring out. War is the occasion that lends an otherwise insignificant man the chance to make himself relevant by demonstrating this virtue.

But the battlefield will show that there is no correlation between valor and manhood. In fact, it will show O'Brien the absence of any valiant deed. He will eventually realize that what kept the soldiers fighting "was not courage exactly; the object was not valor." The object was to behave in such a way as to mask their fear. He and his comrades "were too frightened to be cowards."³²² But sometimes they were unable to keep themselves from behaving like cowards. The fright generated by enemy attacks, for instance, was worse than the fear of cowardice. They tried hard, but under fire the will often wilted.

Being under fire in Vietnam was an especially unsettling experience for Americans. It was like dying a tortured death, a process that no amount of courage could forestall. "You writhe like a man suddenly waking in the middle of a heart transplant," O'Brien recorded that experience, "the old heart out, the new one poised somewhere unseen in the enemy's hands. The pain, even with the ether or sodium chloride, explodes in the empty cavity, and the terror is in waiting for the cavity to be filled, for life to start pumping and throbbing again. You whimper, low and screeching, and it does not start anywhere."³²³ Such an experience had the power to shake any soldier, incapacitating him and wiping out all possibilities for doing deeds of valor. Under fire, a keen observer of the Vietnamese battlefield echoed that same note of terror, "would take you out of your head and your body too."³²⁴ The effect of this unusual type of terror is that the soldiers have "already died more than once, squirming under the bullets, going through the act of death and coming through embarrassingly alive. The bullets stop... You tentatively peek up, wondering if it is the end. Then you look at the other men, reading your own caved-in belly deep in their eyes. The fright dies the same way Novocain wears off in the dentist chair. You promise, almost moving your lips, to do better next time; that by itself is a kind of courage." ³²⁵ Under fire there is no courage. The combatant is paralyzed and unable to perform any kind of daring deed. Courage consists in trying to suppress fear and to avoid shame, but though he is still physically alive, the experience under fire has often left his inner self dead. The blank expression known as the "thousand-yard stare," which could be detected in the faces of many combatants, reflected well their state of mind and decay, "Fed-up, fucked-up, and far from home."³²⁶ The thousand-yard stare expressed no heroic tension.

American soldiers were short of the required courage because the war itself stifled it. War's failure to generate courage defied Clausewitz's belief that fighting on the battlefield is the surest way to create it. Instead of strengthening the soldier and leading him to fight with courage, war created in him a sense of impotence. The hostile environment, the lack of belief in a cause, and death anxiety stood in the way of heroic deeds.

The environment was alien to Americans and, figuratively, conspired to disarm them. No weapon was available to fight the jungle, except defoliation. "Our real enemy is the jungle," a veteran pinpointed the source of danger for Americans.[327] "The trees would kill you; the elephant grass grew up homicidal," and fear seized the soldiers because they were defenseless before these natural enemies. "So, you learned about fear. It was hard to know what you really learned about courage,"[328] because courage was inadequate in overcoming the obstacles posed by the environment. The jungle floor was stifling hot; no breeze got through the vegetation. It rained frequently, and the troops and their equipment became soaked with water and mold. When they got up from sleep, they found that their skin had whitened and wrinkled.[329] The jungle and the bush were harsh, impenetrable, and invincible. In the bush, visibility was no greater than the length of an arm; it acted like a stifling enclosure, where the air was "as thick and stale as an over-inflated tire." It was impossible to break through this kind of enclosure. Walking through bamboo growth, for example, the soldier felt as if he were locked in a closet "packed with broomsticks and rubber raincoats"; it was an "agony."[330] Even the color of the lush vegetation in the jungle, the uniform and unchanging green without any contrast, exerted a depressing effect on the soldier. On the other hand, when the sun shone, Americans became disoriented. They received the impression that the sun and the land were the allies of the Viet Cong, "wearing us down, driving us mad, killing us." Lieutenant Caputo came to realize.[331] In such an environment, courage would be required, but the combatants were unable to summon it, for in the bush they lost their human identity. They went wild, a veteran combatant tells a new arrival, "Wild as hell. You spend a month in the bush, and you are not a Marine anymore. Hell, you are not even a goddamn person."[332] Showing valor in such an environment was out of the question. The environment could not be changed by human courage.

The topography offered the enemy effective concealment, enabling it to launch unexpected attacks from points often impossible to identify. These attacks disconcerted the Americans and turned the war into "a formless" one,[333] a war in which the traditional strategies and tactics were useless. Fighting was often reduced to defending themselves with little chance of hurting the enemy, and little room for showing courage for there was no enemy to shoot at. "Snipers yesterday, snipers today, we did not know which way to shoot, we wanted a foxhole like a basement." This was the kind of desperation that held combatants out in the bush or in some hamlet far from their base.[334] How could they show bravery if the enemy could not be engaged? When the enemy is invisible, courage is irrelevant.

The ground itself, the very same ground that in earlier wars had been the first refuge for a soldier under fire, was an enemy. A reporter with extensive battlefield experience noted the instinctive reliance of the combatant on the ground.[335] In earlier wars, "it was you and the ground; kiss it, eat it, fuck it, plow it with your whole body, get as close to it as you can." The infantryman in particular had a special relationship with the earth. He walks, sleeps, and eats on it; he digs his home and shelter in it. But in Vietnam, mines and booby traps changed the role of the earth in the life of the combatant. The earth no longer was a friendly refuge; it was a deadly enemy. The enemy used it to conceal all sorts of explosive devices. It was impossible for Americans to think and to behave heroically while walking through the jungle, knowing that a hidden mine could suddenly blow up. Fear replaced boldness. They were not waging war; they were simply being murdered. The combatants "had begun to feel more like victims than soldiers."[336] Men marked for death or injury become resigned to their fate, and resignation is the opposite of courage. Because of the expectation of explosions, any soldier who steps on the trail, on large patches of grass, or in the rice paddies, "hallucinates," and courage has no place in hallucinations. Looking ahead a few paces, one wondered what his legs would resemble if one tripped the wire and caused a mine to explode, "Will the pain be unbearable? Will you scream or fall silent? Will you be afraid to look at your own body, afraid of the sight of your own red flesh and white bone?"[337] On the trail, in patches of grass or in paddies, fear ruled. Courage, if it existed, had no place in defending against hidden mines or escaping their lethal effects.

Even so, in the face of a daunting task, the combatant still yearned for the strength that would enable him to soldier on without fear. The war fiction has come up with an image of valor as the function of a mysterious organ in the human body. "The issue, of course, was courage," one soldier ponders, but "the real issue was the power of the will to defeat fear," and how to get hold of this power. The soldier imagines a fantastic search leading to a no less fantastic discovery of valor. The soldier must dig into his biological being, since somewhere inside every man "is a biological center for the exercise of courage," may be a piece of tissue, a chemical, or a chromosome, each in its own way capable, when manipulated properly, to produce "chain reactions of valor."[338] Such a project simply underscores the soldier's desperate need for courage and the impossibility of getting it.

Death anxiety was probably the most significant drawback to the exercise of valor. Combatants in general fear death, but Vietnam combatants feared it with a singular intensity. They became alienated from the idea of valor since its exercise increased the risk of death. For the Americans, death was "the Worst Thing in the World."[339] In Vietnam, "death was taboo... Fear was taboo. It could be mentioned, of course, but it had to be accompanied with a shrug and a poorly concealed grin with obvious resignation and indifference. All this took the meaning out of courage."[340] In the Pacific War of 1941-1945, "courage meant overcoming fear and doing one's duty in the presence of danger, not being unafraid."[341] In that war, stoicism and courage may have been possible, since the thought about dying and the ugliness of death recurred far less obsessively than it did among combatants in Vietnam where the very consciousness of the varieties of death that were possible terrified the soldier, tormenting his imagination and shaping his behavior. "You could die in a sudden blood burning crunch as your chopper hit the ground like dead weight. You could fly apart so that your pieces could never be gathered. You could take one neat round in your lung and go out hearing only the bubble of the last few breaths. You could die in the last stage of malaria with that faint tapping in your ears... You could be shot, mined, grenaded, rocketed, mortared, sniped at, blown up and away so that your leavings had to be dropped into a sagging poncho and carried to Graves Registration."[342]

In the Pacific War a soldier could be sickened at the sight of men getting hurt and killed day after day. He could be drained of emotion and strength, but at the end of the day, he felt that he had accomplished something "special," surviving the intense physical exertion of weeks of combat in extremely muggy heat. The memoirs of that war express a great deal of fear, but also a note of pride. On the other hand, the combatant in Vietnam endured, but he took no pride in enduring. There is only pleasure in escaping the ordeal and in surviving. Putting up with death was a sign of courage in the Pacific. In Vietnam putting up with death is demeaning, humiliating, and destructive; death erases any trace of the nobility of valor in the fallen. In Europe during the Second World War, the presence of death could reconcile the soldier to his fate and even promote a love for it.[343] In Vietnam the presence of death had the opposite effect. Americans who got killed were "wasted," their lives sacrificed for nothing. No amount of courage that the fallen might have shown could improve the survivors' estimate of death as useless, nor could it ennoble the fallen soldier.

The dead lie around the battlefields of all wars, a presence and a spectacle that no combatant can ignore. In past conflicts, however, the dead lacked the power to bring the combatants to dwell so much on the meaning of death as they did in Vietnam. Corpses often display features that upset and traumatize the onlooker. A reporter who lived very close to the troops discovered that "exposure to the dead sensitized you to the force of their presence and made long reverberations, long." Some soldiers were so vulnerable that one look at a dead soldier "was enough to wipe them away." Even hardened veterans who looked at the dead knew that "something weird and extra was happening to them,"[344] something that was far from inspiring the fighting spirit.

    The contemplation of death puts the soldier in its arena, increasing his fear and his resistance to doing any deed that might lead him near, even if it would also make him a hero. One of the duties of Lieutenant Caputo as the "accountant of corpses" for his unit, was to send death notices to the families back home. He had trouble writing them because he perceived them to be expressions of an unspeakable human failure. From the Lieutenant's point of view, the notices in reality said to the parents at home that the work, the hopes, and the values of their sons were suddenly wiped out: "How do you tell parents that all the years they had spent raising and educating their son were for nothing? Wasted." It was impossible to conceive of death as a "noble sacrifice," even if the fallen had died trying to save a comrade's life. For those combatants who were religious, the sight of death had the effect of erasing any justification for war and fighting. The sight of mutilated bodies, of body organs splattered over the ground, destroyed in the mind of the onlooker the value of life and human dignity. It was impossible to look at those bloody messes and still believe that they would be capable of resurrection on Judgment Day, or that they had souls within them, and that these would pass on to a better life. It made no difference to the survivors whether the mutilations and the scattered body organs were those of a hero or of a coward. The state of their remains takes away any meaning from bravery. One cannot think of a soldier whose body is reduced to such a state as having died making a noble sacrifice; the very look of death denies heroism. It defies the belief that man holds a special value because of his kind heartedness, his humanity, a value greater than heroism, and if that value is destroyed, heroism loses its meaning, too. Massacred and annihilated, men no longer are made in the image of God. They are the likeness of "the crushed dogs" seen lying on the side of the highways. The soldiers disfigured by death "were gone for good, body, mind, and spirit." Death in Vietnam was a supremely destructive event. Even the fallen who kept the integrity of their bodies could no longer inspire nobility and pride in those who remembered them.[345]

Lieutenant Caputo conceived death as the result of "noble sacrifices," made in the belief in a cause or of trying to save a comrade's life. But in his memoir, there is no trace of this. He can only think and write of his comrade Sullivan, who died from a sniper's bullet, while filling canteens at the edge of a river. As a result, Caputo's writing will strip death of any noble feature. His comrade died for nothing noble. It was a useless death, a waste of human life.

The spectacle of death caused in some combatants a kind of inner deterioration, a feeling of belonging to the dead, not simply of being in the vestibule of death. The helicopter pilot, Robert Mason, had an eye for the dead too sharp for his own good. Something "weird and extra" was bound to happen to him. One load of troops stepping out of his helicopter during the battle of Ia Drang is completely gunned down and left on the ground dying. The spectacle overwhelms him, creating the expectation that bullets would be coming through the plexiglas and into his bones, "never stopping." As the battle unfolds his contact with the dead grows closer and more disquieting. He drops some wounded soldiers at the field hospital and notices bodies lying outside the tent. He "couldn't believe how many bodies were piling up." Later he walks past the same tent, smells blood and notices "grotesquely contorted" corpses. While transporting the dead back from the battlefield, he is aware that their blood drains on the deck of the helicopter and fills the interior with an unmistakable sweet smell, making "the living retch." No matter how fast he would fly, the smell could not be blown away. Back in camp, he feels "jittery after seeing too much death." He notices that the recovered bodies are placed in one pile and the loose parts in another. In the meantime, the newly wounded and dead come in, and Mason notices the "bellies blown open." On this day of action, he has done his duty and, given the extreme danger he faced, he could regard himself as a courageous combatant. But he does not. The death of others has become his own, and he loses courage. Having come to know death so intimately, he feels he belongs to the dead. And he is right because the expectancy of dying in his outfit is very high. When one of the commanding officers reveals that other companies have had a lot more dead than Mason's, he thinks, "it's our turn now." He and his comrades believe they "were delinquent" in not dying, and that they now need to resign themselves to death, "C'mon you guys, let's get out there and die!"[346]

Both Mason and his co-pilot's endurance had been taxed by the frequent and dangerous helicopter flights. Their fear of death increased. "Scared out of our minds," they confessed, we felt like we were on death row and near the end of our wait. Yet they refused to admit this fear to others. At the end of the narration Mason is a short timer with one month left on his tour. Like all short timers, he now wants to stop flying to avoid risk-taking, injury, or death. There must be a medical reason to gain exemption from flying, and the doctor is willing to grant the exemption, provided the pilot admit his cowardice ("If you tell me, you are afraid to fly, I can ground you"). But no such admission is forthcoming. Mason is more afraid of acknowledging his fear than of the risk itself, revealing himself more heroic than his narration would lead one to believe. In fact, he handles himself well when he is in action. "When I am flying the assaults," he points out, "I start feeling brave, almost comfortable, in the middle of it all. Like a hawk may be."[347]

To be brave in Vietnam one had to be unafraid of death and accept it. The fear of death had stalled Lieutenant Broyles on his way to Vietnam. In Los Angeles, he took several steps toward desertion, but he finally changed his mind as a result of a phone conversation with family and friends, reassuring him that the possibility of his dying in Vietnam was remote. However, he was unable to step on the battlefield like a true Marine and fight and die for valor's sake. In 1984 during a return visit to Vietnam, he realized that to win wars one needs the moral strength to control suffering and fear, a strength that the Viet Cong had but the Americans did not.[348] The soldiers kept coming down the trail from the North "prepared to die," and their families were resigned to mourn the loss. They were willing to go on indefinitely to kill and to be killed, Broyles realizes. "We were brave," he writes of the Americans, but "not brave enough" to prevail over the enemy. "We were afraid of death," and "the Communists were not." They were willing to keep on fighting and "dying" while the Americans were not.[349] This strength enabled the Vietnamese to disregard death. Vietnamese bravery and their willingness to die on the battlefield are shown, for instance, by one of their tactics. American strength was clearly technological. It was "not based on individual bravery or superiority—soldier against soldier."[350] The Vietnamese tried to nullify their technological superiority by engaging the enemy at very close range, as short as thirty meters, thus preventing the Americans from using their air and artillery power for fear of hitting their own men. This tactic naturally produced higher-than-normal casualties for the Vietnamese, who were willing to accept death in defending their cause with the kind of courage that Americans were unable to muster.

In O'Brien's novel, *Going after Cacciato,* Lieutenant Sidney Martin believes that a soldier's duty is to make use of "his full capacities of courage and endurance." Martin holds a view that was common in American military circles, that man is inherently brave and that serving as a soldier affords him the chance to release this virtue. It is a view akin to that of the chaplain who, in an earlier narrative, made the case for war as an occasion to bring out the best in man. But Martin's view is more radical, for he assumes that bringing out what is best in man depends on a competition with death. He believes that neither purpose nor cause counts in battles. In fact, he can't imagine any soldier dying for a higher cause. "Death was its own purpose," he declares. War gives man the "chance to confront death many times and to act with valor. For Martin, fighting bravely and dying are the same thing, a likeness that the great majority of American soldiers in Vietnam rejected, and he is so taken by his idea of courage and death that he sees the candidate for its realization in one of his own men, Paul Berlin. Berlin is dutiful and energetic. He displays "fortitude, loyalty, self-control, courage," the capacity to fight and to die, according to Martin. But Martin is mistaken, for Berlin has no desire "to confront death" on the battlefield. He aims to live a long life.[351]

Confronting death as an expression of courage had no place among combatants in Vietnam. For them, death was the ultimate abomination. To the few who dared resurrect the classical saying that death embodies the ultimate courage, "dulce et decorum est pro patria mori," one veteran replies that this noble saying was an "epitaph for the insane." The aim of the combatants was to avoid death, and the best way to do that was to get a job in the rear. In the face of death, there was "no valor to squander for country or honor or military objectives."[352] But the great majority of soldiers had no choice. They lived and fought in the field, and all they could do was put up a sort of psychological defense, pretending "it was not the terrible thing it was." It was necessary to keep fear under control. When death was mentioned among soldiers, it elicited a shrug, a grin, resignation, or indifference. There was great fear of dying, but a greater one of showing it. They carried all the emotional baggage of men who might die: "grief, terror, love, longing." But they wanted to avoid the blush of dishonor, and so some chose to die quietly rather than live in constant retention. "They died so as not to die of embarrassment."[353] One imaginative veteran depicts a comrade as having "died of fright, scared to death, on the field of battle."[354] One way to fight fear was to imagine oneself to be invulnerable to the thought and touch of death, to be a hero of darkness. The back of some jackets worn by combatants displayed a biblical adaptation: "Yea, though I walk through the Valley of the Shadow of Death, I shall fear no Evil, because I am the meanest motherfucker in the Valley."[355] The soldier mentally enables himself to confront death by bringing out the worst in man, evil being stronger and meaner than death itself. Death in Vietnam could be very ugly, and in a gesture of willful degradation, some soldiers seized on this aspect to ridicule and reject heroism. Having heard of a helicopter pilot carrying a portable toilet aboard, who was shot down and buried under the toilet when his plane crashed, one veteran said that was the "way I would like to die." To be killed by a crashing toilet and buried under human excrement, expressed a profound contempt for heroism. "I did not want to die a heroic death," the veteran explained.[356] The American vision of death was such that it was impossible for the supreme sacrifice to be considered valorous. Dying was a tragic experience and a waste of life.

On the contrary, resignation or indifference to one's fate could produce the disappearance of a death anxiety. On a dangerous search and destroy operation toward the end of his tour of duty, Lieutenant Caputo was marching loaded with gear through an area littered with mines. Nevertheless, he "felt good all over." The reason for such an unexpected state of being was the sudden and mysterious vanishing of the fear of death. "I had ceased to be afraid of dying... I had ceased to fear death because I had ceased to care about it." He calls his emotion, "indifference toward my own death," sublime and liberating. He now cares only about having a quick and painless death. "The big D is the world's most powerful narcotic, the ultimate anesthetic." He conceives of himself and his comrades as mere beetles. "I was a beetle. We were all beetles," trying unsuccessfully to survive in the wilderness. Caputo recognizes his insignificance in the total picture of life and death. He erases his human identity, makes himself worthless, faces death without fear, and becomes a hero by virtue of his fearlessness. He is resigned to die as casually as a beetle crushed under a boot heel. When he and his troops come under fire, he thinks that "it is not bad," that dying is "pleasant," because it is painless.[357] The painlessness is a myth, but death is welcomed because it eliminates once and for all fear from the soul of the soldier. A popular song, and a favorite of the Marines, echoes the feeling of the lieutenant in welcoming the end as the beginning of a period in which dying and killing no longer have a place:

> I am not scared of dyin'
> And I don't really care
> If it's peace you find in dyin'
> Well then let my time be near
> If it's peace you find in dyin'.[358]

The fear of death had a paralyzing effect on the combatant, but it also intensified the desire and effort to survive. Surviving became the name of the game. "The only thing the grunts found to win in Vietnam was 365 consecutive days of life."[359] The troops want to keep themselves alive for the term of service, so that they can go home alive. "The trick of being in Nam," so ran a belief held by the troops, "is getting out of Nam. And I don't mean getting out in a plastic body bag. I mean getting out alive."[360] A savage, but shrewd Sergeant Sace of *The LBJ Brigade* was an expert "on staying alive.". Always before undertaking a mission, he tells his men that they are fighting neither against the Communists, nor against the Viet Cong, nor on behalf of American freedom. "You," he tells them, "are fighting to stay alive."[361]

"You're scared," wrote an infantryman just back from a search and destroy operation, "really scared, and there is no thinking about it." He is pleased with the killing he has done, not because it contributed to the operation's success, but because the killing ensured his safety, "You kill because that little SOB is doing his best to kill you, and you desperately want to live, to go home, to get drunk or walk down the street on a date again."[362] Survival was the coveted goal of the American soldier in Vietnam. Lieutenant Caputo concludes his narrative in a way that summarizes the meaning of the Vietnam experience: "We had done nothing more than endure. We had survived, and that was our only victory."[363]

Because death in war is a "waste" and terribly feared, survival matters a great deal. The soldier craves survival or, if he is safe, he is overwhelmed by the joy of having avoided the worst. In the presence of death, Broyles is happy for just being alive. He has understood how abhorrent death was to Americans and that the only victory for them "was not to die."[364] For those who survive after a fire fight, there is always the "secret joy" of being alive, the "immense pleasure of aliveness," and one is never "more alive" than when he was "almost dead."[365]

Although in the fall of 1965, the war was still in its beginning, the soldiers already "fought for no cause other than [their] own survival," and many were made ruthless by an "overpowering greed for survival,"[366] a need that encouraged the combatant to kill as many enemies as he could, either soldiers or any civilians viewed as dangerous. Even before My Lai, Lieutenant William Calley noted, the men in his unit called themselves the "Dispensers of Death." The soldiers' speech left no doubt that they really meant to kill and kill to survive. They said things that Calley himself could hardly believe. They would have liked to kill "every" man, woman, and child in South Vietnam because they thought that if every Vietnamese were killed, then their own survival would be guaranteed, and they could return home, "If I kill everyone, then I can leave." This was the "logic" that supported the resolve of Calley's men.[367] Although the will to stay alive often induced a combatant to fight with valor, especially when the life of a comrade was at stake, his bravery served his own life and that of his comrade, rather than the aim of the military leadership. There may be heroism in fighting for survival, but heroism has little to do with the primary aim of the military organization, victory over the enemy. Fighting for survival may be heroic, but in a sense, it shows that the soldier has become alienated from the military organization and its objectives, since he is now serving a human end, rather than a military one. Soldiers who fight for survival are obscure heroes.[368]

Some of the problems Americans wrestled with on the battlefields of Vietnam might have been overcome, had they believed in a cause. But few believed in a cause. Most had none. Or if they accepted the official one, the Communist threat, it was felt with insufficient depth and was not enough to produce heroic acts. S. L. Marshall's extensive experience with soldiers on diverse battlefields led him to the discovery that in war the belief in a cause is the basis of the aggressive will in battle. When an army loses faith in its cause, "it is, in fact, defeated and wholly submissive to the enemy."[369] The belief in a cause has the power to create courage; the lack of belief undermines it.

In Vietnam there were examples of courage, but some acts could render courage irrelevant. In one memoir, a Captain Johansen, charges a Viet Cong across a rice paddy and shoots him at close range, after which, he calls himself "brave." The event reinforces the captain's belief in the virtue of courage and of his own in particular. "I'd rather be brave" than almost anything else, he tells one of his men after his supposedly heroic deed. The trooper acknowledges his bravery but notes the similarity of his action to that of the knights of the Round Table who fought to show their prowess and to uphold their reputations. The recklessness with which Captain Johansen's assault was executed cast even more doubt on the quality of his bravery. It displayed unreason and imprudence and had very little military value. Sadly, soldiers who act like that become "heroes forever" in the eyes of the public. The charge "is the first thing to think about when thinking about courage." "It seems like courage," and the public is impressed. The problem with the captain's charge is that it was made for the sake of heroism alone. Courage "is more" than the attack,[370] which was showy, and unsupported by a cause other than to build his reputation. It served Johansen's vanity rather than a military objective.

A cause that would motivate an ordinary man or a soldier to act with courage, would be resistance to bullying in any form and to defend what is rightfully his. The bullying could be a violent individual, or Hitler's blitzkrieg, or the perpetrators of the attack on Pearl Harbor. Such an opposition is reasonable, just, and wise. It is what gave O'Brien courage when, as a teenager, he was challenged by a bully. He fought back, not to prove his physical superiority which he did not have, but out of his conviction that, he needed to defend his freedom. This belief provided him with the will and strength to face a stronger adversary. In his conviction lay his courage.[371] Plato said that "wise endurance is courage." Courage includes temperance, justice, and wisdom. These virtues give meaning to a cause that supports the soldier and makes his deeds heroic. An action unsupported by any of these qualities cannot be considered courageous. To complicate matters, the war itself did not lend itself to heroic deeds. It was "a wrong war,"[372] a war that could not give Captain Johansen any "certain reason" or provide him with any wisdom or sense of justice.

Opposition to Communism could be regarded as a noble cause, but in Vietnam it provided no incentive to fight with valor, because it was not embraced by the majority of soldiers. The war was fought for "uncertain reasons," but the men lived and acted in a vacuum, doing no act of true courage. "Men must know what they do is courageous," and to know what they do is courageous, they "must know it is right." Only this "kind of knowledge is wisdom,"[373] and only wisdom can create valor. The war in Vietnam "drifted in and out of human lives, taking them or sparing them or angering them." It was shaped by the strategy of the enemy, and the Americans could only respond as best they could.

In Tim O'Brien's estimation, Frederic Henry, the protagonist of Hemingway's *A Farewell to Arms,* showed true heroism when he abandoned the war on the Italian front. He "was able to leave war,"[374] an act that could send him before a firing squad. His courage rested on the belief that he was doing the just and wise thing, saying no to the wrong and inhumane strategy of the Italian military, which had conducted the war up to the defeat of Caporetto in 1917. With a fair spin on the heroic code, O'Brien has come to regard any soldier who fights for the side that cannot provide him with an incentive that touches his heart and mind is right to repudiate the war; therein lies his heroism.

Of course, there are questionable causes. The Nazis, for instance, fought well and gained many victories in the Second World War. They must have fought with courage. They did, but their courage in the end was insufficient to win, because the courage of the people who resisted them was superior. Why? Because their cause was superior. Whereas the Nazis were driven by the desire to subjugate entire peoples and nations, those who opposed them were driven by the resolve to resist being bullied. The Nazis were defeated by the defenders of freedom. The quality of the cause is vital in defining and inspiring valor in the combatant. In Vietnam, the Americans' military spirit turned out to be inferior to that of the Vietnamese. The character who in *Going after Cacciato* expounds the value of a cause, reasons that "it was an absence of a clear moral purpose that produced defeat." Without purpose, the soldier is left "without moral imperatives to fight hard, well and winningly." The "absence of a good purpose" affects courage by jeopardizing the soldier's "own ego," and by undermining his performance on the battlefield. He knows that his sacrifices are demeaned and his dignity impaired.. "Without purpose men will run... like animals in stampede. It is purpose that keeps men at their posts to fight. Only purpose." The war in Vietnam was fought "without evident cause," and that is why Cacciato, an infantryman in O'Brien's fiction, has left his unit and the war.[375]

The fictional Cacciato heads for Paris, the stark opposite of the hell which is the Vietnam battlefield. His courage consists in repudiating the war in the name of what the City of Light represents, intellect and civilization. He realizes that the war had no moral purpose that he could believe in. In such a case, a just cause, it turns out, lies in opposing war. Private Berlin, who pursues Cacciato, is unable to see the importance of cause in war. Berlin reaches Paris, for the avowed purpose of capturing Cacciato. But implicitly he, too, is there to redeem himself. "You have been brave beyond your wildest expectations," he is told, and now one more step must be taken, "a final act of courage." But when he is asked to confirm his "salvation" by explicitly repudiating war and embracing peace, timidity and indecision overtake him. He resorts to political and military rhetoric about victory—a peace we can be proud of—but above all, he is afraid of becoming an outcast if he were to abandon the war for good. "I fear being thought of as a coward," he confesses, "I fear that even more than cowardice itself."[376]

The American combatant often acted under forces of habit, self-preservation, and revenge. No one in O'Brien's company, for instance, knew or cared about the cause and purpose of the war. The officers failed to instill in them a cause that would ignite the fighting spirit. They understood the value of courage but failed to grasp its premises. The officers of one battalion promotion board impressed on a private that the biggest incentive for fighting was simply to win without showing him what it takes to win. The soldiers in the unit of *Going after Cacciato* "did not have targets. They did not have a cause. They did not know if it was a war of ideology or economics or hegemony or spite... They did not know how to feel when they saw villages burning. Revenge? Loss? Peace of mind or anguish?" Without a cause, they were disoriented, and in the end, they lost a sense of good and evil.[377]

Despite General Westmoreland's assertion that "we were in Vietnam for serious and moral purposes,"[378] such purposes failed to motivate the combatants and to generate the spirit required to win the war. Evidently, those purposes were neither serious nor moral, or if they were, they had no power to motivate the combatants. On the other hand, the North Vietnamese soldiers possessed a moral certainty capable of overcoming huge suffering and losses. That certainty came from a cause, the belief that they were fighting for a "great goal, one worth dying for."[379] Washington never offered U.S. soldiers in the field a credible justification for American involvement in Vietnam, the kind of justification that combatants would accept with no reservation.[380] Some soldiers could not make any sense of their service and sacrifices. "Who appreciates my sufferings? Who do I suffer for?"[381] Major Blake, the main character of the highly regarded *The Laotian Fragments*, had a "sense of duty," loved his country, and was brave. However, he did not hide the "idiocy of the cause" that sent him and his comrades to fight in Vietnam.[382] Americans, he said, kept on "killing and dying for a cause unworthy of their bravery. They deserved to be heroes, but they were fools."[383] Could it be that the war, fought without any moral certainty "disgraced the name of bravery"?[384] One veteran believed that "to be a patriot is to believe that there are values greater than one's life, values worth dying for. "But in Vietnam patriotism rang hollow."[385] The consensus among veterans interviewed by a psychiatrist was that it was impossible for them as combatants to make an "inwardly convincing association between death and a higher principle," between their sacrifice and a good reason for making it, a reason that would stir mind and heart. Individual survival was "the only purpose or cause" that prompted the actions of many veterans on the battlefield.[386]

Nonetheless, having no cause to inspire them, and their reluctance to engage the enemy, did not mean they were reluctant to kill. On the contrary, killing was done whenever possible and even under circumstances that did not warrant it. The fact that in War World II, seventy-five or eighty percent of riflemen did not fire their weapon at an exposed enemy, while in Vietnam only about five percent did not fire,[387] implies that Americans did a lot more killing in Vietnam than in the previous war. "You men are here to kill VC," General Wallace Greene, the commandant of the Marine Corps spread the word on an inspection tour.[388] Sanctioned by the policy of the "body count," the troopers easily complied. Killing would become a mark of heroism.

One reason for the widespread killing had to do with the political and moral state of Vietnam. Living and warring in an underprivileged and corrupt society gave the Americans a sense of superiority that made them bold to the point where crimes were committed and justified by military necessity. "I had a sense of power. A sense of destruction," related a combatant while serving in Vietnam. "In Nam you realized that you had the power to take a life. You had the power to rape a woman, and nobody could say nothing to you." A sense of moral freedom from the fetters of civilization entitled him to something special. This kind of freedom ("I could take a life. I could screw a woman"), was reinforced by the knowledge that he would not be held accountable to anyone. In his own eyes, he enjoyed this exceptional standing, "It was like I was a god."[389] Here we have the same feelings of power that enabled the heroes in Roman times to tyrannize the people, violate the laws of humanity and finally declare themselves to be gods.

American power was technological, "not based on individual bravery or superiority of soldier against soldier."[390] The combatants relied heavily on technology, which lent them boldness, a powerful incentive to kill, and the illusion of being brave when prevailing over the enemy. Seduced by the spectacle of their own overwhelming military strength, they were confident of achieving domination over the whole of Vietnam. The power of the weapon that Gustav Hasford held in his hands transformed him, "I understood that my own weapon could do this dark magic to any human being. With my automatic rifle I could knock the life out of any enemy with just the slightest pressure of one finger. And, knowing that, I was less afraid."[391] Powerful tools of destruction sometimes enabled the Americans to be less afraid of wounds and death, since they felt confident that they could eliminate the enemy before they were wounded or killed. The "Spooky" gunship, vomiting fire from their guns, the silent power of napalm, causing tree lines or houses to burst out in flame, and the white phosphorous bombs, exploding with "fulsome elegance" changing human flesh into candles assuaged the fear and sense of vulnerability that William Broyles and his comrades felt. Firing a bazooka or an M-60 machine gun and contemplating the results -- the blast and sound of energy that caused a truck or a house to disappear in a second—created in the combatant the feeling of holding a magic sword, "a soldier's Excalibur." That feeling translated into a sense of invincibility.[392] Americans discovered that their superior military technology gave them the chance to accomplish extraordinary deeds, enabling them to feel heroic, doing what they were unable to do when facing the enemy in the jungle, on the trail or in the paddies.

But there was more to boldness and the readiness to kill than weapons and technology alone. With or without superior weapons, facing the enemy brought out fear, and killing, was the primary means for suppressing it. To rid themselves of fear, the combatants performed actions that bore the hallmark of heroism. During an uphill attack, Lieutenant Caputo's men encountered more difficulties than expected and became fearful and frustrated. Pushed to the extremity of endurance, they suddenly turned very violent, but also very successful, and acted like the heroes of old. Their resolve to eliminate the danger worked wonders in the soldiers who advanced irresistibly, driving the enemy out of the village. They rampaged through another village, whooping like savages, torching thatch huts, tossing grenades into cement houses that could not be burnt. The soldiers "did not feel anything." They had no feeling for themselves or others. The whole village was set a fire, and people were burned by a platoon that had become a bunch of arsonists. The platoon achieved the results that a disciplined unit could not do unmotivated by rage. Caputo's men took the hill, and the soldiers were happy with their performance and regained some sort of emotional balance. The killing of the villagers and the destruction of the village "had been a catharsis, a purging of months of fear, frustration, and tension. We had relieved our own pain by inflicting it on others. The resolve to eliminate fear and danger with more killing was the catalyst of heroism. Turning "savage" when facing the enemy was common among the combatants, and it has since been the object of psychiatric studies. These studies show that soldiers who perform memorable deeds, such as routing the enemy singlehandedly, are often in the grip of a special state of mind and body. Such soldiers are regarded by their superiors as having gone berserk, but also among the best; they "have been honored as heroes."[393] Going berserk releases a force that turns ordinary soldiers into heroes.

In Vietnam, it took very little for soldiers to go berserk and to become heroes. In the course of a large operation in the My Lai area, O'Brien's company failed to engage with the enemy. The unit triggered the explosions of one hidden mine after another, frustrating and angering the troops who were "boiling with hatred" as they left the area. A smaller operation was later assigned to the same unit in the same area, and as soon as they entered the territory, they became the target of shots fired from the bushes. Mines exploded, and the invisible enemy caused two casualties. Another futile search in the same region forced the soldiers to run over a bridge exposed to enemy fire concealed in hedgerows and clumps of dead trees. There were no Vietnamese at which to shoot. They were invisible, and the Americans "were becoming angry." The following night, the same unit was mortared and forced to evacuate the village. They layed out in the water of the paddies to avoid the Viet Cong bombs. In the early morning, the enemy no longer posed any danger, but the Americans, who had spent the night in the paddies, were full of hatred, and torched the huts of the village. The destruction gave them a great deal of satisfaction. "It was good," O'Brien recalls, "to walk from Pinkville and see fire behind the Alpha Company. It was good, just as pure hate is good." The unit moved into another village where a mine killed two soldiers. Some of the troops mistreated old men and women. Finally, jetfighters were called in, and the village was leveled with napalm.[394] O'Brien explained elsewhere that "if a man can squirm in a meadow, he can shoot children." This kind of experience brings out the worst in the soldier who survives. Being mean makes one bold, as the well-voiced parody of the psalms, suggests: "I shall fear no Evil, because I am the meanest motherfucker in the Valley." The hurt from having been immensely frightened has brutalized the combatant. Of course, neither the massacre at My Lai, nor the shooting of children, nor the atrocities committed by the Alpha Company on its search and destroy missions "are examples of courage."[395] But others, will have no problem in ascribing that kind of killing to valor.

    Anger, hatred, and heroic deeds can be the result of an encounter with the enemy, either visible or invisible, gone bad. But, independent from the course of an encounter, battle itself has a way of releasing an energy that enables the combatant to become oblivious of his own safety and extremely bold. There is a state of being unconnected to anger and frustration that can yield heroism. Lieutenant David Kramer of *Sand in the Wind* learned of this superhuman energy that propels the combatant into action on the battlefield. The platoon he led through a search and destroy operation comes close to being wiped out by the ambushing enemy. The brush with death turns the platoon on, and it hurls itself against the enemy "like a huge wave." Kramer, "swelled by its impetus into something of ascendant power, experiences within himself a sense of destructive potency both bestial and godlike." He leads the wave of attackers. During the frenzied action, he repeatedly utters a cryptic expression, "I see! Now I see!" He sees nothing, of course, but he understands what is happening to him under fire. Kramer is now acting just like the North Vietnamese soldier he had watched earlier attacking the Americans when, though badly wounded, he kept advancing, and until the last second of his life, tried to toss a grenade. At the time, the North Vietnamese's action impressed him, but its meaning had escaped. His platoon's assault has transformed him, and he sees why the enemy soldier kept coming forward in the face of death. This is what Kramer finally understands in the aftermath of his victorious assault— "the courage in that act" and what was behind it. He intuits that the extraordinary inner experience is something known by many fighting soldiers, and that it is sought after. "It was apparent to him what the lifers lived for, those few seconds of reckless exhilaration that he had so often both glorified and denied." Whether they lived for it or not, it was a fact that experiencing that altered state of being produced positive results for the combatant by unleashing an energy and action that are unmistakably brave.[396]

The energy released in the heat of battle produced the necessary drive for killing and being a hero. Under fire, the combatant was transformed. "No sport I had ever played," Broyles recalls, "brought me to such close awareness of my physical and emotional limits" as warfare. "My mouth immediately went dry," he describes his experience, "I was terrified. I was ashamed," and yet, [I] could not wait for "it to happen again."[397] Fear is overcome while the combatant is taken over by the heroic impulse. Michael Herr, a reporter who shared with the fighting soldiers their experience under fire, corroborates Broyles's diagnosis. "Under Fire," he sums up the experience, "would take you out of your head and your body too." It was an amazing and unbelievable experience that even transcended that of athletes who had played a lot of hard sport. "A lot of what people called courage," Herr explains, "was only undifferentiated energy cut loose by the intensity of the moment, a mind loss that sent the actor on an incredible run. If he survived, he had the chance later to decide whether he had really been brave or just overcome with life, even ecstasy."[398]

Combat fascinated Lieutenant Caputo. He wanted to escape his dreary duties as the "accountant of the dead" at Graves Registration. He yearned to live the "intensity of the moment. . . There was a magnetism about combat," he proclaimed despite the experiences that had made him fear death and detest the war. "You seem to live more intensely under fire. Every sense was sharper, the mind worked clearer and faster... experiencing a headiness that no drink or drug could match." He confirms that "something like the elevated state of awareness induced by drugs" is powering him. "An eerie sense of calm came over me," he remembers as he prepared to lead an attack on a small contingent of the Viet Cong entrenched in a village that had opened fire. His mind was working with remarkable speed and lucidity, while his body "was tensing itself to spring." This intense concentration of physical energy "was born of fear."[399] Determined to eliminate what represented a deadly danger, he focused "on a single end—destroying the thing that frightens him," namely, the men who are the source of the danger. "This resolve, which is sometimes called courage, cannot be separated from the fear that has aroused it. It is, in fact, a powerful urge to rid himself of fear by eliminating the source of it." At the destruction of a village close to Da Nang, Caputo was part of a force assaulting the enemy by helicopters, and for him, it was an experience of dread and courage under fire even more intense than that on the ground. As the helicopter prepared to land on a "hot" zone, the lieutenant was at first very frightened, until he focused on the men who were the source of his fear, and a powerful hostility translated into "a fierce resolve to fight." This hostility can lead a soldier to disregard danger, act with boldness, kill the enemy, and win the fight, in short, deeds that a true hero would do.[400]

There is power in what is instinctual. It can replace weakness and fear, generating a strength that enables the combatant to act with valor. "You feel like you could run around the world." Hasford remembers his transformation into a kind of superman during an assault. He defies death, his resolve to kill intensifies, and he turns into someone who is even more than a hero, "You are fast and graceful, a green jungle cat." You feel and act "like a god." At the same time, he screams: "Die! Die!"[401] The godlike feeling becomes an action that bears the hallmark of extreme valor. It finds its highest expression in the killing of the enemy. Thus, killing becomes for some soldiers a cherished endeavor and an exploit highly satisfactory and admirable.

After the assault, Corporal Chalice of *Sand in the Wind* wanders around and comes upon the crater dug by a grenade he had thrown. He sees three dead enemies lying in it. He contemplates the killing and mutters audibly in disbelief, "I enjoyed it. God, I enjoyed it."[402] Another veteran recalls, "I have to admit I enjoyed killing. It gave me a great thrill while I was there... There was a certain joy you had in killing, an exhilaration that is hard to explain."[403] After killing ten Vietnamese who were sitting in the open unaware of danger, a small group of Americans showed excitement and pleasure. One of the soldiers was "ecstatic" even though it was an easy kill and particularly unheroic. Another was overwhelmed with pleasure in the slaughter. "Shit, I almost shit!" he reported his pride when relating the deed.[404] His pride and satisfaction derive, not from having fulfilled a duty, but for having killed. It became the "thing to do" and many wanted to have a hand in doing something that came to be regarded as routine. Private Fat Jack, who had never shot anyone in cold blood, wanted to have this particular experience. "Jack had this thing." He eyed an old man standing beside his hut in a tiny village along a river. He pointed his rifle at the head of the old man and pulled the trigger.[405]

Groups of soldiers, too, were unanimous in performing and praising any killing. In *Body Count*, a novel written by a marine veteran, the combatants considered their performance, the wholesale slaughter of an enemy contingent, as a singular event. It was for these men, a personal, satisfying experience, not an act done for a broader military end. They celebrated it in a mystical way, worshipping the act and enshrining it heroic. Lieutenant Hawkins figures that he and his men have killed about one hundred North Vietnamese, a signal of success that raises the spirit of the troops. The soldiers gather in small groups, survey the scene of the slaughter and are carried away: "Oh, we killed those sorry bastards. Oh, we were tough. We were hard! We won!" On one of the Vietnamese corpses, a soldier finds a wide leather belt with a heavy brass buckle engraved with a red star. The belt is given to the lieutenant as a trophy, proof that he is "a bad ass" hero. His men urge him to wear it. But before wearing it, a rite is performed. A Marine named Chief bends down, dips the belt in the blood of the dead Vietnamese, lets it dry, and then hands it to Hawkins who slips it on. Then the troops "snapped to attention. Their hands went up in unison. They saluted,"[406] recognizing their hero in the leader of the exploit. The celebration was not a victory for their unit or for American arms. It was to honor their superior ability in killing. This was more than hero-worship; it was killing worship.

Killing, especially at a high rate, came to be recognized as a heroic deed. It was assumed that it diminished the number of enemies and ensured a better chance of survival. Killing reduced their death anxiety—the fewer enemies, the smaller the chance of death for the Americans. "If you wanna live, ya gotta kill,"[407] a commander tells his men, before leading them into the field. Killing was codified and enshrined as a virtue, by the official directive of the "body count," placing a mantle of heroism on the shoulders of the killers. Since it was impossible to distinguish friend from foe, the men soon understood that the best way to protect themselves, was to kill anyone, military or civilian. By this time, all North Vietnamese posed a mortal threat to Americans, and killing them became the hallmark of success. More than simply connected with valor, the act was valor itself, and the body count became the official policy of the military leadership. Killing the largest number of enemies became the main thrust of the American strategy for winning the war. Units were expected to give a high body count to prove that the generals' strategy was right. Supported by the policy of the body count, a high rate of killing, was personally satisfying to the combatant, and gave the leaders the illusion that the war was being won. The policy codified killing as the highest accomplishment of the soldier.[408]

It turned out to be an "infamous measurement of success." It made everyone a bounty hunter and a liar. But the policy was never abandoned. Aside from the fact that it produced distortions and falsifications as it was hard to count the bodies on the field, it was an invitation and justification to kill without discrimination. Any Vietnamese killed could be counted as an enemy. Killing was the name of the game. Even the simple soldier felt this way, especially when angry and frustrated under fire, knowing that he could not fight back when a booby trap blew the point man up. The shock reinforced his and his comrades' resolve to kill. They were "looking to kill" every time they went on a search and destroy mission.[409]

Body count fitted the mindset of the American combatant, who wanted to protect himself by destroying as many enemies as possible. It also fitted the instructions given to the Marines. They were eminently suited to assassinate by virtue of their training. They were not given a cause. They were trained to make killing the supreme purpose of their service on the battlefield. One Marine in the field surmised that the purpose was to instill contempt for human life and arouse the instinct to destroy it. They seemed to mind Clausewitz's warning that a belief in a cause could hinder prowess, because if they disagreed with the purpose, the training and indoctrination would be wasted. They were trained to generate the "killer instinct," making them "fearless and aggressive like animals." A good Marine turned himself into a "minister of death, praying for war."[410] Training came down to a "deification of killing," which gave the recruits the purpose "to be brave," "to fight well," and "to kill people."[411] They were destined to be "professional killers in the service of the United States government."[412] Even so, the training did not erase in some Marines the truths learned at home that human life is precious and the taking of it wrong, but in many others it did erase it. The responsibility of Lieutenant Robert Santos, the highest decorated veteran from the state of New York, "was to kill," he wrote, and to "be good at it." He did his best, but eventually realized that a high body count and a high kill ratio was "a fucking way to live your life."[413]

If training failed to convert the soldier to the religion of killing, the body count helped him see the light. "Our mission," Lieutenant Caputo understood very well, "was not to win terrain or seize positions, but simply to kill, to kill Communists and to kill as many as possible."[414] The official demand for killing embodied in the body count put pressure on unit commanders and the troops to produce Vietnamese corpses. That pressure revealed that "one of the most brutal things in the world is your average nineteen-year-old American boy."[415] Those boys gradually turned into excellent killers. Reporter Michael Herr is probably the first and only writer to call American soldiers killers. He was struck by the mentality and life of the Marines in besieged Khe Sanh. "They got savaged a lot and softened a lot, their secret brutalized them and darkened them and very often made them beautiful. It took no age, seasoning, or education to make them know exactly where true violence resided. And they were killers. Of course, they were; what would anyone expect them to be?" The knowledge that they were killers "absorbed them, inhabited them, made them strong in the way that victims are strong, filled them with the twin obsessions of Death and Peace, fixed them so that they could never again speak lightly about the "Worst Thing in the World."[416] They became victims not because the enemy struck them hard, but because the killing tore their lives apart against their own wills. Still, they regarded their deeds not as evil but proof of their valor. They recorded kills with notches on their rifles as "evidence of one's prowess" and counted the corpses that were part of a body count as "evidence of a warrior's prowess."[417]

The value of the body count as a military tactic was sometimes underscored by the public display of corpses. After the enemies were shot, their bodies would be piled up, and the Quartermaster Corps would call the news people, NBC or CBS. "They wasn't out there when we was shooting, but they was out there when it was over for the body count,"[418] complained a soldier about the propaganda and public relations aspect. A general wanted a pile of dead enemies which were headed for the cemetery, left where they were in the open outside the morgue. Even though he knew that in a short time the stench would be unbearable, he wanted them to be seen by his officers. To the general, it was vital that his following "get used to the sight of blood." To see the results firsthand would testify, he thought, to the success of American arms.[419]

In a dramatic fashion, the deeds of twenty-four-year-old Lieutenant William Calley Jr. and those of his platoon at My Lai in March 1968 froze killing and heroism in the same frame. The massacre was mainly the result of the Americans' frustration and anger caused by several soldiers killed, and an entire squad destroyed by a booby trap. It was a gruesome and unsettling spectacle. Calley's troops became very hostile, and as they approached to search the village of My Lai, the order went out "to kill everything in the village." The troops interpreted the order as meaning "to kill every man, woman, and child in the village." It was their chance for revenge on these people for the losses suffered earlier. Calley's superior, Captain Medina, gave the men the impression that they "could kill the people," that they "could kill anybody they saw." As a result of being all psyched up, one soldier from the company reported, the shooting started almost as a chain reaction. The killing produced a high body count—347 bodies, including old men, women, and children—but only three weapons were found,[420] a sign that the villagers represented no danger to the Americans. When it became clear that the enemy could not be identified as such, then all Vietnamese became the enemy, and the reason for the massacre became more plausible and urgent. That was the rationale for indiscriminate killing. "You can't tell who's your enemy. You got to shoot kids, you got to shoot women."[421]

Lieutenant Calley, who supervised, and participated in the killing at My Lai, was turned into a hero, and the massacre into a heroic performance. When he marched out of the courthouse door at Fort Benning many spectators at the trial and millions of Americans who had followed the trial proclaimed him "not a murderer of the innocent but a hero—a hero of our time." Instead of being recognized for what he really was—the murderer of unresisting, unarmed, innocent old men, women, children, and babies—Calley was transformed into "the symbol of the American soldier in the world—into a hero."[422] Congress and some sections of the public took up Calley's defense and strove to glorify him. Congressional activities were directed to defend him and denigrate his accusers. They reached the height of their attacks with a House resolution praising each serviceman and veteran of the war for "his individual sacrifice, bravery" and devotion to duty, regardless of the truth.[423] After the court-martial, the expression "Lt. Calley is a hero" was heard throughout the country.[424] It was not the military alone that up-held Lieutenant Calley. It was a nation, or at least a good part of it, that bandied about his figure "as hero and symbol." At the same time, the lack of any widespread outrage at him filled the minds of many others with gloom and foreboding for the future.[425]

By rewarding and praising as valiant the soldiers who did the killing at My Lai, the military rewarded their callousness, their suppression of moral scruples, their denial of civilized behavior, and their defiance of the commandment that holds humanity together. A new kind of valor was born, the power of the combatant to suppress his own conscience and to perform any deed whatsoever in an effort to prevail over the enemy.

In the aftermath of My Lai, General Westmoreland sent a message of congratulations to the officers and the men of Calley's company "for outstanding action."[426] Since the idea and practice of killing had been raised to the rank of the highest military virtue by the policy of the body count, it is easy to see why the commanding general praised a performance that produced an enormous number of Vietnamese dead in less than a day. Though he refrained from explicitly calling the troops heroes, they considered themselves to be heroes. Indeed, later discussions and interviews conducted by Robert Lifton with My Lai veterans showed that "they were recreating My Lai, as a great battle and a noble victory, and themselves as if they were all-powerful warrior-heroes who had magnificently carried out their ordeal."[427]

These delusions cover up the military reality—lack of strength in the combatant and true heroism. Because of these deficiencies, General Westmoreland himself pointed out, Vietnam was lost. He believed that in every war, a time is reached when both sides become discouraged by the endless requirement for more effort, more resources, and more faith. "At this point, the side which presses on with renewed vigor is the one to win," he declared.[428] At the crucial point, the Americans missed the necessary vigor to go on fighting to victory. The display of a renewed vigor would have been an act of true valor. But by the time that point was reached, true valor no longer existed and the murderous acts that replaced it proved inadequate to gain a military victory.

War in Vietnam did indeed "disgrace the name of bravery."[429] Even though "gallantry" impressed witnesses, Americans returned home as "losers" because they fought on "ignominy's side."[430] That My Lai proved to be a turning point of the war is shown by the fact that from the end of 1969 on, the army deteriorated. The soldiers escaped into marijuana and heroin, and men died because their comrades were stoned on these drugs that profited the Chinese traffickers and the Saigon generals. "It was an army whose units in the field were on the edge of mutiny, whose soldiers rebelled by assassinating officers and noncoms with accidental shooting and fraggings with grenades."

Demoralization continued as General Creighton Abrams kept on pursuing the attrition strategy begun with Westmoreland.[431]

Over time it has become harder and harder to be a hero. Good causes are hard to find and very few individuals are willing to do deeds that create a reputation for valor, such as the heroes of early ages and of the Renaissance. In those times, the desire to be a hero was intense. The cause for fighting and the sacrifice asked was irrelevant. Only the hero was relevant. In our time, soldiers have become reluctant to risk life in order to be recognized as heroes. Valor in battle has lost its mystique while abhorrence of death and the love of life have grown.

ENDNOTES

1. Aristotle, *Nicomachean Ethics*, tr. M. Ostwald (Indianapolis, 1962), pp. 69-71.
2. Thomas Carlyle, *On Heroes, Hero-Worship, and the Heroic in History* (New York, 1904), pp. 31-32.
3. Konrad Lorenz, *On Aggression*, tr. M. Wilson (New York, 1970), p.275.
4. John Keegan - Richard Holmes, *Soldiers. A History of Men in Battle* (New York, 1985), p. 49.
5. Robert Hanning, *"Beowulf as Heroic History,"* Medievalia et Humanistica, no.5 (1974), 77.
6. All quotations are from Beowulf. A New Verse Translation by Seamus Heaney (New York, 2000). Numbers in the text refer to verses.
7. Laisse 82. All citations from *The Song of Roland* are from the D. Sayers' translation (New York, 1982), and refer to laisse number.
8. Marc Bloch, *Feudal Society*, tr. L. Manyon (Chicago, 1964), II, 294.
9. Aristotle, *Nicomachean Ethics*, pp 69-71.
10. Philippe, Contamine, *War in the Middle Ages*, tr. M. Jones (New York, 1984), p. 253.
11. Quoted by Bloch, *Feudal Society*, II, 293
12. Chrétien de Troyes, *Cligés, in Arthurian Romances*, tr. W. Comfort (New York, 1928), p.146.
13. Yvain, in *Arthurian Romances*, p.184.
14. Id., Erec and Enide, in *Arthurian Romances*, pp. 32-33, 36, 84.
15. Id., Yvain, in *Arthurian Romances*, p. 212.

16 Richard Barber, *The Knight and Chivalry* (Suffolk, 1995), p. 52.

17 Howard Bloch, *Medieval French Literature and Law,* (Berkeley, 1977), p. 199.

18 Ludovico Ariosto, *Orlando Furioso,* tr. G. Waldman (Oxford, 1974), p. 36.

19 Arthur Ferguson, *The Chivalric Tradition in England* (Washington, 1986), pp. 71, 72.

20 Johan Huizinga, *The Waning of the Middle Ages* (New York, 1954), particularly chapter VII and in "The Political and Military Significance of Chivalric Ideas in the Late Middle Ages" in Men and Ideas (New York, 1959), pp. 196-206.

21 Peter Saccio, *Shakespeare's English Kings* (Oxford, 2000), p. 109.

22 Ibid., p. 104.

23 Ibid., p. 109.

24 Norman Rabkin, *Shakespeare and the Problem of Meaning* (Chicago, 1981), p. 88.

25 Theodor Meron, *Henry's Wars and Shakespeare's Laws* (Oxford, 1993), p. 36.

26 Alvin Kernan, "The Henriade," in Modern Critical Views. William Shakespeare. Histories and Poems, ed. H. Bloom (New Haven, 1986), p. 237.

27 R. A. Foakes, *Shakespeare and Violence* (Cambridge, 2003), p. 167.

28 "Manhood or manliness was in the Renaissance a popular synonym for valor": C. Brown Watson, *Shakespeare and the Renaissance Concept of Honor* (Princeton, 1960), p. 245.

29 On fear of cowardice generating an indiscriminate display of valor in *Troilus and Cressida* cf. Jean Gagen, "Hector's Honor," *Shakespeare Quarterly* 19 (1968), 137.

30 Jan Kott, "Amazing and Modern," in *Troilus and Cressida, a Casebook,* ed. P. Martin (London, 1976), p. 145.

31 Robert Kimbrough, *Shakespeare's Troilus and Cressida and Its Setting* (Cambridge, Mass.,1964), p. 121.

32 Montaigne, *The Complete Essays*, tr. D. Frame (Stanford, 1965), P 47.

33 Robert Ornstein, "The Ethic of the Imagination: Love and Art in *Antony and Cleopatra*," in *Shakespeare. Modern Essays in Criticism* (Oxford, 1968), p. 396.

34 The meaning of "heart" is here "courage, spirit." Arden Shakespeare edition of *Antony and Cleopatra*, ed. M. Ridley (London, 1967), p.142

35 Ornstein, "The Ethic of the Imagination," p. 397.

36 Miguel de Cervantes Saavedra, *Don Quixote de la Mancha*, tr. S. Putnam (New York, 1949), pp. 611-18.

37 Ibid., pp. 27-28, 146

38 Ibid., pp. 62-64, 70, 76, 131-34.

39 Ibid., pp. 611.

40 Thomas Mann called this adventure the "climax of Don Quixote's exploits" and of the novel. "Voyage with Don Quixote," in *Essays of Three Decades*, tr. H. Lowe-Porter (New York, 1957), p. 452.

41 Miguel De Unamuno, *The Life of Don Quixote and Sancho According to Miguel de Cervantes Saavedra*, tr. H. Earle (New York, 1927), p. 178.

42 *Don Quixote*, pp. 611-18. p. 984.

43 W. H. Auden, *Lectures on Shakespeare* (Princeton, 2000), p. 250.

44 Jan Kott, *Shakespeare Our Contemporary*, tr. B. Taborski (New York, 1966), p. 194.

45 Harley Granville-Barker, "Coriolanus: Introduction," in *Twentieth Century Interpretations of Coriolanus*, ed. J. Phillips (Englewood Cliff s, 1970), p. 40; Eugene Waith, *The Herculean Hero* (New York, 1962), pp. 124, 126; Philip Edwards, *Shakespeare. A Writer's Progress* (Oxford, 1986), p. 140.

46 Rabkin, *Shakespeare and the Common Understanding* (New York, 1967), p. 129

47 Plutarch, *The Lives of the Noble Grecians and Romans*, tr. J.

48 Quoted by P. Brokbank, "Introduction" to the Arden edition of Coriolanus, (London, 1996) p.40.

49 Coppelia Kahn, *Man's Estate. Masculine Identity in Shakespeare*, (Berkeley, 1981), p. 162.
50 Kott, *Shakespeare, Our Contemporary*, p.190.
51 Waith, *The Herculean Hero*, p.142.
52 Some observations on the ethic and esthetic of violence in Jean Charles Payen, "Un poétique du génocide joyeux: devoir de violence et plaisir de tuer dans la *Chanson de Roland*," *Olifant*, 6 (1979), 229.
53 Steven Runciman, *The First Crusade* (London, 1980), p. 229.
54 Torquato Tasso, *Jerusalem Delivered*, tr. E. Fairfax (New York, 1964), pp. 40-41, 427, 443.
55 Francis Bacon, *The Essays of Counsels Civil and Moral, in Works*, eds. Spedding-Ellis-Heath (Boston, 1860), 12: 177-179.
56 Quoted by J. R. Hale, "Incitement to Violence? English Divines on the Theme of War, 1578-1631," in *Renaissance War Studies* (London, 1983), p. 494.
57 Quoted by Paul Jorgensen, *Shakespeare's Military World* (Berkeley, 1956), p. 186.
58 Thomas More, *Utopia*, ed. E. Surtz, (New Haven, 1972), p. 120.
59 Gordon Zeeveld, "Food for Power—Food for Worms," *Shakespeare Quarterly*, 3 (1952), 249.
60 Derek Cohen, *Shakespeare's Culture of Violence*, (New York, 1993), p.73.
61 Jorgensen, *Shakespeare's Military World*, p.163.
62 Kernan, "The Henriade," in *Modern Critical Views*, p. 239.
63 John Keegan, *The Face of Battle*, (New York, 1976), p. 110.
64 Cf. Goddard, *The Meaning of Shakespeare*, I, 236.
65 Stephen Greenblatt, "Invisible Bullets: Renaissance Authority and its Subversion, *Henry IV*, and *Henry V*," in *Political Shakespeare. New Essays in Cultural Materialism*, eds. Dollimore—Sinfield (Manchester, 1985), pp. 42, 43.

66 Keegan, *The Face of Battle,* p. 79.

67 Goddard. *The Meaning of Shakespeare,* I, 257.

68 The Arden Shakespeare editor writes that Henry's "physical courage" is ignored. Shakespeare could have shown Henry's combat with Alençon, but he chose not to. *King Henry V,* ed. J. Walker (London, 1961), p. XXX|V.

69 *Johnson on Shakespeare,* eds. Bronson - O'Mear, (New Haven, 1986), p. 201.

70 Thomas Milles, *The Treasury of Ancient and Modern Times,* (London, 1613), p. 260.

71 Walter Raleigh, *The History of the World, in The Works,* (New York, 1829), V, 380-81.

72 Thomas Hobbes, *Leviathan,* ed. C. Macpherson (Harmondsworth, 1971), p. 717.

73 Matthew Proser, *The Heroic Image in Five Shakespearian Tragedies* (Princeton, 1965), pp. 139, 148.

74 Or, as a commentator puts it, "make quarreling the height of valor." *Timon of Athens,* ed. G. R. Hibbard, (Harmondsworth, 1981), p. 197.

75 *Henry VI,* Part II, 5.2.37.

76 Oscar Campbell, "Coriolanus," in *Shakespeare. Modern Essays in Criticism* (London, 1968), p. 407.

77 Michael Davis, "Courage and Impotence in *Macbeth,*" in *Shakespeare's Political Pageant. Essays in Literature and Politics* (London, 1996), p. 223.

78 Proser, *The Heroic Image,* p. 59; Kahn, *Man's Estate,* p. 180.

79 *Johnson on Shakespeare,* pp. 263-64.

80 Ibid., p. 263.

81 Edwards, *Shakespeare,* p.139.

82 Kenneth Muir, *Shakespeare's Tragic Sequence* (New York, 1979), p. 145. Cf. Goddard, *The Meaning of Shakespeare,* I, 494: men who have been "valiant on the battlefield" may come home to act like "criminals in time of peace."

83 Commentators ignore the meaning of "insane root." The Arden Shakespeare, for instance, refers to root only in its literal sense, the Mekilwort berries, mentioned by Holinshed, *Macbeth*, ed. K. Muir (London, 1974), p. 17.
84 G. Wilson Knight, *The Wheel of Fire* (London, 1969), p. 150, notes that the Weird Sisters "are related to the bloodshed of battle" and have been waiting "to instigate a continuance of bloodlust" in Macbeth.
85 Waith, *The Herculean Hero*, p. 268.
86 A. C. Bradley, *Shakespearean Tragedy* (New York, 1992), p. 88.
87 Anne Barton, "Introduction" to *Hamlet*, ed. T. Spencer (New York, 1988), pp. 39, 41.
88 Ibid., p. 44.
89 Frederick Nietzsche, "The Birth of Tragedy," *The Philosophy of Nietzsche*, Random House, Inc. (New York, 1954), p. 984.
90 Montaigne, *The Complete Essays*, pp. 157, 277.
91 Ibid., pp. 500, 502.
92 Ibid., pp. 209-11, 213, 229-33.
93 Ibid., pp. 154-57.
94 Giambattista Vico, *The New Science. Revised Translation of the Third Edition* (1744), tr. Bergin-Fisch (Ithaca, 1968), pp. 195,196.
95 Ibid, pp. 197, 218.
96 Isaiah Berlin, *Vico and Herder. Two Studies in the History of Ideas* (London, 1976), p. 61.
97 Vico, *The New Science*, pp. 157, 237, 277.
98 Ibid, pp. 239, 353, 385, 398.
99 *An Essay on Man*, ed. M. Mack (London, 1951), pp. 147-48.
100 Vico, *The New Science*, pp. 19, 239, 241.
101 John Milton, *Paradise Lost*, 11: 689-90, 695-96.
102 *The History of Britain*, in *The Works of John Milton* (New York, 1932), 10: 324-25.

103 Vico, *The New Science,* pp. 252- 55, 267, 315, 324, 338.

104 Ibid., pp. 20, 133, 144, 237.

105 On archaic Roman History's relevance to Vico's concept of the heroic age, see Arnaldo Momigliano, "Vico's *Scienza nuova*: Roman 'bestioni' and Roman 'eroi'," *History and Theory,* 5 (1966), 15.

106 Vico, *The New Science*, pp. 211, 253-54.

107 Ibid, pp. 336-39, 423.

108 Momigliano, "Gibbon from an Italian Point of View," in *Edward Gibbon and The Decline and Fall of the Roman Empire*, eds. Bowersock-Clive-Graubard (Cambridge, Mass., 1977), p. 78.

109 François Furet, "Civilization and Barbarism in Gibbon's History," in *Edward Gibbon and The Decline and Fall of the Roman Empire*, p. 164, 165.

110 Frank Manuel, "Edward Gibbon: Historien-Philosophe," in *Edward Gibbon and The Decline and Fall of the Roman Empire*, p. 170.

111 Edward Gibbon, *The Decline and Fall of the Roman Empire*, ed. J. Bury (London,1909), 4: 173. All quotations from this work are from this edition.

112 Ibid., 1: 2-7.

113 Ibid., 1: 10-12, 62. On this conclusion, cf. Giuseppe Giarrizzo, *Edward Gibbon e la cultura europea del settecento* (Naples, 1955), 253.

114 Gibbon, *Decline and Fall,* 1: 69, 80 115, 167-69.

115 Patricia Craddock, *Edward Gibbon, Luminous Historian 1772-1794* (Baltimore, 1989), p. 228.

116 Gibbon, *Decline and Fall,* 1: 251, 389; 3: 74; 6: 146.

117 Ibid., 3: 77; 4: 176, 178; 6: 104-05.

118 Ibid., 1: 244, 245, 248-49; 3: 94; 6: 105.

119 Ibid., 1: 233, 235, 251; 3: 74, 79-80.

120 Tacitus, *Germany and its Tribes, in The Complete Works of Tacitus,* tr. Church-Brodribb (New York, 1942), p. 718; Machiavelli, *The Discourses,* Book 1, chapter 55.

121 Gibbon, *Decline and Fall*, 1: 235, 251.

122 Furet, "Civilization and Barbarism in Gibbon's History," in *Edward Gibbon and The Decline and Fall of the Roman Empire*, p. 164.

123 Momigliano, "Gibbon from an Italian Point of View," in *Edward Gibbon and The Decline and Fall of the Roman Empire*, p. 78.

124 Michael Howard, *War in European History* (Oxford, 1979), p. 70; Theodor Ropp, *War in the Modern World* (New York, 1962), pp. 55-56. Cf. Voltaire's description of recruitment methods in the age of Frederick the Great in *Candide*, and *Candide and Other Writings*, ed. H. Block (New York, 1984), p.113.

125 Peter Paret, *Clausewitz and the State* (Oxford, 1976), p. 246.

126 Quoted by Paret, *Clausewitz*, p. 341; Hans Rothfels, "Clausewitz," in *Makers of Modern Strategy. Military Thought from Machiavelli to Hitler*, ed. E. Earle (New York, 1969), p. 98.

127 Carl von Clausewitz, *On War*, ed., and tr. M. Howard-P. Paret (Princeton, 1984), pp. 86, 137, 227, 260. All quotations are from this English edition.

128 Ibid., pp. 76, 100, 140, 190-92, 282.

129 Ibid., p. 76. In a review of a new English edition of *On War*, strategist Harry Summers caught the importance of passionate hatred, pointing out that "the passions of the people" is central to Clausewitz's thought. But Summer is reluctant, understandably, to acknowledge that the passions Clausewitz writes about have to do with turning back the clock of civilization. Harry Summers, "What is War?" *Harper's Magazine*, 268 (May, 1984), p. 77.

130 Clausewitz, *On War*, p. 76.

131 Ibid., pp. 138, 189, 253.

132 Ibid., pp. 101, 187-89.

133 Raymond Aron, *Clausewitz, Philosopher of War*, tr. Booker - Stone (London, 1983), p. 125.

134 *Tolstoy: Miscellaneous Letters and Essays*, tr. L. Wiener (Boston, 1905), 13: 279-281; Id., "The Kingdom of God is Within You," in *The Kingdom of God and Peace Essays*, tr. A. Maude (London, 1936), p. 371

135 Tolstoy, "The Raid," in *Tales of Army Life*, tr. L. A. Maude (Oxford,1935), p. 2.
136 Ibid., pp. 5-6, 79-80.
137 Tolstoy, "The Wood-Felling," in *Tales*, pp. 60-61, 70-71.
138 Ibid., pp. 73-75.
139 Tolstoy, "The Raid," in *Tales*, pp. 4-6.
140 Tolstoy, "Sevastopol in May 1855," in *Tales*, pp. 112-15, 129-32, 139. Tolstoy, "Sevastopol in August 1855," in Tales, pp. 169-73, 188 -92, 209-25.
141 Ibid., pp. 222-23.
142 Quoted by Ernest Simmons, *Leo Tolstoy. The Years of Development 1828-1879* (New York,1960), I, 125.
143 Tolstoy, "Sevastopol in May 1855," in *Tales*, pp. 139-42.
144 The influence of Sevastopol, (part of *Tales of Army Life*), on *The Red Badge of Courage* as noted by Edmund Wilson, *Patriotic Gore: Studies in the Literature of the American Civil War* (New York,1962), p. 684.
145 Joseph Conrad, "His War Book," in *Stephen Crane: A Collection of Critical Essays*, ed. M. Bassan (Englewood Cliffs, 1967), p. 125.
146 Stephen Crane, *The Red Badge of Courage*, ed H. Binder (New York, 1982), pp. 7, 10, 15, 17, 18.
147 Ibid., pp. 27, 30, 32, 78-79, 88-89, 102-03.
148 Ibid., pp. 3, 6, 7, 20.
149 Perry Lentz, *Private Fleming at Chancellorsville. The Red Badge of Courage and the Civil War* (Columbia, 2006), p. 123.
150 Donald Gibson, *The Red Badge of Courage. Redefining the Hero* (Boston, 1988), p. 77.
151 James T. Cox, "The Imagery of The Red Badge of Courage," in *The Red Badge of Courage. An Annotated Text Background and Sources. Essays in Criticism* (New York, 1962), p. 320.
152 Crane, *The Red Badge*, pp. 56, 78-80.
153 Ibid., pp. 80.

154 Ibid., pp. 86.

155 Chester Wolford, *The Anger of Stephen Crane* (Lincoln, 1983), p. 46.

156 M. - E. Marcus, "Animal Imagery in *The Red Badge of Courage*," in *The Red Badge of Courage* (New York, 1962), p. 312.

157 Clausewitz, *On War*, pp. 100, 189, 192.

158 Crane, *The Red Badge*, pp. 37, 38.

159 Ibid., pp. 39, 42.

160 Ibid., pp. 42, 44, 45, 48. Henry's response to death contrasts with Peza's, the Greek volunteer protagonist of the semi-fictional piece on the Greco-Turkish War, done about three years after *The Red Badge of Courage*. The dead on the battlefield cause Peza to flee, escaping the seduction of death, valor, and glory: "He was being drawn and drawn by these dead men, slowly, firmly down, as to some mystic chamber under the earth, where they could walk, dreadful figures, swollen and blood marked. He was bidden; they had commanded him; he was going, going, going." Peza "bolted for the rear" never to come back. "Death and the Child," in *The War Dispatches of Stephen Crane*, eds. Stallman-Hagemann (New York, 1964), p. 102.

161 Crane, *The Red Badge of Courage*, p. 49.

162 Ibid., pp. 101.

163 Ibid., pp. 101.

164 Crane, *The Red Badge*, pp. 3-4, 6.

165 Tolstoy, "The Wood-Felling," in *Tales*, pp. 60-61, 70-71.

166 Tolstoy, *War and Peace*, tr. C. Garnett (New York), pp. 163, 166-67, 178, 1010-11.

167 Ibid, pp. 158, 162, 166, 172, 173, 179.

168 David Bell, *The First Total War: Napoleon's Europe and the Birth of Warfare as We Know It* (Boston, 2007), p. 201.

169 Renato Poggioli, "Tolstoy as Man and Artist," in *Tolstoy, a Collection of Critical Essays*, ed. R. Matlaw (Englewood Cliffs, 1967), p. 22.

170 Tolstoy, "Sevastopol in December 1854," in *Tales*, pp. 92-96, 105-06.

171 *War and Peace*, pp. 610-11.

172 Ibid, 256

173 Ibid, 267

174 Bell, *The First Total War*, p. 211.

175 Tolstoy, *War and Peace*, p.256.

176 Ibid, pp 265-67, 761, 1058.

177 Tolstoy, "The Raid," in *Tales*, p. 4.

178 Tolstoy, *War and Peace*, pp. 963

179 Tolstoy, "The Raid," pp. 22-23.

180 Tolstoy, "Hadji Murat," in *Master and Man and Other Stories*, tr. P. Foote (New York, 1988), pp. 225-26.

181 Tolstoy, War and Peace, p. 752.

182 Isaiah Berlin notes, Tolstoy "sometimes seems almost deliberately to ignore the historical evidence and more than once distorts the facts in order to bolster up his favorite thesis," *The Hedgehog and the Fox: An Essay on Tolstoy's View of History* (New York, 1957), p. 46.

183 Tolstoy, *War and Peace*, pp. 750-53.

184 Berlin, *The Hedgehog and the Fox*.

185 Tolstoy, *War and Peace*, pp. 764, 960, 1013.

186 Tolstoy, *War and Peace*, p. 962-3.

187 Ibid., pp. 564-65, 768, 1011.

188 R. F. Christian, *Tolstoy's War and Peace, a Study* (Oxford, 1962), p. 111.

189 Christian, *Tolstoy's War and Peace*, p. 107, 109

190 Tolstoy, *War and Peace*, p. 963.

191 Ibid. p. 962

192 Tolstoy, "Hadji Murat," in *Master and Man*, p. 226; Tolstoy, "The Raid," in *Tales*, p. 23.

193 Tolstoy, "The Raid," pp. 32-33.

194 Tolstoy, *War and Peace*, p. 964

195 Ibid., pp. 962-63. The Russian critic Boris Eikhenbaum caught some of the spirit of that sentence in his *Tolstoy in the Sixties,* tr D. White (Ann Arbor, 1982), p, 184. In *War and Peace,* the novelist wrote about war "as inspiration for the people's moral powers."
196 Alan Clark, *The Donkeys* (New York, 1965), p. 114.
197 Frederic Manning, *Her Privates We* (New York, 1958), p. 160.
198 S.L.A. Marshall, *World War I* (Boston, 2001), p. 73.
199 Manning, *Her Private We,* p. 18.
200 Attilio Frescura, *Diario di un imboscato* (Milan, 1981), pp. 9798.
201 Lieutenant Ghisalberti quoted in Piero Melograni, *Storia politica della Grande Guerra 1915-1918* (Bari, 1969), p. 99.
202 Frescura, *Diario di un imboscato,* p. 98.
203 Robert Graves, *Good-bye to All That* (New York, 1998), p. 131.
204 Andrew Rutherford, *The Literature of War: Five Studies in Heroic Virtues* (London,1978), p. 93.
205 Siegfried Sassoon, "Memoirs of an Infantry Officer," in *The Memoirs of George Sherston* (New York, 1937), p. 148
206 Graves, *Good-bye to All That,* pp. 145, 148-49, 151, 157-58, 162, 170.
207 Ibid., pp. 164, 165, 257, 260.
208 *Men Who March Away: Poems of the First World War,* ed. I. Parsons (New York, 1965), p. 171.
209 Sassoon, *Diaries 1915-1918* (London, 1983), p. 254.
210 Manning, *Her Privates We,* pp. 14, 17, 18, 45, 219, 221.
211 Ibid., pp. 221-222.
212 *War Letters of Fallen Englishmen,* ed. L. Housman (Philadelphia, 2002), p. 121.
213 Sassoon, "Remorse," in *Collected Poems,* p. 91
214 Ibid., "The Hero," p. 29.
215 Ibid., "Glory of Women," p. 79.
216 Ibid., "Conscripts," p. 31.
217 Henri Barbusse, *Under Fire,* tr. W. Wray (London, 1974), pp. 5-6, 17.

218 Jean Norton Cru, *Témoins* (Nancy, 1993), p. 558.

219 Barbusse, *Under Fire*, pp. 241-42.

220 Ibid., pp. 247-50.

221 Ibid., pp. 247, 250-257, 340-342.

222 Erich Maria Remarque, *All Quiet on the Western Front*, tr. A. Wheen (New York, 1982), p. 22.

223 Rudolf Binding, *A Fatalist at War*, tr. I. Morrow (Boston, 1929), p. 78.

224 Remarque, *All Quiet on the Western Front*, pp. 13, 26, 113-15.

225 Ibid., pp. 56, 113, 114, 138-39, 273-74.

226 Ibid., p. 130.

227 Ibid., pp. 263, 272, 274, 294.

228 Benedetto Croce, *L'Italia dal 1914 al 1918. Pagine sulla guerra* (Bari, 1965), pp. 111-12, 221, 224, 233-34.

229 Adolfo Omodeo, *Lettere 1910-1946* (Turin, 1963), p. 142.

230 Enrico Corradini, *Il nazionalismo italiano* (Milan, 1914), pp. 1516, 230, 231; Id., *Discorsi politici* (Florence, 1923), pp. 114, 303, 305.

231 Alfredo Rocco, *Scritti e discorsi politici* (Milan, 1938), 1: 99, 215.

232 Giovanni Papini, "Campagna per il forzato risveglio," *La cultura italiana del '900 attraverso le riviste* (Turin,1960), 1: 314.

233 Papini, "Un uomo finito," in *Opere. Dal Leonardo al Futurismo* (Milan, 1977), pp. 136, 244-48, 264-66, 278, 328. Papini, "Amiamo la guerra!" "La vita non è sacra," *Lacerba, in La cultura italiana del '900 attraverso le riviste,* (Turin,1961), 4: 208, 329.

234 Filippo Marinetti, *Guerra sola igiene del mondo* (Milan,1915), p. 147.

235 Benito Mussolini, *Il mio diario di guerra* (1915-1917), in *Opera omnia*, ed. E. Susmel (Florence, 1962), 34: 69.

236 Luigi Capello, *Note di guerra,* (Milan, 1921), 1:318-19; 2: 147; Id., *Caporetto. Perchè?* (Turin, 1967), pp. 25, 34.

237 Carlo Salsa, *Trincee. Confidenze di un fante* (Milan, 1982), pp. 60-63; Marshall, *World War I*, p. 174.

238 Mario Puccini, *Davanti a Trieste (Esperienze di un fante sul Carso)* (Milan, 1919), p. 137.

239 Giuseppe Prezzolini, *Diario 1900-1941* (Milan, 1978), p. 224.

240 Giulio Dohuet, *Diario critico di guerra* (Torino, 1921), 1: 411-12. 2: 141.

241 Agostino Gemelli, *Il nostro soldato. Saggi di psicologia militare* (Milan, 1917), pp. 4, 27, 37, 104.

242 Emilio Gadda, *Il castello di Udine* (Turin, 1961), pp. 31-33, 5253.

243 Adolfo Omodeo, *Momenti della vita di guerra. Dai diari dalle lettere dei caduti* 1915-1918 (Turin, 1968), p. 213.

244 *Tutta la guerra. Antologia del popolo italiano sul fronte e nel paese*, ed. G. Prezzolini (Milan, 1968), p. 295.

245 Keegan, *The Face of Battle*, p. 326.

246 Melograni, *Storia politica della Grande Guerra*, pp. 245, 247.

247 Emilio Lussu, *Un anno sull'altipiano* (Turin, 1964), pp. 94-95.

248 Paolo Monelli, *Scarpe al sole* (Milan, 1966), pp. 52, 55-57, 194.

249 Ernest Hemingway, *A Farewell to Arms* (New York, 1957), p. 185.

250 Samuel Hynes, *A War Imagined. The First World War and English Culture* (New York, 1990), p. 436.

251 Gabriele D'Annunzio, *Prose di ricerca* (Milan, 1958), 1: 812, 816.

252 *Gabriele D'Annunzio combattente al servizio della regia marina*, ed. G. Po (Rome, 1931), pp. 22, 23, 24, 25. D'Annunzio,

253 *Notturno* (Milan, 1989), pp.169, 240.

254 D'Annunzio, *Prose di ricerca*, 1: 587, 806, 879, 886, 917, 935, 1023.

255 Ernst Jünger, *The Storm of Steel*, tr. B. Creighton (New York,1975), pp.1, 27, 28, 29, 38-39, 70, 254-255, 262-263, 285, 316.

256 Jünger, *Copse 125: A Chronicle from the Trench Warfare of 1918*, tr. B. Creighton (London, 1930), pp. 190-191.

257 Benito Mussolini, *Opera omnia* (Florence, 1962), 11:121; 34:70, 348.

258 Ibid., 10:345; 13:148, 151,153.

259 Ibid., 18:413, 433.

260 Ibid., 34:124, 125.

261 Ibid., 11:132.

262 Ibid., 31:47, 142, 144.

263 Giuseppe Bottai, *Diario 1935-1944* (Milan, 1982), p. 412.

264 Remarque, *All Quiet on the Western Front*, pp. 263, 264, 274, 294, 296.

265 Barbusse, *Under Fire*, p. 257.

266 Herbert Read, *A Coat of Many Colors* (London, 1956), p. 21.

267 John Mack, *A Prince of Our Disorder: The Life of T. E. Lawrence* (Boston, 1976), pp. 456, 457.

268 T. E. Lawrence, *The Seven Pillars of Wisdom. A Triumph* (New York, 1935), pp. 29-32.

269 Arnold Lawrence, ed., *T. E. Lawrence by His Friends* (London, 1937), p. 272.

270 Mack, *A Prince of Our Disorder*, p. 242.

271 Hemingway, *A Farewell to Arms*, p. 249.

272 Hemingway, *For Whom the Bell Tolls* (New York, 1968), pp. 43.

273 Ibid., pp. 91, 162-163, 235, 236.

274 Ibid., pp. 369-70.

275 Ibid., p. 21.

276 Ibid., 41-42, 196, 197, 304.

277 Ibid., pp. 10, 14, 26, 90, 103.

278 Ibid., pp. 312-13.

279 Ibid., pp. 467, 471.

280 Paul Fussell, *Wartime. Understanding and Behavior in the Second World War* (New York, 1989), p. 273: "In contrast to the expectation of heroic behavior which set the tone of the earlier war, now it was recognized that the fact of fear had to be squarely faced."

281 Hemingway, *Across the River and into the Trees* (New York, 2003), pp. 126, 127, 205, 206.

282 Ibid., pp. 222, 229, 230, 234.

283 Ibid., p. 26-27

284 Philip Young, *Ernest Hemingway, a Reconsideration* (University Park, 1966), p. 120.

285 D'Annunzio, *Prose di ricerca*, 1: 70, 814; Id., *Notturno*, p.130.

286 Hemingway, *Across the River and into the Trees*, pp. 53-54, 229.

287 Keegan, *The Face of Battle*, p. 324.

288 Joseph Heller, *Catch-22* (New York,1963), pp.16-17, 30, 46-47, 51, 69, 127.

289 Norman Mailer, *The Naked and the Dead* (New York, 1948), pp. 3, 18, 24, 35, 37, 113, 115, 122, 123, 297.

290 Ibid., pp. 495, 510, 514, 644, 661, 698.

291 Ibid., p. 708.

292 Ibid., pp.175, 322-323, 717.

293 Richard Foster, "Norman Mailer," in *Norman Mailer, the Man and his Work* (New York, 1971), p. 27.

294 Ibid., p. 27.

295 A certain type of criticism has recognized in Croft and Cummings the only two protagonists of the novel who are endowed with "courage": Norman Podhoretz, "Norman Mailer: the Embattled Vision," in *Norman Mailer*, pp.66, 67.

296 Mailer, *The Naked and the Dead*, pp. 28, 143, 153, 156-164.

297 William Manchester, *Goodbye, Darkness. A Memoir of the Pacific War* (New York,1982), pp. 16-18.

298 Ibid., pp. 22-24.

299 Ibid., pp. 272-78.

300 Ibid., p. 96.

301 Ibid., p. 282.

302 Ibid., p. 436.

303 Ibid., pp. 394, 414, 421.

304 Ibid., pp. 22, 300.

305 Ibid., p. 451.

306 Ibid., pp. 291-94, 298.

307 Ibid., pp. 341-342.
308 Ibid., p. 289.
309 E. B. Sledge, *With the Old Breed at Peleliu and Okinawa* (New York, 1990), pp. 63, 74.
310 Ibid., pp. 91, 121.
311 Ibid., pp. 60, 125, 128, 137, 164, 170, 235, 247.
312 Harold Moore and Joseph Galloway, *We Were Soldiers Once... and Young* (New York, 2002), pp. 133, 214, 218, 373-74, 408, 445.
313 William Westmoreland, *A Soldier Reports* (New York, 1989), p. 297.
314 Moore and Galloway, *We Were Soldiers Once*, p. 2.
315 Ron Kovic, *Born on the Fourth of July* (New York, 1976), pp. 63, 73.
316 Ibid., pp. 54, 55, 63, 218-19, 222.
317 Philip Caputo, *A Rumor of War* (New York, 1984), pp. 5, 6, 14.
318 William Broyles, *Brothers in Arms. A Journey from War to Peace* (New York, 1986), pp. 80, 81, 200.
319 Michael Herr, *Dispatches* (New York, 1978), p. 102.
320 Broyles, *Brothers in Arms*, pp. 22, 91.
321 Eric Schroeder, "Two Interviews: Talks with Tim O'Brien and Robert Stone," *Modern Fiction Studies*, 30 (1984), 145.
322 Tim O'Brien, *If I Die in a Combat Zone* (New York, 1973), pp. 37, 57; Id., *The Things they Carried* (New York, 1998), p. 22.
323 O'Brien, *If I Die in a Combat Zone*, p. 130.
324 Herr, *Dispatches*, p. 63.
325 O'Brien, *If I Die in a Combat Zone*, p. 141.
326 Caputo, *A Rumor of War*, p. 93.
327 Gustav Hasford, *Short-Timers* (New York, 1979), p. 129.
328 Herr, *Dispatches*, p. 66.
329 Malcolm Browne, *The New Face of War* (New York, 1986), p. 334.
330 Stephen Wright, *Meditations in Green* (New York, 1983), pp. 276-78.
331 Caputo, *A Rumor of War*, pp. 92, 100.

332 James Webb, *Fields of Fire* (Englewood Cliffs, 1978), pp. 59,187.

333 Caputo, *A Rumor of War,* p. 89.

334 O'Brien, *If I Die in a Combat Zone,* pp. 1, 2.

335 Herr, *Dispatches,* p. 63.

336 Caputo, *A Rumor of War,* pp. 272-73.

337 O'Brien, *If I Die in a Combat Zone,* p. 120.

338 Ibid., pp. 101-02.

339 Herr, *Dispatches,* p.103.

340 O'Brien, *If I Die in a Combat Zone,* p. 136.

341 E. B. Sledge, *With the Old Breed at Peleliu and Okinawa* (New York, 1990), pp. 91, 121.

342 Herr, *Dispatches,* pp. 133-34.

343 Glenn Gray, *The Warriors* (New York, 1970), p. 128.

344 Herr, *Dispatches,* p. 9.

345 Caputo, *A Rumor of War,* pp. 121, 153, 170, 209-210.

346 Robert Mason, *Chickenhawk* (New York, 1985), pp. 212, 214, 217, 218, 221, 223, 224, 228, 279, 299-300.

347 Ibid., pp. 243, 451.

348 Broyles, *Brothers in Arms,* p. 267.

349 Ibid., p. 91.

350 David Halberstam, *The Best and the Brightest* (New York, 1972), p. 613.

351 Tim O'Brien, *Going after Cacciato* (New York, 1978), pp. 201-03.

352 O'Brien, *If I Die in a Combat Zone,* pp. 167-68.

353 Id., *The Things They Carried,* pp. 20, 21, 238.

354 Id., *Going after Cacciato,* p. 13.

355 Herr, *Dispatches,* p. 87.

356 Robert Lifton, *Home from the War* (New York, 1973), p. 223.

357 Caputo, *A Rumor of War,* pp. 246-48, 258.

358 Webb, *Fields of Fire,* p. 262.

359 Charles Anderson, *The Grunts* (Novato,1983), p. 201.

360 O'Brien, *If I Die in a Combat Zone,* pp.135-36.

361 William Wilson, *The LBJ Brigade* (Los Angeles, 1966), pp. 11, 56.

362 A letter by George Olsen, in *Dear America. Letters Home from Vietnam,* ed. B. Edelman (New York,1985), p.118.

363 Caputo, *A Rumor of War,* pp. XVII, 320.

364 Broyles, *Brothers in Arms,* pp. 202-03, 254.

365 O'Brien, *The Things they Carried,* pp. 81, 175

366 Caputo, *A Rumor of War,* pp. XIV, XIX.

367 John Sack, *Lieutenant Calley. His Own Story* (New York,1971), pp. 124-125.

368 Samuel Hynes, *The Soldiers' Tale* (New York, 1997) p. 214.

369 S. L. Marshall, *Men against Fire* (Norman, Oklahoma, 2000), pp. 161, 162.

370 O'Brien, *If I Die in a Combat Zone,* pp. 128-29.

371 Ibid., pp. 129-32.

372 Ibid., p. 140.

373 Ibid., pp. 133-135.

374 Ibid., p. 137.

375 O'Brien, *Going after Cacciato,* pp. 237-41; Id., *If I Die in a Combat Zone,* p. 133.

376 O'Brien, *Going after Cacciato,* pp. 45, 357, 375, 377.

377 Ibid., pp. 320-21; Id., *If I Die in a Combat Zone,* p. 76.

378 Westmoreland, *A Soldier Reports,* p. 423.

379 Broyles, *Brothers in Arms,* pp. 200, 267.

380 Michael Shafer, "The Vietnam Combat Experience: The Human Legacy," in *The Legacy. The Vietnam War in the American Imagination,* ed. M. Shafer (Boston, 1990), p. 84.

381 Webb, *Fields of Fire,* p. 172.

382 John Pratt, *The Laotian Fragments* (New York, 1974), p. 37.

383 Mason, *Chickenhawk*, p. 474.
384 William Styron in a review of Caputo's book in *The New York Review of Books*, 24 (1977), 6.
385 Broyles, *Brothers in Arms*, p. 76.
386 Lifton, *Home from the War*, p.225.
387 David Grossman, *On Killing* (New York, 1995), p. 250.
388 Caputo, *A Rumor of War*, p. 112.
389 Mark Baker, *Nam. The Vietnam War in the Words of the Men and Women who Fought There* (New York, 1981), p. 152.
390 Halberstam, *The Best and the Brightest*, p. 613.
391 Hasford, *Short-Timers*, p. 110.
392 Broyles, *Brothers in Arms*, pp. 200-201 ,204
393 Jonathan Shay, *Achilles in Vietnam. Combat Trauma and the Undoing of Character* (New York, 1994), pp. 77, 80.
394 O'Brien, *If I Die in a Combat Zone*, pp. 113-16.
395 Ibid., pp. 131, 141.
396 Robert Roth, *Sand in the Wind* (Boston, 1973), pp. 330-33.
397 Broyles, *Brothers in Arms*, pp. 200-201.
398 Herr, *Dispatches*, pp. 63, 66.
399 Caputo, *A Rumor of War*, pp. XVII, 218.
400 Ibid., pp. 251, 252.
401 Hasford, *Short-Timers*, p. 84.
402 Roth, *Sand in the Wind*, pp. 333-334.
403 Baker, *Nam*, p. 163.
404 O'Brien, *If I Die in a Combat Zone*, p. 79.
405 M. P. McCusker, "The Old Man," in *Free Fire Zone* (Coventry, 1973), p. 1.
406 William Huggett, *Body Count* (New York, 1973), pp. 302-06.
407 Wilson, *The LBJ Brigade*, p. 56.

408 Richard Hammer, *The Court-Martial of Lt. Calley* (New York, 1971), p. 258.

409 David Hackworth, *About Face: The Odyssey of an American Warrior* (New York, 1989), pp. 467, 572, 778. Baker, Nam, pp. 63-64.

410 Hasford, *The Short Timers*, pp. 4, 12, 13, 15.

411 Roth, *Sand in the Wind*, p. 79.

412 Caputo, *A Rumor of War*, p. 117.

413 Robert Santos, "My Men," in Al Santoli, *Everything We Had* (New York, 1983), p. 110.

414 Caputo, *A Rumor of War*, p. XIX.

415 Ibid. p. 129

416 Herr, *Dispatches*, p. 103.

417 Lifton, *Home from the War*, pp. 45, 64.

418 Baker, *Nam*, pp. 56-57.

419 Caputo, A Rumor of War, p. 164.

420 Seymour Hersh, My Lai 4. A Report on the Massacre and Its Aftermath (New York, 1970), pp. 33, 40-42, 51, 77.

421 Baker, Nam, p. 171.

422 Hammer, *The Court-Martial of Lt. Calley*, pp. 3-4, 6.

423 Hersh, *My Lai* 4, p. 157.

424 Wayne Greenhaw, *The Making of a Hero* (Louisville, 1970), p. 191.

425 Hammer, *The Court-Martial of Lt. Calley*, p. 389.

426 Hersh, *My Lai* 4, p. 80.

427 Lifton, *Home from the War*, p.56.

428 Westmoreland, *A Soldier Reports*, p. 409.

429 William Styron in a review of Caputo's book in *The New York Review of Books*, 24 (1977), 6.

430 Walter Capps, *The Unfinished War* (Boston, 1982), p. 86.

431 Neil Sheehan, *John Paul Vann and America in Vietnam* (New York, 1988), p. 741.

www.ingramcontent.com/pod-product-compliance
Lightning Source LLC
LaVergne TN
LVHW042249070526
838201LV00089B/86